The
British State
since 1945

for my parents
Syd and Kathleen Ling

The
British State
since 1945

An Introduction

Tom Ling

Polity Press

First published in 1998 by Polity Press in association with Blackwell Publishers Ltd.

2 4 6 8 10 9 7 5 3 1

Editorial office:
Polity Press
65 Bridge Street
Cambridge CB2 1UR, UK

Marketing and production:
Blackwell Publishers Ltd
108 Cowley Road
Oxford OX4 1JF, UK

Published in the USA by
Blackwell Publishers Inc.
Commerce Place
350 Main Street
Malden, MA 02148, USA

ISBN 0-7456-1140-0
ISBN 0-7456-1141-9 (pbk)

A CIP catalogue record for this book is available from the British Library.

Library of Congress Cataloging-in-Publication Data

Ling, Tom.
    The British state since 1945 : an introduction / Tom Ling.
        p.   cm.
    Includes bibliographical references and index.
    ISBN 0-7456-1140-0 (alk. paper). — ISBN 0-7456-1141-9 (alk. paper)
    1. Great Britain—Politics and government—1945– I. Title.
JN231.L56 1997
351.41—dc21   97-39510
                                                                                    CIP

Typeset in 10½ on 12 pt Sabon
by Ace Filmsetting Ltd, Frome, Somerset
Printed in Great Britain by T.J. International Ltd, Padstow, Cornwall

This book is printed on acid-free paper.

Contents

* * * * * * * * * * * * *

List of Figures and Tables   vii

Acknowledgements   ix

Introduction   1

1 State Management and the Post-war Settlement   15
2 State Management and Economic Policy from the
   1940s to the 1970s   45
3 Managing the British Welfare State   72
4 Professional Interests and the British Welfare State   97
5 The Emergence of 'New Managerialist' Approaches
   towards the Civil Service in the Transition to Thatcherism   118
6 The New Technologies of State Management   138
7 Two Case Studies of the Changing British State: Youth
   Training and the Instruments of Urban Intervention   171
8 The British State: Interpretations and Prospects   211

Bibliography   253

General Index   271

Author Index   274

List of Figures and Tables

Figures

3.1 Outline of the national structure of the CDPs   86
3.2 Outline of the local structure of the CDPs   87
6.1 The regulatory hierarchy in the financial services industry, 1996   164

Tables

1.1 Shares of major British exports going to empire markets,
1870–1934   19
2.1 Balance of payments, current account, 1946–1952   49
2.2 Balance of payments, current account, 1952–1973   50
2.3 Volume indices of GNP at market prices   51
2.4 Volume indices of GNP per capita   51
2.5 General indices of industrial production   51
3.1 The relative growth of different categories of public
expenditure, United Kingdom, 1910–1975   75
3.2 Estimates of public expenditure on goods and services,
1945–1951, as a percentage of GDP   77
5.1 Public administration and the new managerialism   120
5.2 The response to Fulton by 1983   124
5.3 Industrial and non-industrial staff in the civil service,
1979–1986   126
5.4 Summary of non-departmental bodies, 1979–1986   135
7.1 ITB levy income (net of expenditure) and exchequer support   173
7.2 Composition of YOP, 1978–1983   174
8.1 The growth of real GDP and real GDP per capita   224
8.2 Comparative levels of GDP per head   224
8.3 The differences between Fordism and post-Fordism   232

Acknowledgements

* * * * * * * * * * * * * * *

Whilst writing this book I have incurred many intellectual debts. Bob Jessop has been a source of both inspiration and knotty problems during the past twenty years. Kevin Bonnett has gone beyond the requirements even of friendship in reading drafts, asking the right questions and nudging me towards possible answers. The final member of the 'gang of four' from the 1980s, Simon Bromley, was especially helpful at the early stages of this book. Colin Hay and I swapped ideas over many years from which I, at least, have benefited. From my time at the Open University, I particularly appreciated the ideas of Grahame Thompson, Allan Cochrane and John Clarke. David Held, through his writings has encouraged me to address the democratic question, and as a very gentle editor both helped to make the project possible and never appeared to lose his faith in it. David Goldblatt and Paul Sanderson have both provided helpful comments and guidance. Jennifer Speake provided exceptionally helpful copy-editing support. I have also been inspired by, in very different ways, the application of theory to practice in the work of Geraldine Ling, Andy Gibson and Philip Hadridge. I alone take responsibility for the content of this book.

Teaching is also a great way to learn. The friendship and support of the excellent teaching staff at Anglia Polytechnic University, and the active participation of APU students in the learning business, have allowed me to propose ideas and receive forthright feedback. Over the years, students at Cambridge University have also helped me separate serviceable arguments from the untenable.

A book cannot be produced by ideas alone. Rowena and our daughters, Anna and Rebecca, have had to put up with me constantly disappearing at weekends and evenings, cutting short the children's bedtime stories and generally being less calm and cheerful than would otherwise be the case. My parents, to whom this book is dedicated, have always given their unlimited support, and sections of the book were written at their house during the summer vacations of 1995 and 1996. Both my sisters, Corrie and Geraldine, helped me to maintain forward momentum, and Bill Monteith's incredulous looks told me when I'd gone too far.

More formally, grateful acknowledgement is made to the following for permission to reproduce material in this book:

Chapter 1   Table 1.1: Schlote, W. (1952) *British Overseas Trade from 1700 to the 1930s*, Oxford: Blackwell. Reconstruction Committee's summary of the 1944 White Paper on Employment (© Crown) reproduced with the permission of the Controller of Her Majesty's Stationery Office (PRO, CAB 124/214).

Chapter 2   Table 2.1: Cairncross, A. (1985) *Years of Recovery: British Economic Policy 1945–51*, reprinted by permission of Allen and Unwin; Table 2.2: Tomlinson, J. (1990) *Public Policy and the Economy Since 1900*, by permission of Oxford University Press.

Chapter 3   Table 3.1: Sleeman, J. F. (1979) *Resources for the Welfare State: an economic introduction*, reprinted by permission of Addison Wesley Longman Ltd.

Chapter 4   Summary of White Paper 'Working for Patients': Pollitt, C. (1993a) 'Running Hospitals' in Maidment, R. and Thompson, G. (eds) *Managing the United Kingdom*, reprinted by permission of Sage Publications Ltd.

Chapter 5   'Aims of the incoming Conservative Government' Pyper, R. (1991) *The Evolving Civil Service*, reprinted by permission of Addison Wesley Longman Ltd. Table 5.2: Drewry, G. and Butcher, T. (1988) *The Civil Service Today*, by permission of Blackwell Publishers.

Chapter 6   'Models of the social consumer': Warde, A. (1994) 'Consumers, consumption and post-Fordism' in Burrows, R. and Loader, B. *Towards a Post-Fordist Welfare State?* by permission of Routledge Publishers. 'Implications of *Working for Patients*': Pollitt, C. (1993a)

'Running Hospitals' in Maidment R. and Thompson, G. (eds) *Managing the United Kingdom*, reprinted by permission of Sage Publications Ltd.

Chapter 8 Tables 8.1 and 8.2: Temple, P. (1994) 'Overview: understanding Britain's economic performance: the role of international trade' in Buxton, T., Chapman, P. and Temple, P. (eds) (1994) *Britain's Economic Performance*, reprinted by permission of Routledge Publishers.

Introduction

The purpose of this Introduction is:

- to clarify what the state is;
- to explain why an understanding of the state is central to an adequate account of politics;
- to introduce how the British state will be examined in the following chapters.

What is the State?

Students of politics at all levels have failed to provide a short and workable definition of the state. This is not because of a persistent stupidity on the part of political scientists. Rather, it is because the state itself is inherently complex and ambiguous. Every state has a number of aspects and these overlap in a variety of ways. Sometimes one aspect will be in tension with another, or even undermine it. Thus all states tend to be fluid, changing and unsettled. At the most general level, states have the following characteristics:

Institutional   all states depend for their existence on institutions and all institutions have their own formal and informal rules and structures.

Legitimacy   all states are associated with the claim that state action is in significant ways different from and superior to the actions of any other organization or individual. States claim the right to be obeyed not because of any agreements willingly entered into by individuals or organizations but simply because they are the state.

Coercion   all states have access to coercive capacities with which to enforce order and under-pin the claim to obedience.

If we turn to the modern state in particular, which took shape in Europe in the sixteenth to the eighteenth centuries, we can take these general characteristics a little further.

Institutional   From modest beginings the modern state developed administrative capacities which provided the building blocks for complex military structures, tax-raising powers and civil bureaucracies. It also developed an institutional specialization during this time reflecting its growing range and number of activities. The specialization into legislative, judicial and executive functions is perhaps the most common example of this. These institutions were increasingly staffed by full-time permanent bureaucrats who had no direct ownership over the institutions and whose success or failure was not directly linked to the success or failure of the institution within which they worked. Their calculations and actions, however, would be strongly shaped by the rules and practices of the institution within which they worked. The state, however, was and is more than just a collection of institutions.

Legitimacy   Legitimacy in the early modern age is increasingly connected to, first, a legal claim to sovereignty and, secondly, to a democratic claim to represent the general interest of a whole nation. In the first case, the right to be obeyed is derived from the legal entitlements of the state. This is not just a cloak to disguise the 'real' power of the state; the actions of state agencies are strongly shaped by the requirement of state institutions to remain within the law. Secondly, the claim to legitimacy is connected to a given territory. Importantly, such claims stop at the border, where another legitimate sovereign power is recognized as a theoretically equal member of an international system of states. Furthermore, the claim to be a legitimate sovereign power began to be associated with the claim to be acting in the interests of the people as a whole. In some sense, all 'the people' should be represented by the state and not just one section. The problem of how such interests should be represented became a central problem of political theory and practice. One reason why nationalism flourished in the modern world was because nationalism offered an answer to this problem; if we all share a common interest as nationalists then representing our interests is easier.

Coercion If the representation of economic and social interests and the requirements of nationalism led modern states towards a concern with the welfare of the people, no state abandoned its control over the ultimate sanction of coercion. This capacity for coercion is deeply embedded in the institutions of state (see Giddens, 1985). During the modern age, the expression of such a coercive power was to shift from punishment (symbolized by the overt and violent spectacle of the public execution) and towards discipline (symbolized by the file, case notes, the rise of the 'expert', the bureaucracy and the clinic) (see Foucault, 1969). It should be noted that where such disciplinary capacities are lost those managing the modern state are rarely slow to apply its more bloody capacities.

This then, provides us with the basic vocabulary for discussing the dimensions of the modern state. It is simultaneously a collection of institutions, a sovereign power claiming the right to act in the public interest (however defined) and a uniquely well-organized coercive force. There are just two further aspects of the modern state which should be touched on here; first the relationship between the state and capitalism, and secondly the relationships within the state between its core agencies and those on its periphery.

The State and Capitalism

Implicitly or explicitly the classical traditions of monetarist, Keynesian and Marxist political economy are all concerned with the relationship between capitalism and the state (this question is discussed at length in Jessop, 1990). For the purposes of this introduction, however, we do not need to enter this whole debate, and we will briefly highlight its implications for the approach pursued here. These implications can be considered in relation to our three dimensions.

Institutional In a capitalist regime there is an institutional separation between the public sector and private economic firms. However, since the public and private sectors are mutually interdependent, each constantly searches for new ways to influence the other. In this sense, the public and the private spheres are institutionally separate but functionally intertwined. For example, firms require that the state secures law and order, a skilled work-force available for work, a monetary system which is usable and predictable, and an international system within which trade can take place. Equally, the state requires of firms that they generate a tax base and a productive system which meets widespread expectations of acceptable living standards. Thus the institutional separation between the capitalist economy and the state creates a boundary which is constantly challenged and transgressed (in both directions). Both public and private sector policy-makers therefore behave, to use an old Scots expression, like a dog in a butcher's doorway, caught between the benefits of state intervention and the costs of an overextended state and politically driven markets. However, it is neither in the interests of state personnel to take over the private sector, nor in the interests of the private sector to directly run the state, and so the boundary (however challenged) remains both in theory and in practice.

Legitimacy When political movements seek legitimacy they appeal to conceptions of the national interest, to a shared history and culture, and to common threats and enemies. When capitalist firms make strategic choices, on the other hand, they do so with the pursuit of profit as a primary goal. It may be on some occasions that these distinct calculations are mutually compatible (as in 'what's good for General Motors is good for America') but it may also be that on other occasions there are tensions or even direct conflicts (as in firms selling arms to regimes which are potentially hostile). Therefore the requirements of legitimation may suggest one set of policies, and the requirements of the capitalist sector another. We might therefore anticipate that those parts of the state system which are close to, and influenced by, the capitalist sector may have a different set of priorities and values to those agencies which are more concerned with legitimation, responding to perceived social interests and reflecting more popular aspirations.

Coercion The coercive capacities of the capitalist state today involve the public and private sectors in relationships which go way beyond the so-called industrial-military complex (important though this may be). More recently, information technologies, management capacities and the generation of 'expert knowledge' have all involved the public and private sectors in increasingly dense relationships. However, the image of a unified 'big brother' at the core of an increasingly coercive 'information society' ignores the conflicting needs of different public agencies and different private companies (leaving to one side the problems of legitimacy associated with such a move). Such a development, were it to arise, would need to cohere with a much wider marginalizing of all but a few interests within the core of an 'information state'. Whether such a state could fulfil the more general requirements of a capitalist state is questionable. However, without assuming the existence of a secret, string-pulling state-within-a-state, it is predictable that those agencies most closely associated with the coercive capacities of the state are likely to have an agenda which is different from that found in other state agencies.

The state we are examining in this book is a capitalist state and this, we argue in future chapters, is an important dimension of the British state since 1945. However, it certainly does not exhaust the nature of the British state and nor is any primacy attached to this dimension of the state. Modern societies are too complex, their various subsystems too diverse and interlocked, to defend the claim that the economy is the single force driving forward change (see Jessop, 1990, p. 365).

Equally, however, the significance of the long boom of the 1950s and 1960s, the retrenchment of the 1970s, the restructuring and apparent 'globalization' of the 1980s and 1990s should not be underestimated. This turmoil of economic activity threw up new players and interests which had to be accommodated, challenged or marginalized within the state. It also generated new problems of economic management and, with these, questions about the most appropriate agencies through which changing economic policies could be pursued (and, subsequently, questions about how such agencies should themselves be managed). Understanding the complex relationships which bind together the state and the capitalist firm, and the consequences of these relationships, remains an important key to understanding the British state.

Core and Periphery

The final aspect of the state which needs to be 'flagged up' in this Introduction is the relationship between the core and the periphery of the state. This is a relationship which embodies many of the tensions within the state. It will also be an important part of the 'story' in the chapters which follow.

Finding the 'core' of the state is a largely empirical matter. It is the cluster of institutions which makes, and is entitled to make, the key determining decisions of state. The precise location of the decision-making forum within this cluster of institutions varies from issue to issue. The term 'periphery' on the other hand, is not intended to imply a geographical dispersal of agencies (although they may well have a spatial aspect) but to indicate the point at which intervention in non-state activities and organizations takes place. These agencies will have a different set of skills, different calculations about how the world works and different dependencies from agencies at the core. They will also be more open to influence (or 'colonization') by non-state inter-ests and organizations. Whilst they are often dependent upon the core, they often enjoy at least some legitimacy of their own (perhaps focused only on one set of functions). Also, they may be able to generate their own financial and other resources, and they may be able to mobilize wider support from outside the state to strengthen their position in relation to the core. Thus, whilst the core can usually hope to impose its objectives on any single part of the periphery, it cannot simultaneously challenge whole sections of it without damag-ing its own legitimacy and capacity to secure economic and social order.

An important part of the story to be told in this book concerns how the core of the British state (along with all other post-war states) was compelled to develop new agencies at its periphery but failed to maintain strategic direction over the state as a whole. This, however, is to go beyond the purposes of this Introduction. First, if we are to study a book about the British state, we should at least consider the question 'why is the state important?'

Why is the State Important?

The construction of the state is one of the remarkable achievements of the modern age. Out of an assortment of relatively simple organiz-ations there emerged in early modern Europe a complex set of social institutions, linked together by novel legal, financial and ideological practices (for example, the state as a legal entity upholding the King's peace through a system of criminal law, the development of public accountancy practices and the identification of the state with the symbols of nationalism). The development of this state was to both shape and transform the nature of political power. It was this state which was to harness the capacities of industrialization to the means of warfare to create the most dramatic and potentially destructive concentration of coercive power in history. But it was also this state which was to create systems of public welfare capable of meeting a diverse range of human needs and systems of law which could protect the weakest members of society against the arbitrary actions of the powerful.

The state was therefore a collection of institutions with a novel organizational form. It also became one of the primary means through which social relationships were organized. The law, the military, the electoral process, lobbying, central and local government, welfare agencies and so forth all provided a variety of fields upon which interests were privileged and norms were upheld. Furthermore, states were to cultivate the affection and loyalty of the people, providing a focus for nationalism and a sense of identity.

The state was therefore never only a collection of institutions; it was also a necessary part of the wider circuits of power which shaped the social relationships of the modern world. The institutions of the state are part of the circuits of power in modern societies. They also transform the nature of that power. The relationship between men and women in the modern world, for example, is profoundly changed by state agencies mediating and policing it. We might therefore ask of the post-war British state:

- who did it empower to do what?
- who was marginalized by state agencies and how?
- which interests were privileged and why?

As we have seen, states operate with a variety of competing logics and the questions posed at the end of the previous paragraph would be answered differently in different parts of the state system. What firms require, for example, might not cohere with the longer-term requirements of legitimation. Neither of these might help to secure social order, adequate birth-rates or the socialization of children. And none of these might protect the nation from the threat of military invasion. These conflicting logics are institutionalized within the various agencies of the state.

These agencies may be organized variously according to geographical region, representative purpose or function. Within these separate agencies, distinctive views of the world emerged which contained both priorities and an understanding of the world which the agency inhabits. Within the state, therefore, there are tensions, conflicts and alliances across the different parts of the state system. How these are avoided, solved or suppressed will shape the wider functions of the state.

The complexity and variety of intra-state discourses, and the complexity of relationships between public agencies and wider circuits of power, both increased dramatically during the post-war period as Britain, in common with other liberal democracies, witnessed a massive expansion of the proportion of the national economy which is (in one way or another) spent by the state. Coinciding with this is the growth of the state as an employer and provider of goods and services. Underlying each of these is the growth of public agencies and policies specifically intended to manage the process of economic change or to alter the life experiences of citizens.

These developments have accelerated the proliferation and variety of discourses within the state. Economic agencies have had to recruit economists, negotiate with employers, incorporate trades unionists, establish training agencies and so forth, and to do so at both national and local levels. Welfare agencies have had to engage in complex assessments of risk and cost-benefit analysis and to sift through complex data. Many employees with distinctive skill sets such as doctors, teachers and social workers cannot easily be managed within conventional public bureaucracies.

One consequence of this extension of activities has been a growth in the complexity and number of organizational linkages between public and private bodies. The outcome is not an expansion of a unified, hierarchical state but, rather, the extension of public responsibility and accountability over an interdependent network of agencies which lacks any necessary and inevitable coherence. Hood expressed such a tendency in this way:

> Modern Government is multi bureaucratic rather than mega bureaucratic, meaning that the patterns of behaviour by agencies towards one another in the process of 'policy delivery' can become increasingly complex and that the manipulation of the overall system from the centre can become more difficult to achieve and dangerous to the system's professed values if it is achieved. Much of current thinking in public administration and policy analysis is directed to this issue. (Hood, 1982, p. 67)

As a result of these trends, more and more public policy is concerned with reorganizing the state itself. As Offe (1975) emphasizes, producing policies for the successful management of state agencies is never easy. The rational bureaucratic structures which are effective at restricting the excessive autonomy of state agencies are also poor at allowing the flexibility and responsiveness which such agencies often require. But equally, the lack of rational bureaucratic structures can create a very heavy dependence upon less formal structures (such as the co-option of a group of professionals) which may become unmanageable or which may also be inflexible. As Poggi (1990, p. 133) suggests, 'the much increased, differentiated and increasingly autonomous administrative apparatus becomes in turn the site of a different kind of politics . . . – bureaucratic politics.'

The attempt to secure both central control and local responsiveness has had a number of consequences. For example:

- the elaboration of a variety of new forms of administrative law intended to provide a legal framework within which these new agencies operate;
- new forms of public sector accounting, intended to provide systems for both regulating in advance public sector activities and scrutinizing it after the event;
- more recently we have seen a wide-ranging attempt to introduce a 'new managerialism' into the public sector which will be responsive both to clients and customers and operate within the quasi-contractual controls of the centre.

In short, these developments have seen the rise of a panoply of public sector management techniques with its own knowledge bases, languages, priorities, assumptions and values.

Returning to the question 'why should we study the state?' we might therefore answer:

- the state is an important part of the organization of social power and through it some interests and groups are privileged and others are weakened;
- how states do this is unpredictable and often unstable because the state is inherently complex and contains a variety of conflicting agencies and discourses; we therefore need to study the peculiarity of each state if we are to understand its consequences.

Before leaving this point, and to avoid exaggerating the tendency for states to fragment over the countervailing tendency for states to cohere, we should briefly explain why the complete fragmentation of a state is so unusual.

Why Don't States Collapse All the Time?

Whilst recognizing the importance of these changes in post-war Britain we should remember that managing intra-state tensions has been difficult throughout the modern age. Maintaining the order of the state has always been difficult but manageable and there is no overwhelming reason to suppose that the current tensions cannot be managed for the foreseeable future (although with what consequences is an important question). It will be claimed here not that the British state as we know it is about to collapse, but rather that its internal tensions and management provide an important clue to the nature of post-war British politics and to political choices in the future.

The state, then, is structured by a variety of distinctive logics. We have argued that on occasions, these may be in tension with each other but it is also the case that on other occasions these may bind together a variety of public agencies and sustain order. Law is perhaps the clearest example of such an intra-state discourse* which has its own construction of legal facts, its own definition of admissible evidence, its own construction of a legal subject. Only those things defined by the legal system as law can be part of the law. This circularity is captured by Ewald who suggests 'a norm is legal only on condition that it derives from a norm that is itself legal' (Ewald, 1988, p. 36). It is therefore a discourse which in certain respects is closed and self-referential.

However, like other discourses, these constantly bump up against, influence and respond to others. In this situation, core institutions seek to impose some degree of state-wide leadership (a meta-discourse, if you like) with which to avoid financial incontinence, arbitrary and illegal acts and the undermining of overall strategic objectives by state agencies pulling in different directions. Conflict between parts of the state system is further contained by the extent to

---

* The term 'discourse' is used here to suggest the ensemble of institutions, practices and 'knowledge' which makes action meaningful and which structures such action. It implies that such institutions, practices and 'knowledge' are not founded on secure 'truths' but that they are the product of changing and often fragile expressions of power and antagonisms. Discourses, in the sense used here, are very varied and include legal, medical, accountancy and welfarist discourses. The important thing to recognize is that such discourses are historically produced, they provide actors with a frame of reference, and they are intimately related to power (indeed, they are an expression of power). For an introduction to discourse theory, see Howarth, 1995.

which state agencies are interdependent (each agency depending upon the resources of other agencies) even when competing for limited resources (see Rhodes, 1988 for more detail).

State managers in the core institutions can therefore impose an order and direction upon the state system. The state system may be potentially fragile but the core agencies also have considerable capacities with which to secure some degree of intra-state order. Most importantly, their resources include hierarchical and bureaucratic controls, financial controls, legal controls, the capacity to shape the calculations of state agencies through influencing their recruitment practices, establishing terms of reference, requiring training procedures and ensuring that certain interests are represented within particular agencies. Consequently, whilst, the strategies of state managers to impose intra-state order vary over place and time, complete 'meltdown' is rare.

It is for these reasons that the term state *management* is used in this book. The term captures more accurately than *'public administration'* the sense of active decision-taking and the need for strategic oversight which is more characteristic of a management role than an administrative function.

In the sense used here, who carries out the state management function? State managers may spend much of their working lives engaged in activities other than state management but they function as state managers when they act to secure a degree of co-ordination and coherence across the state as a whole. When core agencies monitor and manage aspects of the state system in order to ensure the coherence of the state system as a whole, this is state management. These functions are located within the 'core' agencies of the state. They are concerned with the coherence of the state as a whole and not simply with managing one department or agency. We are concerned with the relationship between this function and wider political strategies.

It has been suggested here that there are factors which tend to fragment state systems, but that fragmentation has historically been met with political action to regain central direction over the state, and that this has given rise to a variety of techniques of financial management, political direction and judicial regulation which provide countervailing tendencies. However, pressure to maintain the coherence of the state comes not only from within the state system itself. It might also be helpful to remind ourselves of the wider consequences for non-state organizations and interests if states cannot control public expenditure, if they fail to provide some administrative coherence, if state agencies collapse into lawlessness and arbitrary action, or if the state cannot recruit personnel (especially the senior administrative cadre). In any of these cases the capacity of the state to function as a cohesive and leading force is weakened. As a result of this weakening of the state's capacity to manage its own affairs, powerful economic, social and political interests are directly threatened. Typically, even the beginnings of intra-state collapse precipitate countervailing trends in which interests are mobilized to reconstitute the state as a relatively cohesive force. If there are few examples in the modern age of states surviving without the support of powerful interests, there are also few examples of powerful interests surviving without a relatively cohesive state.

How will the British State be Studied in this Book?

For reasons which I hope are now becoming clearer, the focus of this book is on how the core institutions of the British state have sought to secure a degree of coherence on the rest of the state system since 1945. There are, of course, many other ways in which this state could have been studied but my intention was to avoid a descriptive narrative by posing an important and interesting analytical question which could drive the story forward. This book is not, therefore, simply a descriptive outline of the institutions of state. Pursuing the analytical questions raised in this Introduction allows us to understand the state in question rather better, whilst also providing insights into British politics more widely.

These questions take us into both general considerations of the post-war British state as a whole and also into more detailed examples and case studies. Inevitably, however, addressing the analytical questions posed has shaped the choice of material and examples. Some students may want more information on particular topics and I try to provide some guidance on this through the references to, and comments on, other texts. Other aspects arise only in relation to the key themes of the book. The territorial question in general, for example, and devolution in particular, are not addressed as issues in their own right but are dealt with as one aspect of more general problems of state management. Another aspect of the state not examined in this book is the coercive and security state. The role of the secret state, the evolution of policing and military strategies and the question of civil rights are put to one side in an account which focuses more on the social and economic functions of the state system. I am particularly aware that the absence of a territorial focus and lack of attention to the coercive agencies of the state mean that the question of the British state in Northern Ireland has not been addressed. However, I believe that the approach offered here provides a fruitful way into many of these aspects (including, as it happens, the territorial and coercive questions). I also felt the need to limit the number of theoretical debates entered into.

It might help to have a sense of the overall development of the argument to come. Stated in its most stark form it can be outlined in three brief statements.

1 After the Second World War the British state was rebuilt in a way which was not compatible with the wider objectives of the post-war settlement. It privileged interests and practices which inhibited the development of a progressive response to the growing problems of the 1960s and 1970s.
2 Despite a growing taste for public sector reform, the British state presented a barrier to effective crisis-management in the 1970s. This culminated in a determined attempt to re-engineer the state during the 1980s.
3 The reforms of the 'long decade' from the late 1970s to the early 1990s left an inherently unstable legacy which has provoked much agitation but failed to reconnect the state to the wider purposes of politics. What to do with the state remains a central, if insufficiently theorized, question facing British politics at the turn of the millennium.

Summary

At the more abstract level, we can say that the modern state is both a collection of institutions and an agency through which social relationships are organized. As a collection of institutions, it is constantly faced with the prospect of its own fragmentation and considerable energy is directed towards sustaining a degree of coherence across its different institutions. The price of failure in this respect would be the collapse of the state and with it the breakdown of those social relationships organized through it.

At the more substantive level, we can say that the way in which order is pursued and resisted within the state will be a driving force shaping the wider conduct of politics. States are connected or de-connected to wider politics not only through their external linkages but also through their internal organization. We will now look in more detail at these complex interrelationships in British politics since 1945, starting with the political settlement after the Second World War.

1

State Management and the Post-war Settlement

The purpose of this chapter is:

- to outline those main features of the post-war settlement which are relevant to the organization and management of the state;
- to examine the main institutional continuities and innovations within the British state following the Second World War;
- to consider the relationships between the internal organization of the state, the coupling of state agencies with non-state interests and the pursuit of the wider objectives of welfarism and full employment.

The Post-war Settlement

The 'post-war settlement' is a term used to describe the strategic choices which led all of the most powerful interests and organizations in post-war Britain to modify, accommodate and tolerate the main political institutions and policies of the British state after the war. (Detail on this process is provided in the following chapters.) This accommodation was to persist through to the 1970s. The key organized interests were:

- the Conservative and Labour Parties;
- employers and their representatives;
- trades unions and their organizations;
- the City;

- the media; and
- the 'Establishment' still dominant in the civil service, the Church and so forth.

The settlement is usually said to have had two pillars. These are Keynesian economic policies and a commitment to a universal welfare state. This 'package' is often called the 'Keynesian welfare state'.

The nature of this so-called settlement is the subject of both theoretical and historical debate. There is no need to assess this debate in detail here but it might be helpful to outline the broad areas of argument. First, was there a consensus? Supporters of the claim that there was a consensus point to the similarity of the main parties' manifestos and the policies of successive governments, the similarity of declared preferences amongst trades unions and employers' organizations, and broad public opinion data showing widely shared views on the means and ends of politics (see Addison, 1975; Kavanagh, 1992). Others point to continuing areas of profound disagreement over the creation of the welfare state and the implementation of Keynesian economic policies and emphasize that when action was required to support broad agreements it was often not forthcoming (Pimlott, 1989). One of the few areas of agreement currently (reflecting an interesting change of historical perspective) is that if there was a consensus, then it was probably a bad thing, worsening Britain's decline and inhibiting a realistic focus on Britain's problems (see, for example, Marquand, 1988; Middlemas, 1986, 1990, 1991).

For our purposes, it is important to note that the Keynesian welfare state brought with it a range of new agencies and ways of thinking about welfare and economic intervention. In economic policy, industries such as coal, railways and the Bank of England were nationalized. The Treasury was given a new responsibility to manipulate overall levels of demand through a judicious use of public spending, through manipulating the cost and form of state credit, and through the taxation system. In welfare, not only were local governments given new or extended responsibilities for areas such as child protection and housing, but central government also took over much greater powers when the National Health Service (NHS) was established, an extended system of social insurance and social security was created, and the school-leaving age was raised to fifteen. In principle, there was a commitment to provide basic security for citizens and to equip all citizens with the basic resources required to participate as equal members of society.

Constructing these commitments required not only new agencies but also new public sector discourses. Plans for the NHS were to be underpinned by a more sophisticated epidemiology, educationalists were to construct strategies for combating ignorance, national insurance required a wider use of actuarial calculations, new economists versed in Keynesian arguments were required in the Treasury, and accountancy systems had to be developed to cope with the expansion of purposes and ways of spending. New management techniques were required to handle the new types of public sector employee and (slowly) judicial instruments and legal mechanisms were to be adapted to provide a legal framework within which the expanding public sector could operate. To understand the impact of this on state management, we can put to one side some of the major debates on the post-war settlement (although these are addressed in passing). Shortly we will focus on the core of the British state which was to have ultimate responsibility for managing the newly emerging state system. Before this, however, we briefly consider the international context of which the British state was a part.

The International Context

The international context matters for state management in at least two ways. In the first place there is a clear, if complex, relationship between external supports and challenges facing a nation and the internal organization of its state. Thus the various international contexts within which states first industrialized were associated with different linkages between state and economy and with different styles of state management. Perhaps most obviously, different international contexts are associated with the military playing greater or lesser roles within the state (the military was not only an important source of ideas about how to manage a state in the early stages of state formation but it also often provided key state officials). The existence of empires, for example, produced a cadre of officials with administrative experiences which they frequently brought back to the imperialist state. In the second place, states actively learn from one another and this is especially true in the field of state management. For a hundred years from the 1880s onwards, official reports in Britain looked first most often to Germany, later to France then Sweden enjoyed official attention for a while but more recently they have looked especially to the US. That the proposed reforms often ignored the peculiar national circumstances which made a particular national administrative approach work, does not detract from the significance of this sort of learning.

Of relevance to us here is that in the second half of the nineteenth century the civil service in Britain emerged in a unique international situation. The external supports which Britain's international position provided by empire, treaty and economic relationships provided the context within which a broadly *laissez-faire* approach could persist. Most other European states had actively to lead the modernization and industrialization of their nations and this produced a different type of senior administrator. Furthermore, occupation or military defeat forced other European nations to radically reconsider their state forms (and with it state management) in the twentieth century. This was a painful luxury which was denied to the British. It left a legacy in the culture of the post-war British politico-administrative elite of three main things:

1 keeping options open;
2 responding to individual problems with specific policies rather than providing a general framework for future action;
3 a general preference for incremental over radical change.

These preferences, we will argue in future chapters, were largely insulated from the sorts of pressure which might have driven forward changes by the particular set of circumstances after the war. This is to get ahead of the argument, however, and we should briefly consider why Britain's international position facilitated the persistence of such a 'mind-set'.

Economically, benefits were maximized by trading first with European countries prior to their industrialization and then, when they were in a position to compete effectively, switching towards the Empire and (later) the Commonwealth. The pursuit of 'easy pickings' was in many ways a rational strategy for British exporters to pursue in the short run but in the long run it created an economy which did not compete with the best. Satisfactory rates of growth and enough revenue to run an empire could be sustained without the more positive role by the state seen in most other industrializing nations. Evidence of this shift into the markets of the Empire can be seen in table 1.1.

Whilst exporters were shifting their attention to the relatively protected environment of the Empire, Britain was simultaneously offsetting a growing negative balance of visible trade with overseas investment earnings and invisible trade (see Mitchell and Deane, 1962, pp. 333–5; quoted in Leys, 1989, p. 19).

Table 1.1 Shares of major British exports going to empire markets, 1870–1934 (%)

	1870	1880	1890	1900	1913	1929	1934
Textiles	26.6	36.8	37.2	39.9	43.9	42.2	
Iron and iron goods	21.7	31.2	33.5	36.1	48.2	51.4	55.3
Machinery	19.0	18.3	24.6	22.3	32.5	43.5	51.2
Locomotives	16.0	67.5	27.8	49.5	58.6	43.8	65.3

Source: Schlote (1952, pp. 166–7); quoted in Leys (1989, p. 19)

These figures suggest that not only was British manufacturing avoiding the competition of the most advanced economies but also the economy as a whole was increasingly kept afloat by income from foreign investment earnings. The Second World War had a direct impact on this situation. First of all, income from overseas investment was slashed as most foreign-held assets were lost or liquidated. Secondly, although the extent of Britain's technological backwardness is a matter of some debate (see Barnett, 1986, for the case for the prosecution) the war undoubtedly increased the gap between the US and the UK. The increase in output during the war was achieved by using existing technologies and work-place organizations more intensively rather than adopting new technologies and processes. Thirdly, the Commonwealth countries increasingly looked elsewhere for their goods. The practical expression of this was the massive external deficit during the 1945–51 period and the 'dollar gap' in particular. In 1938, Britain's output per head stood at 90 per cent of the US equivalent. By 1948 it had slumped to just 51 per cent (see Warner, 1995, p. 99; Woytinsky, 1953, pp. 389, 392). With hindsight we can see that, economically at least, Britain would have to compete in Europe or face bankruptcy.

Despite this, the post-war Labour government sought to prop up its supposed 'special relationship' with the US and its links with the former Empire and Commonwealth. It gave at least as much priority to these as to Europe in its thinking. This was largely a consequence of a calculation that the USSR was a significant threat to European peace and stability and that only the US was in a position to balance this threat. But it was also based on a deeper suspicion of the institutions and practices of continental Europe which – according to the logic of the time – had led to fascism or military defeat whilst the

British and American Anglo-Saxon way had led to a remarkable focusing of national energies on the war effort and the New Deal (in the US) and welfarism (in the UK) (see Middlemas, 1993, p. 16).

One consequence of this attitude towards continental Europe was a reluctance to accept that Britain's future was as a European nation rather than as a world power. There were good reasons for this (in addition to simple-minded anti-European sentiment). Whilst withdrawal from India had long been envisaged and was widely regarded as inevitable, Britain still had substantial areas of influence across the Middle East and Africa potentially providing supplies of raw materials (in particular oil) and expanding markets. It still had a powerful military force, setting it apart from other European nations and involving it in a distinct (if not 'special') relationship with the US. For the time being, closer ties with Europe offered neither economic opportunities nor a military alliance capable of addressing the perceived Russian threat.

Britain in 1945 was therefore placed in an unusual situation by its position in the global market and emerging international security system. There were strong military and economic factors pushing strategists toward the US and the Commonwealth in the short run but these choices inhibited the development of a coherent response to Britain's long-term future in Europe. Meanwhile, victory and the trappings of world power weakened the small chorus of voices asking for a more radical look at British institutions.

The international context in 1945, then, provided both a legacy of values and assumptions sedimented in the core of the British state, and an immediate set of circumstances which inhibited a decisive response to the changed realities of Britain's global position. Energies and resources which should have been directed towards securing the success of the domestic post-war settlement were therefore dissipated. Worse still, the cultural assumptions, of which world leadership was one part, were allowed to persist. To understand how this happened more fully we must look at the core institutions of the British state, the civil service and the statutory framework within which they operated.

The Core Institutions in the Post-war Settlement

As indicated in the Introduction, by the 'core institutions' of the state we mean those parts of the state system which are responsible for developing overall policy objectives and ensuring that the activities of particular state agencies fit with these objectives. Obviously, we may find that core institutions are only partially successful in this project and it cannot be assumed that, by definition, all states have competent cores. What we can assume, following the comments made in the Introduction, is that a progressive breakdown of the state system is typically associated with strong political pressure to strengthen the core.

In the British case, the 'core' is usually taken to involve the Cabinet/ senior civil service nexus (and the Prime Minister/Treasury nexus within that). This core provides political direction and administrative co-ordination. Within this core the dominant force has tended to be the Treasury (particularly when it is not opposed by the Prime Minister). To understand how the core changed after the Second World War, and more importantly how it did not change, it would be helpful to glance briefly at the background of the civil service prior to 1945.

The Civil Service in 1945

Prior to the 1850s the core administration of the state was carried out in a haphazard manner by a mixture of politicians' friends, competent careerists and people who could find no other source of gainful employment. There were at least two reasons why this situation came to be regarded as untenable; the first was a nationalist and techno-cratic claim that it was damaging the efficiency of the whole nation, and the second was the perceived need to put the running of the country in 'safe hands' prior to the inevitable arrival of democracy.

These concerns found their expression in the Northcote-Trevelyan Report of 1854 which shaped the massive subsequent growth of the state's administration after 1870. According to Leys, this was 'probably the most rapid peacetime expansion in its history (before or since)' (Leys, 1989, p. 280) He goes on to note that in 1873 there were some 55,000 employees in the central civil service. By 1914 there were 280,000 (figures from Smellie, 1950, pp. 162, 328). The Northcote-Trevelyan Report suggested at least six things which were to shape the civil service until the latter part of the twentieth century. Dowding, (1993, pp. 236–7) helpfully summarizes these as:

1 The civil service should be divided between superior and inferior posts according to intellectual and mechanical tasks.

2 Entry into the civil service should be for young men who are then trained 'on the job'.
3 Recruitment should be on merit based upon competitive examination overseen by an independent central board.
4 The examinations should be based upon the arts (rather than the sciences) and for the superior positions be on a par with university education.
5 All promotion should be on merit.
6 The civil service should become less fragmented and allow individuals to move from department to department and be given a more uniform pay structure.

By 1914 three grades of civil service had emerged the 'Intermediate class' being added to the First and Second Divisions in 1912. Recruitment to the First Division was strongly geared towards a public school/Oxbridge intake. This was Britain's response to the problem of how to recruit an administrative cadre capable of managing an increasingly complex state which also had sufficient cultural, political and social cohesion. Rather than being unified by specialist schools of administration, conspicuous privileges or military-style titles, the British civil service elite was unified by its shared background, shared objectives, shared clubs and shared culture of being 'good chaps'. The problem of the supply of recruits to the Intermediate class was partially solved by the extension of the public school ethos to the growing grammar school sector. This pattern of recruitment was broadly the same for both the military and the judiciary.

The style of management associated with this is well described by Norman Chester, a dominant academic figure in post-war public administration who was also a member of the wartime civil service. Along with most other observers and practitioners, he was deeply impressed by the importance of personal contacts and shared values. Characteristic features of a system can often be most clearly seen when it is under stress, and this is true of the British style of state management during the Second World War. Describing these wartime circumstances, Chester wrote:

> The formal apparatus of communication was the minutes of the committee meetings from the War Cabinet downwards; and in addition when Mr Churchill was Prime Minister, a series of directives. But the most effective method was the close personal contact which existed between a comparatively small number of Ministers and civil servants – permanents and temporaries. From their daily attendance at this or that

committee they took back to their departments the current attitude. By lunching, dining or even breakfasting together, during the long days worked during the war they not merely kept in touch with what was happening . . . but also developed a corporate thought which was more effective than any series of minuted decisions . . . Notwithstanding the vastness of the machine and the many stages which might have to be gone through before a decision could be reached, it could be galvanised into sudden action or the course of policy dramatically changed by the actions of a comparatively small number of people. In the sphere of general economic policy there were probably twenty to fifty people in Whitehall who, if their views coincided, could do almost anything. (quoted in Hennessy, 1993a, p. 44)

Civil servants believed that they were part of the insiders' club – the Establishment as it came to be called in the 1950s – and that it was their right, indeed their duty, to ensure that their values and assumptions found their way into the policies of the elected government of the day, and into the administrative practices of the public sector as a whole. The 'soft' systems of culture and values were as important as the 'hard' structures of formal rules and institutional structures. As Sir Edward Bridges, then head of the Home Civil Service, could write in 1950:

> It is . . . precisely on broad issues [of policy] that it is the duty of a civil servant to give his Minister the fullest benefit of the storehouse of departmental experience; and to let the waves of the practical philosophy of the Department wash against the ideas put forward by his political master. (Bridges, 1950, p. 19; quoted in Elcock, 1991, p. 6)

This view is not an expression of the formal role of the civil servant, and Elcock is surely right to ask 'at what point waves washing against Ministerial wishes begin to wash over them' (Elcock, 1991, p. 6). Did these values conflict with the values of the incoming Labour government?

Morgan (1984, p. 92) insists that the civil service and its values were no barrier to the Labour government. Indeed, Attlee told the House of Commons in 1948 that the civil service behaved with 'exemplary loyalty' (see Fry, 1986, p. 540). Morgan included the civil service within the wider institutional matrix of the Press, the City, the House of Lords and the monarchy and concluded that '(T)he general view that emerges, then, is of the institutional framework of the time, both in terms of internal party cohesion and external structural restraints, as being generally favourable to Attlee's government at the start of its tenure of power'. (Morgan, 1984, p. 92). It is, however, worth contrasting this with the view of Hennessy, who describes Lord Plowden and his Central Economic Planning Staff as 'management consultants to the existing way of doing things' and insists more broadly that in 1945 'we simply lacked the institutional infrastructure for the modern state' (Hennessy, 1993b, pp. 7, 10). Similarly, Keith Middlemas argues that by 1945:

> at the level of the machinery of government, the questions of how decisions would be made and by whom had ceased to be a matter for discussion . . . The state apparatus bequeathed to the Labour government of 1945–51 was not only susceptible to amendment; it contained within itself a blueprint for economic management intrinsically hostile to the decisions of the 1944 Labour Party conference and to the spirit if not the letter of Let Us Face the Future. (Middlemas, 1986, p. 111)

This is a claim which we evaluate more fully in future chapters but it is clearly of central importance to an analysis of the post-war British state. However, Middlemas's claim goes beyond the concern with the so-called 'soft' features of the values and cultures dominant in the core of the British state. It is also concerned with the institutions of the state and their articulation with each other. Alongside the bureaucratic structures of the civil service was a statutory and legal framework which was to structure the operation of the post-war British state.

The Statutory and Legal Framework

It is a characteristic of liberal states that they establish legal limits to their own action which, if transgressed, may be challenged by their citizens and other legal subjects. If the new public organizations were to create greatly increased state capacities to influence and condition the life of its citizens, we might expect this newly extended state power to be hedged around by new and appropriate legal instruments. Without this, one important mechanism for shaping and managing the operations of state agencies would be undermined.

The debate in Britain over how best to regulate the expanding public sector was already well developed by the 1920s, especially in relation to the possible benefits of the development of administrative law. Robson (1928), for example, pressed the case in favour of a system of administrative law. As Hayek expressed it a little later on:

The very idea of separate administrative courts . . . came to be regarded in England . . . as the denial of the rule of law. Thus, by his attempt to vindicate the rule of law as he saw it, Dicey in effect blocked the development which would have offered the best chance of preserving it. He could not stop the growth in the Ango-Saxon world of an administrative apparatus similar to that which existed on the continent. But he did contribute much to prevent or delay the growth of institutions which could subject the new bureaucratic machinery to effective control. (Hayek, 1960; quoted in Graham and Prosser, 1988, p. 17)

Others took a contrary view, with Lord Hewart in the 1920s insisting that administrative courts would break down the separation of powers by combining executive and judicial functions.

Much toil and not a little blood have been spent in bringing into being a polity wherein the people make their laws and independent judges administer them. If that edifice is to be overthrown, let the overthrow be accomplished openly. Never let it be said that liberty and justice, having been with difficulty won, were suffered to be abstracted or impaired in a fit of absence of mind. (Hewart, 1929, pp. 16–17)

Behind each side of the argument, in their different ways, is the difficulty of applying a nineteenth-century conception of the role of law to the conduct of a twentieth-century state. This 'classical' form of legal regulation of the state involves any member of the public using the courts to circumscribe the actions of public bodies. Particular legal devices intended to achieve this in the British system include injunctions, declarations and three prerogative orders described by Greenwood and Wilson as '*certiorari* (which removes decisions of administrative authorities, tribunals or inferior courts to the High Court for review); prohibition (which requires a public body to desist from unlawful – *ultra vires* – acts); and *mandamus* (issued by the High Court, which compels public bodies to perform their statutory duties)' (Greenwood and Wilson, 1984, pp. 240–1).

In Britain, as elsewhere, the expansion of the state posed a growing problem for this form of regulation. The courts came to be seen as too expensive, time-consuming, formal and inaccessible to resolve the growing variety of disputes between the private citizen and public agencies. One way of managing this problem would have been to give the minister greater powers to settle such disputes (as, for example, the Home Secretary can do in certain disputes over immigration) but this has generally been seen as undesirable both because government ministers would become overburdened and because the executive would often be resolving disputes to which it was a party. In practice, therefore, this problem has increasingly been managed through the use of tribunals whose piecemeal development continued throughout most of this century. The Labour governments of 1945–51 did little to alter the course of this development and it was not until the 1950s that the question of administrative tribunals was again directly addressed.

Like the dog that didn't bark, the importance of this lies in what did not happen rather than what did. The absence of a clear legal framework capable of regulating the operations of the state as a whole meant that the law played a less important (but not trivial) role in managing intra-state relationships within the British state than was the case in, say, the US. Consequently, despite later attempts to use the law more forcefully, we must look for additional factors which conditioned the management of the post-war state. These factors can be studied at three levels.

Three Levels of Analysing the Core of the Post-war State

Morgan regards the absence of overt conflict between the incoming Labour government and the civil service as evidence of a wider harmony of interest. Similarly, Addison maintains that a shift took place during the war which was both significant and largely consensual (Addison, 1975). Middlemas, on the other hand, is concerned to show that interests competed within the state, and that these conflicts influenced the trajectory of policy in the post-war period. Furthermore, for Middlemas at least, these conflicts were expressed not only through overt conflicts between self-conscious rivals, but also through the institutional form of the state itself. Particularly as it is expressed in *Power, Competition and the State, Vol. 1*, we are presented with an image of a state within which conflicting interests achieved a balance (rather than a more deep-seated agreement) which was to be increasingly disturbed from the 1960s onwards (Middlemas, 1986).

There are obvious methodological and theoretical differences between these two positions; the first focuses on the actions and conflicts amongst discrete, observable agents, whilst the second imputes interests to certain groups and asks 'under what circumstances could these interests be realized?' There might, for example, be a high level of interpersonal agreement but a low level of institutional congruency amongst a collection of organizations. In the latter case we might expect to find that even where individuals within a number of organizations can agree at a personal level, their organizations are ordered in such a way that it is difficult for one organization not to threaten the interests of neighbouring organizations when it pursues its own.

This points to the embedded nature of inter-organizational relationships (see Keohane and Nye, 1977) which are different from both the study of interpersonal relationships and what Jessop calls the '"societal" embeddedness of functionally differentiated institutional orders . . . in a complex, de-centred societal formation' (Jessop, 1996, pp. 6–7). In the approach pursued here we are interested in conflicts working at all three levels and, in particular:

- the values and culture of the core institutions and the wider state system;
- the ordering of relationships between organizations within the state and between state and non-state agencies;
- the relationships between the various functionally differentiated parts of the state system such as the judicial, financial, economic, and legitimizing functions.

Drawing on this three-fold typology to suggest an oversimplified hypothesis (which has yet to be properly evaluated), we might argue that in 1945 values and assumptions which had been dominant before the war re-emerged at the centre of the British state (despite the much-heralded arrival of the 'new Jerusalemists'). Secondly, external demands, political challenges and legal requirements were all insufficient to secure an organizational change within the core of the state compatible with the far greater complexity and differentiation of state organizations as a whole. Thirdly, the wider economic and social functions required of the state by the objectives of the post-war settlement were incompatible with the institutional orders of its economic and social agencies. Let us consider some of the evidence.

Power within the Expanded British State in 1945

Of particular importance in shaping the post-war state was the ability of the Treasury to dominate the wartime discussions about the shape of the future machinery of government (see Middlemas, 1986, p. 79). By November 1944 the Cabinet was prepared to put the Treasury at the centre of economic planning and management, albeit with responsibility for a more flexible taxation system and with new responsibilities in the market for state credit. Of equal importance was the fact that the Treasury also secured for itself the right to be the coordinator of public expenditure and public sector management more widely. Thus techniques of state management which had evolved to manage the bureaucratic and legal modes of calculation typical of the nineteenth century were called upon to manage an increasingly different state.

However, contrary to what may be imagined, this characteristic was not a mere oversight, an error on the part of the British Establishment to be swept away by a consensual programme of modernization, but a key part of the process through which that Establishment exercised power. The apparent archaism of the British state is not simply a consequence of benign neglect; it is part of a pro-active strategy in which institutions and practices were maintained because they condensed within them certain power relationships. Without such a strategy, new agencies, new interests and new people would have been brought into the core of the British state. Archaism, in this sense, was not a product of the stupidity of the British ruling class but of its tactical political skill.

A necessary part of the Treasury, regaining its administrative dominance after the war was that the state system should be brought under much firmer and more formal political control. During the war itself the focus on the war effort provided a normative basis for at least some unity of purpose amongst state agencies and officials (see Chester's comments above). Changes after the war included attempts to ensure that the newly extended parts of the state system (nationalized industries, the NHS and so forth) could all be kept under central control. The first step towards achieving this was taken when the Cabinet itself was brought more firmly under the direction of Prime Minister Attlee (see Hennessy and Arends, 1983).

In doing so, Attlee created 157 standing committees and 306 *ad hoc* committees organized in a pyramid with Attlee at its apex. Morgan sees this as a remodelling of the cabinet structure (Morgan, 1984, p. 49). However, such remodelling was limited to reorganizing the relationships between the Prime Minister and key individuals in and around the Cabinet. It was not a part of a more radical overhaul of the executive. There was no reconsideration of the relationship between the core and other state agencies. Thus, where new agencies were created such as the National Health Service and nationalized industries, they were grafted onto the existing core institutions.

However, through non-radical changes in accountabilities and relationships within the core, a degree of flexibility was created. It was sufficient to allow the revived Treasury-dominated structure to function but was insufficient to overcome the constraints of this essentially Victorian state. The most overt weaknesses of the pre-war system survived intact (for example, endemic secrecy, civil service anonymity, inadequate scrutiny of departments, weak individual rights for redress against maladministration and so forth). New weaknesses became apparent as the post-war years unfolded (the inability to intervene purposefully in the economy and society). As problems arose they were typically dealt with by attempting to modify existing practices or institutions.

This preference for fiddling enjoyed full expression in the 1946 Ministers of the Crown (Transfer of Functions) Act which gave the government the power to transfer functions across departments with just an order in council. The then assistant secretary to the Machinery of Government Committee later told Christopher Pollitt that this 'opened the gates' to painless structural change (see Pollitt, 1984). However, on the contrary as we shall see, in practice it was used to avoid structural change.

In conclusion, knowing what was implied by commitments to managing the economy and a greatly expanded welfare state, it is hard to believe that the senior civil service did not believe that there was a need for a fundamentally reorganized core and widespread public sector restructuring. Hennessy notes that, despite two meetings in May 1946 to discuss the future management and training needs of the civil service, the permanent secretaries rejected the idea of a new-style civil service to cope with the extended functions of the state (Hennessy, 1993a, p. 181). We have suggested, however, that, far from being inexplicable, the decisions taken by Bridges and his fellow mandarins were in one sense highly understandable. Hennessy assumes a high degree of technical rationality towards public sector change. We have suggested that selecting the most technically rational institutions is only one objective of state managers.

On the face of it, a determined Labour government willing to prioritize questions of the machinery of government had the opportunity for radical reform. However, it would have required a more radical political explosion than that registered at the ballot boxes of 1945 to have dislodged the key participants in the British state and these players were unlikely to give up power willingly. The pressures and constraints arising from the wider context help to explain why these players were not dislodged. To put a little more detail on these claims, we will examine first the expansion of welfarism and then the management of economic intervention.

Managing Welfarism

The nineteenth-century form of the British state involved all members of society (and especially those from the working-class) in only a limited relationship with the state. When they were so involved it was frequently in the formal setting of courts of law or the military. The knowledge required by the state of the population in general and of individuals in particular could therefore be kept to a high level of generality and a low level of detail. The collection of information and the compiling of data could be managed within the confines of the emerging discipline of statistics. Similarly, the fabric of daily experience required the average member of society to know little about the operation of the state.

The developments during and immediately after the Second World War helped to accelerate trends which changed much of this. Changes in social security, health, education, housing and the personal social services stood alongside the commitment to full employment to offer the individual protection against the 'five giants on the road to recovery' of the Beveridge Report. Famously, these were 'want, disease, ignorance, squalor and idleness' (HMSO 1942, p. 6). More than at any previous time in its history, the legitimacy of the British state was influenced by its ability to defeat these giants. The consequence of mobilization for total war was that social reform became as much a matter of national survival as the battlefields of the Second World War (see Cronin, 1991, p. 131). Marshall was not alone in believing that the development of the welfare state heralded a profound change in the relationship between the citizen and the state (Marshall, 1950). These ideological commitments found at least some expression in the main developments in welfare after 1945.

The Main Developments in Welfare 1945–1951

In this section we quickly glance over the main developments in welfare at this time before discussing their implications for the state in the following section. In the symbolism of post-war reconstruction, the Beveridge Report is a pivotal document. The Report which identified the five 'giants' (although sadly it did not slay them) was a combination of technical argument, populist slogans and sexist pomp

State Management and the Post-war Settlement

which captured well the spirit of the time. It committed the post-war government to a system offering workers insurance against illness, accident, old age and unemployment in return for a National Insurance contribution. The contributory element was fundamental, for Beveridge at least, because it underscored the reciprocal nature of the new citizenship. In return for participating as responsible citizens, the state would guarantee certain rights. The participants were to be men, women and children in their roles as workers, housewives and dependants respectively. Quite clearly the image uppermost in Beveridge's mind was one of fully employed males and their families.

Alongside National Insurance was to be a National Health Service. Beveridge emphasized in his Report that a successful social insurance system depended upon a coherent service of health care (as well as full employment). The idea of a state-led national system of health-care goes back to the pre-First World War Liberal government and it had been raised again by the Second World War coalition government. What proved controversial was Bevan's willingness both to take on the medical profession and challenge the existing decentralized management of the hospitals. The British Medical Association (BMA) fed the Conservative opposition as much ammunition as it could muster and it fought a continuing battle up to and even after the passage of the National Health Service Act. Bevan eventually won their grudging support through a combination of concessions, brinkmanship and (as he is rumoured to have said of the consultants) 'stuffing their mouths with gold'. In contrast to the argument that post-war change was largely consensual (see Addison, 1975), Webster argues that, for health at least, change was a product of conflict (Webster, 1988, 1991; Smith, 1995, p. 41). The medical profession's stubborn resistance was rewarded by an administrative system which left them, as a profession, broadly beyond the control of NHS management – at least for forty years.

With education policy, the leaderships of the two main parties were remarkably united. This may be because both parties had worked closely together during the passage of the 1944 Education Act (especially over securing the non-religious aspects of the Act) and the leadership of both parties appeared to accept a tripartite secondary system and its corollary that children could be examined after primary education and then despatched to three distinct types of secondary school. Perhaps the consensus was aided by the strong representation of public and grammar school products on both sides of the House. The Labour manifesto pledge in 1945 committed it only to introducing the Act as quickly as possible and to raising the school-leaving age. The debate over comprehensive education was not to build up a head of steam until the 1950s.

The manifesto was much more forceful in its commitments to housing and these were reinforced by Bevan's promises. It would have been a problematic brief for any minister because of shortages of both labour and raw materials, but the Conservative opposition delighted in their attacks on Bevan remembering well his many verbal assaults on their party and its members. Bevan's approach was that the assault on the housing shortage should be publicly led (and not led by the speculative builder), centrally funded and administered through local authorities. In addition, he insisted that council housing should be of a standard that would be attractive to all members of society:

> We should try to introduce in our modern villages and towns what was always the lovely feature of English and Welsh villages, where the doctor, the grocer, the butcher and the farm labourer all lived in the same street. I believe that it is essential for the full life of a citizen . . . to see the living tapestry of a mixed community. (Foot, 1975, p. 76; quoted in Hill, 1993, p. 37)

The final aspect of the welfare state was the least widely discussed at the time; the development of the personal social services. The Children Act of 1948 gave the Home Office the overall responsibility for children's services, and it gave local authorities the responsibility for delivering these at the local level. The National Assistance Act also gave local authorities responsibility for providing residential homes for older people but it does not appear to have been envisaged that these functions should be unified within a social services department. This development had to await the arguments for a generic social work function in the 1950s and 1960s. The final piece of legislation which was to influence the development of the personal social services was the National Health Act which gave local authorities responsibility for providing home help services.

Social Citizenship and the Developing State–Society Relationship

The changes outlined above were intended to bring about a new set of relationships between the state and society. To only a very small degree did the incoming Labour government actively mobilize support for these measures. These policies reflected the pre-existing wartime mobilization of the population (see Anderson, 1992, p. 163) and, as Hay points out, they usually reflected the least radical currents of popular opinion (Hay, 1996, p. 31). Even so, they produced a significant and lasting shift in the relationship between the state and civil society and one which was to have lasting implications for the problems of state management.

Predominantly bureaucratic or legalistic ways of managing that relationship were no longer sufficient. To put it simply, when the citizen asks a state official 'why?', the bureaucrat answers that the rules must be followed, the judge says that the law must be obeyed, but the welfarist must answer 'because it's good for you'. The 1945–51 social policies therefore involved the state in sanctioning a whole new set of calculations and values. State agencies demanded and secured vast new sources of data about the population. Medical or educational knowledge was used to legitimize one set of policies or another and their very presence within the state sanctioned their power still further. Professionals from environmental health officers to town planners were authorized to take more and more decisions on behalf of the public and in pursuit of public 'welfare'. Obviously, this professional logic does not begin in 1945 but it does become a far more important source for both legitimizing state action and conditioning it. Morgan and Evans maintain that, despite the relatively unchanged social backgrounds of the elite groups in society,

> something had changed with the war. The idea of 'citizenship' promoted within the armed forces and on the home front expressed a qualitative change in relations between individuals and the state. Official pamphlets, broadcasts and the activities of the wartime Army Bureau of Current Affairs emphasised reciprocity and fairness, decency and trust which caught and endorsed the current mood. The state at war was a moral as well as a legal entity; its legitimacy was based upon a consensus of patriotic sentiments and common aims. (Morgan and Evans, 1993, p. 61)

This new relationship with civil society, we should note, was one which both returned women to their subordinate pre-war position (see Summerfield, 1993, p. 69) and one which excluded the bulk of the population (and women in particular) from decisions about the planning and delivery of welfare. But to return to the particular question of state management, as the state took on responsibility for the welfare of its citizens in new and extended ways, it required new forms of knowledge in order to act. This included a substantial extension of the state's data collection activities in policy areas such as health, education, the skills of the workforce and housing. Interpreting the data and identifying causal relationships also required the state to develop new patterns of recruitment and training. New forms of calculation increasingly rubbed against the older legalistic and bureaucratic discourses which, in turn, resisted by seeking to bureaucratize or juridify social policies. In some places they (broadly) kept incipient professionals at bay (as with social workers) whilst in others they had to accept many defeats (as with health) until the 'new managerialism' of the 1980s and 1990s provided them with (only partially successful) new technologies of control (see ch. 6).

If governments only had to worry about managing the new agencies of intervention they would have had difficulties enough, but the qualitative changes in the relationship between the state and society also provided the basis for new forms of political mobilization and pressure group activity. Especially where these pressure groups had information or other resources which the state lacked, or could obtain only with difficulty, pressure groups in the field of welfare often found themselves on the inside of the policy process rather than pressuring it from the outside. Alternatively, the state may benefit from 'legitimate' charities and pressure groups sanctioning interventions which might otherwise be challenged (in child-care cases, for example). In this way new inter-organizational policy networks emerged amongst professionals, bureaucrats and pressure groups, and these gave rise to a growing tendency to conduct politics outside the parliamentary process. As we shall see, managing these new relationships, given the core state agencies and culture operating in the 1940s and 1950s, was to become an increasingly haphazard and desperate business.

Managing Growth and Full Employment

The 1944 White Paper on Employment is to post-war economic policy what the Beveridge Report is to post-war welfare: one of the central symbols of the post-war settlement. It therefore repays the effort of looking at the circumstances of its production with some care. Its contents were neatly summarized by officials from the Reconstruction Committee in an outline produced for Churchill immediately before the White Paper's publication (Public Records Office, CAB 124/214; quoted in Hennessy, 1993a, pp. 186–7). It is worth quoting this in full:

1 Government accept responsibility for maintenance of high and stable level of employment after the war.
2 *First condition* to be satisfied: maintenance of total national expenditure, both by investors and consumers, at high level.
3 Means of satisfying this first condition:
    (a) Varying the rate of interest.
    (b) Timing of public investments to offset swings in private investment.
    (c) Raising when trade is brisk (and reducing when trade slackens) rate of weekly social insurance contributions, without impairing actuarial basis of new insurance scheme.
    (d) Deferred income tax credits (payable in times of depression) might also be used.
    (e) Balancing Budget over period of years, but not necessarily each year.
4 *Second condition*: stability of prices and wages and avoidance of inflation, by means of
    (a) Moderate wage policy (responsibility of employers and organised labour).
    (b) Industrial policy of expanding output, not increasing prices (chiefly responsibility of private enterprise).
    (c) Cost of living subsidies, on certain conditions.
5 *Third condition*: mobility of labour to be achieved by
    (a) Individual initiative and adaptability.
    (b) Training and re-settlement schemes.
    (c) Divorce of unemployment benefit from training allowances.
    (d) Availability of low rented houses.
6 *Fourth condition*: balanced distribution of industry, to maintain employment in 'development areas' (pre-war 'special areas' policy to be superseded), by means of
    (a) Influencing location of new factories and factory extension.
    (b) Policy regarding munitions' factories and Government contracts.
    (c) Government erection of factory premises for smaller firms.
    (d) Financial assistance by Government.
7 *Transitional Period:* measures
    (a) to forestall danger of unemployment resulting from switchover from war to peace production;
    (b) to ensure priority for essential needs (eg exports);
    (c) to prevent inflation.
8 *Machinery* for applying policy:
    (a) Better statistics and other information from private enterprise.
    (b) Small central staff to interpret facts and figures.
    (c) Annual Capital Budget of total national investment.
    (d) Complementary Man-Power Budget.

Behind this apparently straightforward set of commitments lay some bitter disputes. The Treasury was not won over to the idea of using public works as a form of demand management and they remained much more reluctant than the Cabinet Office's Economic Section to accept that budget deficits should be used to combat unemployment. Based on a careful consideration of official sources and diaries, Hennessy is persuaded that the 'rearguard action' against Keynesianism was continuous, even after the 1941 'Keynesian' budget (Hennessy, 1993b, pp. 8–9).

Worse still, whilst it was widely acknowledged that there were fundamental problems with the economic settlement after the war, these were left largely unresolved. For example, there was a recognized conflict between full employment policy and wage stability but the response to this was little more than hopes that reasonable behaviour from the trades unions might resolve this impasse. In a parallel example, whilst training was accepted as crucial to the objective of labour mobility (and therefore of securing growth) it was simultaneously accepted that the employers' 'right to manage' should free them from any obligations under a national training system. Similarly, the Labour government sought the cooperation of employers in pursuit of growth and modernization with the introduction of Development Councils. However, employers neither supported this initiative nor suggested any alternative means of achieving shared objectives. Writing on the subject of Development Councils, Mercer argues that '(H)aving few coherent policies themselves, either for an overall industrial policy, or for the future of individual industries, businessmen simply defended the status quo against the "big black cloud of nationalization" and against any other policies which, in their eyes, were half-way houses to nationalization, or challenged industrial self-government' (Mercer, 1991, p. 72).

The point is not simply that the 1944 White Paper was flawed but that many of the officials contributing to its production knew it to be flawed (see Hennessy, 1993a, pp. 186–90). For example, the anti-statist sentiment of British employers is less surprising than is the production of a White Paper which pretends to the contrary. Most later historians agree with the contemporary view that the White Paper was inadequate. Middlemas sees the White Paper as an outcome of the rivalry of different interests within a broadly corporatist framework (Middlemas, 1986, ch. 3) whilst Morgan comments that 'compared with the expectations aroused, [the White Paper] was a timid and unenterprising document. It was disappointing to Keynesian economists, and progressive Conservatives in the Tory Reform group as well as to the Labour Party' (Morgan, 1984, p. 22). How was it possible to produce such an important document that was so flawed, and what does this tell us about the management of the British state?

Part of the answer to this question is suggested when we remember that the purpose of the White Paper was to maximize agreement rather than to stimulate a serious discussion about how best to achieve growth, low prices and full employment. At one level, the deliberate suppression of critical points and the avoidance of difficult questions emerge from this example as features of the civil servants' art. The 'club culture' which allowed the British Establishment to respond quickly and cohesively in certain situations (especially where there were few conflicts of interest) also encouraged an inability to do anything which might threaten the rules of the game. What held the senior civil service together culturally was not that they all agreed (contemporary records make it clear that they did not) but that disagreements produced compromises in which, as far as possible, no particular interests lost out.

At another level, however, the White Paper is an expression of the conflicting (and often contradictory) nature of organized interests in Britain in 1944 as these were understood by senior civil servants. They wanted to set a consensual agenda for post-war economic reconstruction and they did this by ignoring the most difficult problems. The dire circumstances of the immediate post-war situation may explain this and, indeed, justify it in the short term. In the long term it produced a style of economic management which was more concerned with conflict-avoidance than with conflict-resolution, and more concerned with evading problems than addressing them.

The post-war management of the state thus reflected both the preferences of the politico-administrative leadership and the wider context of unresolved conflicts and contradictions amongst organized interests. The fact that this managerial style was never challenged was to become a Trojan horse for British social democracy. The style itself was not an accidental aberration. On the contrary, it was an inherent part of the state system in Britain. Politicians and senior civil servants appear to have embraced contradictions and inconsistencies rather than face a wholesale restructuring of the core of the state and its relationships with organized interests. In the short run at least, neither politicians nor civil servants saw a significant advantage in creating new structures to reflect the changed role of the state. Indeed, to change a relatively small thing, such as, for example, ministerial responsibility (according to which a minister is responsible for everything happening in his or her department), would immediately have raised fundamental constitutional questions to which there were no easy answers. The paradox of an unwritten constitution is that it can create great inflexibilities where a small formal change (making civil servants more accountable, for example) quickly becomes a constitutional problem (without ministerial responsibility the key *formal* constitutional mechanism for securing parliamentary control over the executive is lost).

Nationalization

Full employment and the 1944 White Paper were only one part of the economic strategy of the incoming Labour government. Another was nationalization and the mixed economy. The lack of preparedness of the incoming Labour government for this task is well known. It is often argued that no clear plans existed, and the form of nationalization subsequently adopted has usually been explained as a consequence of Morrison's influence who, in turn, drew on his experiences in the London County Council and the London Passenger Transport Board.

This explanation is not entirely convincing. In the first place, as Hennessy points out, far from one 'Morrisonian' model being introduced everywhere, a wide variety of forms of public ownership were adopted (compare the Bank of England, the British Electricity Authority and the London Port Authority, for example), and Hennessy quotes a leading civil servant working on nationalization with Morrison insisting that Morrison liked innovation and actively sought a variety of forms of nationalization (Hennessy, 1993a, p. 200). In the second place, the outcomes were neither as accidental nor as arbitrary as is often implied (despite the story of Shinwell rumaging around the files at Transport House in search of a blueprint). What all the nationalizations shared in common was their consonance with the existing forms of managing the state. They were based on the myth that it was possible to make the key strategic choices about the running of an extended state from an insulated core of institutions, serviced by 'good chaps', leaving the day-to-day activities up to (relatively poorly paid) administrators. Workers and consumers had no more real influence over the nationalized industries than they had over the earlier private companies (despite Labour Party commitments to the contrary) (see Cronin, 1991, p. 190). This also produced the formula that ministers were responsible for the long-term strategies of the nationalized industries whilst the industries themselves dealt with day-to-day problems. The sole positive thing to be said of such an arrangement was that it could easily be grafted onto the existing departmental structure of ministerial responsibility. It should come as no surprise that support for any extension of this form of public ownership had all but evaporated by 1951.

The general problem was one of establishing clear institutional mechanisms by which objectives could be set, achievements monitored and responsibilities assigned. These problems are highlighted by the fate of economic planning. We briefly mentioned the failure of the Development Councils and this failure was underlined at the national level by the failure of the tripartite Economic Planning Board to have any discernible impact on policy. Consequently, ministers stopped attending and the Board fizzled out. Its failure was because of the absence of effective machinery which might have linked strategic choices to changes at the point of production. The enormously difficult question of how to link strategic economic thinking to practical day-to-day action can never be fully resolved, but in Britain after the war it seemed to be a question which was wilfully avoided. Part of the reason for this lies with the peculiar nature of British corporatism.

Corporatism and the Post-war British State

In many ways, the post-war settlement required a degree of corporatism which it never got. Corporatism, at least in the sense used here, involves the institutionalization of the representatives of the main functional groups in society (unions and employers in particular) within public bodies in pursuit of the more or less clearly articulated economic interests of society as a whole. Corporatism was needed because the economic objectives suggested in the 1945 Labour Manifesto, and indeed the objectives of the 1944 White Paper on Employment, presupposed that employers and trades unions could be called upon to collaborate in a series of policies such as wage restraint, the introduction of new technology, the relocation of industry to areas of high unemployment, the training of the work-force and so forth. It was accepted that these were essential if Britain was to overcome its massive balance of payments deficit, since the only way to solve this in the medium term was to increase exports, and that increasing exports required the 'modernization' of industry. However, neither was the Labour government willing to use compulsion to achieve this 'modernization', nor was it able to secure the voluntary support of employers. By 1950, Harold Wilson, President of the Board of Trade, could say 'this problem of the relationship between Government and Private industry is almost a vacuum in Socialist thought' (CAB 124/1200, 4 May 1950; quoted in Mercer, 1991, p. 71).

This 'vacuum' was not monopolized by socialist thought. As we shall see in later chapters, when Conservative governments set themselves major goals, such as the pursuit of a trained and skilled workforce, they could do little without the active support of private employers. The post-war Labour government sought to create corporatist bodies capable of co-ordinating the work of the private sector in pursuit of 'modernization'. The fate of these bodies, and of Development Councils in particular, is well outlined by Mercer, who concludes that Labour's reluctance to challenge the private enterprise system 'prompted an inevitable reliance on voluntary and co-operative methods of control, an inability to compel, and the necessity for retreat in the face of opposition, and failure to sustain, therefore, "modernizing" programmes' (Mercer, 1991, p. 84).

If Labour's relationship with private employers was largely poor, then what of its relationship with the trades union movement? According to Tomlinson, '(I)f 1945 was the apogee of the Labour Party's electoral fortunes, it was also in the late 1940s that trade unions in Britain reached the peak of their influence' (Tomlinson, 1991, p. 90). He goes on to show how this power was broadly used in support of attempts to secure modernization.

However, there were real limits to the impact of the trades union movement. In the first place, corporatism necessarily involves a process of bargaining about common interests. If one side (the employers) associates the common interest exclusively with their own perceived sectional interests, and acts on this basis, then the willingness of the other side to make concessions will most likely diminish. This is largely what happened in the case of wage restraint, for example. In 1945 a significant section of the left within the trades union movement would have accepted the idea of a wages policy as part of an overall approach to planning for growth and recovery (see Tomlinson, 1991, pp. 93–4; Panitch, 1976, ch. 1). By 1948, demands for wage restraint had been divorced from any commitment to wider economic planning and consequently the left came into line with the more traditional and workerist commitment to free collective bargaining and the right to push wages as high as they could go. In the absence of either 'corporatist-minded' employers or a strong and determined state, trades unions had little to gain in return for a policy of wage restraint.

In the second place, if employers were reluctant to play the corporatist game, it was open to the trades union movement to become a modernizing force itself. However, this would have required organizational resources which were not available to the TUC. With a large number of crosscutting unions, with very limited central control over TUC members, with inadequate research and information facilities, the union movement could not play this role.

These are all relatively well-understood problems with British corporatism. Of particular interest to us, however, is the reaction of the British state to this situation. In France at the same time, where the institutional bases of corporatism were at least as weak, the state drew on a cadre of administrators who already adopted a pro-active approach and added to this supply with the creation of the *École Nationale d'Administration*. Following Monnet's leadership, the French state was to embark on a state-led process in which it would be the state which established the terms of the public interest and led the institutions designed to secure this interest. By contrast, the British state was reluctant to go far beyond creating the bodies within which sectional interests could arrive at a conception of the public interest through a process of bargaining; the 'public interest' under these conditions usually became the lowest common denominator amongst the competing groups. Very often, public officials saw no role for themselves in promoting a sense of the public interest and, indeed, with bodies such as the Anglo-American Council on Productivity, the Labour government appeared to support with enthusiasm the idea of bipartisan talks in the absence of the state.

One reason for the apparent timidity of the 1944 Employment White Paper noted above was that it was designed to produce something to which no one could object. Therefore, as Middlemas points out, it never addressed the problems of institutionalized self-interest, restrictive practices, resistance to investment and innovation, the reluctance of firms to seek out new markets or the inevitable problems of regional economies (Middlemas, 1986, p. 83). Similarly, David Marquand is surely right to lament the absence of a state able and willing to play a developmental, modernizing role (Marquand, 1988). It is important to note that this absence was not a result of the ignorance of the main participants; the problems identified here were all widely debated problems at the time and the authors of the White Paper would have been familiar with them (Middlemas, 1986, p. 83).

The explanation is not to be found in a sudden attack of amnesia but in the basic way in which the state viewed itself, managed itself and related to the two sides of industry. If there was a failure to develop such a state system it was because there was a gulf between what was required in the interests of a progressive welfarist capitalism and the interests of the dominant cadres of the state system. However, the preferences of the senior civil servants were supported by the values and strategic thinking of British employers. Whilst some sections of the trades unions may have advocated an alternative approach in the early stages of the post-war Labour government these became increasingly muted. Neither was the international context one which might have encouraged the application of financial, organizational and political resources to a state-led industrial growth project.

Conclusions

What does a state-focused account of the post-war settlement have to offer? It is clear that the key participants in the settlement (industrialists, trades unionists, the City and the politico-administrative elite) all wanted rather different things. They had conflicting views about the desirability of Keynesianism, about the appropriate extent and form of welfare and about Britain's international role. Not surprisingly, these differing views are represented variously within separate public agencies, and the state as a collection of agencies has no uniform set of values and purpose. Whilst such conflicting views found their niches within the state, the state system as a whole was clearly not neutral between them. The core of the state was recomposed around the pre-war Treasury-dominated model with a conception of the means and ends of politics which drew more from Victorian England than post-war Britain. As we shall see, this systematically privileged financial calculations over industrial calculations, the short term over the long term, the external deficit over domestic productivity, the bureaucratic over the professional, and the Establishment over other networks.

However, the state was not impassive in this process. It was not simply a 'sieve' which removed certain interests from the policy agenda and let others through. The structures and personnel of the state exerted their own independent influence on this process; interests have political effects primarily through being mediated and simultaneously transformed by state officials and state agencies. The creation of the National Health Service, for example, reflected not only the competing interests of the various groups involved but also the perceptions and values of key political and administrative figures involved. One characteristic of these calculations was a systematic preference for policies which left the core of the state as unchanged and unchallenged as possible. Where the logic of policy commitments required alternative agencies and policies (such as were required by the 1944 White Paper, for example) such implications were evaded. Objectives were obscured and men (and they were almost all men) who otherwise regarded themselves as hard-headed and pragmatic signed up to pious hopes and gentle exhortations. Given that such soft-headedness was reserved almost exclusively for the protection of the institutional *status quo*, we can draw our own conclusions.

State management was not only important for the immediate post-war years. The newly extended state was going to have to be managed. As new forms of intervention were introduced in pursuit of the fully employed, economically vibrant, welfarist society, new questions were to be asked of public sector management. As we shall see, these were to be questions to which the core of the British state had few answers.

Indeed, the leading politicians in 1945 were not greatly concerned with the creation of a restructured state. Morgan comments: 'The Attlee cabinet was essentially a cabinet of veterans, most of whom were in their sixties or even seventies. Their instincts were conditioned largely by the history of their party in which they themselves had often played significant roles (Morgan, 1984, p. 7). Indeed, the Labour Party had never shown a great deal of interest in how a socialist state would be managed. Concern with the nature of the state can be found in Cripps's *Where Stands Socialism Today?* (1933) which proposed a centralized socialist state. There were also grassroots demands for nationalization throughout the Labour movement, and the Socialist League's demands for centralized planning, but these were sporadic and often vague. Even these sporadic and vague demands began to dissipate as the 1930s progressed. This is in marked contrast, for example, to the active debates and thinking about how socialist strategy might be integrated with Keynesian economic arguments to deliver growth, full employment and social justice (see Hugh Dalton's *Practical Socialism for Britain*, 1935, Douglas Jay's *The Socialist Case*, 1937, and Evan Durbin's *The Politics of Democratic Socialism*, 1940).

The result was the failure to construct a form of state management which could facilitate and shape the emergence of a vibrant social democracy in Britain. In short, the British state in 1951 was managed in a way which was inherently damaging to the development of a social democracy. It lacked the necessary managerial culture, legal systems, financial controls and calculations. In this context, it is hard to escape Middlemas's conclusion that the men of the 1930s who had power in the 1940s 'saw in the reconstruction process a way to incorporate new methods, like tripartite consultation or demand management, as techniques to ensure stability without altering a more fundamental and ancient disposition of power' (Middlemas, 1986, p. 37).

Summary

The state at the centre of the post-war settlement in Britain was never one which could actively promote a productivist and welfarist strategy associated with successful social democracies. The so-called post-war consensus was significant and genuine but it was the product of a strategy of avoiding the most difficult questions. This strategy was actively promoted by those within the core of the state, thus securing for themselves continuing influence and power but fundamentally weakening the long-term prospects for the Keynesian welfare state.

2
State Management and Economic Policy from the 1940s to the 1970s

● ● ● ● ● ● ● ● ● ● ● ● ● ●

The purpose of this chapter is:

- to briefly explore the meaning of 'economic policy';
- to consider the implications of economic policy for the state in the context of both the international and the domestic economies of the 1940s–1970s;
- to explore these implications further through a closer look at the fate of economic planning and training policy in the 1940s–1970s;
- to begin an assessment of the role of the British state in the political economy of the 1940s–1970s.

What is 'Economic Policy'?

In the widest sense of the word, 'the economy' is the arena within which goods and services are produced, exchanged and consumed. This definition would obviously include the provision of services in the home (child care and cooking, for example) as well as the provision of social services such as education and health. In capitalist societies, however, it is conventional to define 'the economy' in terms of producers (who own the means of production and purchase labour) and consumers being brought together through markets and with the primary objective of producers making profits and purchasers satisfying perceived needs.

'Policy' is the pursuit of explicit or implicit objectives through the deliberate application of resources. It presupposes the belief that appropriate resources (financial, organizational, and so on) are available and that these resources can be systematically applied. Resources are needed both to monitor and, if necessary, to compel and reward. Each new policy therefore requires an adjustment of the state system. Without this, the state has a 'wish list' rather than a set of policies.

Arguably, the nineteenth-century state had such limited resources with which to influence interest rates, employment figures, growth and so forth that the term 'economic policy' can only be applied with some care. More arguable still is the claim that today governments must content themselves with governance, rather than policy, because all of the objectives which it hopes to secure can only be secured with the partnership of a variety of organizations. The skills of the strategist, accordingly, become more concerned with negotiation, trust and diplomacy. This claim will be considered in chapter 8 of this text.

The period under review, then, was a period in which public sector strategists believed that states had the necessary capacities to pursue economic policy objectives; it might be seen as a golden age of policy-making during which confidence in the capacity of the state to secure policy outcomes was greater than before or (probably) since. These economic objectives were, broadly, growth, price stability, full employment and a sustainable balance of payments. The potential instruments were: interest rate variations, counter-cyclical public investment programmes, counter-cyclical variations in taxation, counter-cyclical public borrowing, industrial policy, a wages policy, training and labour mobility systems and a regional policy. Each of these instruments required, at the very least, certain powers of compulsion and reward and the capacity to monitor outcomes.

There are two questions to be answered here. First, were these instruments sufficient to achieve the economic objectives of post-war governments? Second, was the core able to control the instruments in a way which was compatible with its economic objectives?

Economic Policies and the State

Economic engagement created particular problems for state management. For a start, the whole way in which calculations within the state were made began to change. The rise of economics as a social science discipline during the nineteenth century brought a new conception of the social world into the heart of the state. Over time, statistics transformed vague, often moralistic, impressions of product-ion and consumption into generalizable bases for economic policy-making. The increasing specialization of economic functions (both within civil society and amongst state agencies) brought differing calculations about the 'real economy' in different parts of the state system; industry, trade, monetary management, banking and so forth. This debate about the appropriate role for economic policy (if any) was raised to new levels of sophistication with the intervention of Keynes during the inter-war period, although had Keynes never put pen to paper, post-war economic policy would have developed in much the way that it did.

During the sixty years leading up to the Second World War, the relationship between economic success and the availability of a fit and skilled work-force was recognized. This required new calculations ranging from the definition and codification of skills and skills aquisition through to actuarial analyses for the purposes of National Insurance. Furthermore, accountancy developed in new and import-ant ways in the nineteenth century and increasingly sophisticated techniques redefined the economic world into discrete categories of current and capital, profit and loss, taxable and non-taxable and so forth in a way which both redefined past economic actions and shaped future actions. Taxation systems had to attempt to match the sophistication of these accounting techniques.

Being able to make calculations about the economy is not a suffi-cient condition for economic policy. A further condition is the exist-ence of state agencies, equipped with not only the necessary modes of calculation, but also the organizational capacities necessary to impact upon the 'real' economy. Both the modes of economic calculation and the institutions of economic intervention exert their own influence over economic policy. Chapter 1 outlined the re-emergence of the post-war state system with the Treasury at its heart. This contributed to both an institutional configuration and an economic discourse which not only reflected policy preferences of economic policy-makers but also constrained and shaped these choices. This config-uration inhibited some political strategies and supported others, privileged certain interests and marginalized others. In the following sections two aspects of economic management are considered sep-arately in order to provide a context for a discussion of state manage-ment and economic policy in post-war Britain.

Foreign Trade, Overseas Investment and the New International Order

In 1931 Britain came off the gold standard. The great advantage of the gold standard for national governments was that (in theory at least) it involved automatic stabilizers which obviated the need for government intervention (and therefore government policy). The theory went like this: if a country imported more than it exported, more gold would leave the country to pay for imports than came in as payment for exports. The net loss of gold would mean that the domestic money supply would contract (either because it was gold or because its quantity was linked to gold). As the amount of money in the domestic economy decreased, less money would chase the same number of goods and so prices would fall. Finally, if prices fell, then domestically produced goods would become relatively cheaper on the home market and overseas, exports would tend to rise, imports would fall and the imbalance of trade would rectify itself. In theory, therefore, the government of the day could safely avoid any direct involvement in foreign trade and consequently it would pose no problems for state management.

There were a number of reasons why this system broke down (one being that the quantity of money was not linked to gold and another being that prices were insufficiently flexible). However, whatever the reasons, the inter-war collapse of the international trading system encouraged a much more interventionist approach, and for much of the 1930s British governments adopted an active policy of managing foreign trade, including the use of tariffs to protect domestic industry from the slump. After the Second World War, a new international economic order was created. In the Conservative Party, in particular, the protectionists of the 1930s were defeated and a liberalized international trading order was embraced (not without a significant element of compulsion from the US). This was to pose problems for domestic economic management which were arguably more acute in Britain than elsewhere, but before considering these it might be worth briefly outlining how the new international settlement was supposed to work.

With the UK playing the role of junior partner, the US put together a system known after the place where the relevant talks took place: the Bretton Woods agreement. Under this system, the potentially disastrous situation where countries tried to 'out-devalue' other countries in order to increase exports and decrease imports should be replaced with a more stable system of exchange rates. If a country ran a mild deficit, it should be encouraged to resolve this by increasing exports rather than by decreasing imports. This would therefore stimulate a general expansion of demand in the international economy and this would 'fit' with domestic (Keynesian or not) full employment policies. Exchange rates should only be changed where a country showed signs of running a permanent deficit (or surplus), in which case it should be allowed to devalue (or revalue). For the US, who sponsored this new order, there were two advantages; first it would help to provide a degree of economic stability throughout the capitalist world and so limit the (alleged) Soviet threat, and second it would create a capitalist world open to US goods.

For Britain, the first implication of this liberal trading order was that it removed certain policy options. It meant that Britain could address its balance of trade problems neither by bilateral agreements with other countries nor by resurrecting a protected sterling free trade area with the countries of the Empire and Commonwealth. Yet the problems caused by importing more than was being exported were great and they demanded a policy response. During the war, only £6bn of its £16bn worth of imports had been paid for by exports (Tomlinson, 1992, p. 133), with much of the gap filled by lend-lease money from the US. In addition, massive debts had built up in countries such as Burma, Egypt and India where British troops had been deployed during the war. As we saw in chapter 1, a key characteristic and support of the pre-war British economy was that Britain was a creditor nation. However, by 1945 debts stood at £3.5bn and

Table 2.1 Balance of payments, current account, 1946–1952 (£m)

	Overall	With dollar area
1946	−230	−301
1947	−381	−510
1948	+26	−252
1949	−1	−296
1950	+307	−88
1951	−369	−436
1952	+163	−173

Source: Cairncross (1985, p. 201); quoted in Tomlinson (1992, p. 159)

debts were still as high as £2.5bn in the 1960s. As tables 2.1 and 2.2 show, the current account difficulties improved after the war but they did not go away altogether.

From these figures we can see why the so-called 'dollar gap' was so central to the post-war government's concerns (and also why Marshall Aid was so important). From table 2.2 we can see that the situation improved for much of the 1950s before worsening down to the devaluation of 1967.

Table 2.2 Balance of payments, current account, 1952–1973 (£m)

1952	+163	1963	+124
1953	+145	1964	−382
1954	+117	1965	−49
1955	−155	1966	+84
1956	+208	1967	−313
1957	+233	1968	−280
1958	+344	1969	+449
1959	+152	1970	+707
1960	−255	1971	+1,093
1961	+ 6	1972	+114
1962	+122	1973	−1,210

Source: Tomlinson (1990, p. 242); quoted in Tomlinson (1992, p. 159)

However, the improvement in the balance of payments current account should be placed in context. By 1950, there was every reason to suppose that Britain could exploit important and expanding markets where it appeared to enjoy a strong position. Interventionist policies in the 1930s and 1940s had produced some real benefits. 'Britain had a strong aerospace industry and a flourishing chemical industry, and was represented across the range of high technology manufacture – a partial recovery of the position that had been eroding since the 1870s' (Hutton, 1995, p. 130). The improvement in the 1950s, however, should therefore be contrasted with the comparatively greater improvements from other economies which, in 1950 were generally weaker (see tables 2.3, 2.4 and 2.5).

This relatively poor performance gave rise to the so-called stop-go policies of the 1950s in which an upturn in the economy was associated with an increased demand for imports, more imports led to a

Table 2.3 Volume indices of GNP at market prices (1953=100)

Country	1951	1955	1960
OEEC (average)	92	111	137
Germany	86	120	161
France	93	111	137
UK	96	108	121

Table 2.4 Volume indices of GNP per capita (1953=100)

Country	1951	1955	1960
OEEC (average)	94	110	129
Germany	87	117	148
France	96	109	128
UK	97	108	117

Table 2.5 General indices of industrial production (1953=100)

Country	1951	1955	1960
OEEC (average)	94	119	155
Germany	85	128	180
France	99	117	130
UK	98	114	130

Source: OEEC *Twelfth Annual Report,* Paris, 1961; quoted in Porter (1995, p. 20)

balance of payments crisis which in turn was followed by a dampening down of demand and an economic downturn. The deficit of 1960 shown in table 2.2, for example, prompted Lloyd's emergency measures intended to dampen down demand and inflation. The package included a 2 per cent rise in bank rate and a public sector pay pause. The intention was to hold down wage settlements below the level of productivity improvements and reflected the OEEC view that wage-cost inflation was undermining Britain's competitiveness (see Porter, 1995, p. 18). In other words, without government intervention, British industry was unable to maintain a balance of payments equilibrium if the level of domestic demand was sufficiently high to maintain full employment. The policies utilized reflected the paucities of both the agencies of intervention and the dominant calculations of the policy-makers (and, as we shall see, especially the former).

However, the cyclical nature of economic growth was not, in itself, a problem. The real problem was the lack of investment during the 'stop' phase and the failure to restructure and modernize the economy throughout the cycle. During the period 1953–60, industrial investment as a percentage of GDP was 8.9 per cent whilst in Germany the figure was 14.6 per cent (Middlemas, 1990, p. 13). Higher domestic investment in manufacturing would have expanded the productive base of the economy so that the following 'go' phase would be longer and stronger. However, as we shall see, the government lacked the sort of influence over investment decisions which might have facilitated this. The alternative policy would have been to use devaluation to boost the profits of exporters, who could then reinvest out of their additional profits and thereby improve their international competitiveness. This could then have provided the platform for export-led growth, creating the conditions for both full employment and a comfortable balance of payments. In the absence of such a policy, the UK's share of total exports of manufacturing goods fell from 20.9 per cent in 1953 to 15.9 per cent seven years later (Middlemas, 1990, p. 13). Why was this latter option not pursued?

Resistance to devaluation came from, amongst other places, the Bank of England. For the Bank, not only was there the danger that, as a debtor nation, uncertainty about the future of sterling might prompt Britain's creditors to call in their loans, but also the belief that devaluation would not have led to greater investment and improved productivity. Rather, it was believed, devaluation would provide an excuse for a cycle of wage rises followed by price rises followed by a loss of competitiveness followed by a balance of payments deficit. Indeed, as Woodward has suggested, a credible case could have been, and was, made against devaluation (at least up until 1966 and, less persuasively until 1967) (see Woodward, 1995, pp. 82–3). It could well have been argued, for example, that the immediate problem of price competitiveness was less significant than the long-term failure to match productivity improvements elsewhere and to secure industrial restructuring. For the Treasury and the Bank the fear of devaluation lay partly in the belief that devaluation would encourage govern-ments to be even less financially disciplined and that one devaluation would be followed by another.

> There was no way to prevent slipping into a pattern of deficit financing except to stand firm on the exchange rate; to deny even the possibility of another devaluation, in the hope that a fixed exchange rate and eventual convertability would, in the long run, help to restrain government borrowing, and state industries' wages and costs, and also keep the reserves high enough to prevent such a crisis as 1951–52 recurring. (Middlemas, 1986, p. 244)

As the Bank made clear in its contributions to the Radcliffe Com-mittee on the 'Working of the Monetary System' (HMSO, 1959), it believed that resistance to devaluation was one of the few ways to maintain discipline amongst government, trades unionists and em-ployers alike. The Bank and its supporters in the Treasury may not have been the perversely malign influence of popular mythology but it appears that they lacked the imagination to envisage any institutional mechanism other than fixed exchange rates through which to impose an order on employers, trades unions and the state.

The recognition of the extent of the problem is important. It is not the case that a late Edwardian languor had descended upon the governing classes (however much Macmillan chose to portray himself in this way). The shelves of the bookshops groaned under the works of Anthony Sampson, Michael Shanks, Nicholas Davenport and Graham Hutton all of whom emphasized the need for immediate and radical 'modernization'. Even the Duke of Edinburgh felt obliged to contribute to the debate in 1961 with his famous, if not altogether helpful, suggestion that it was 'about time we pulled our fingers out' (see Porter, 1995, p. 23). It is not possible to read contemporary accounts of the 1950s and 1960s without being struck by the sense of urgency with which they debated the economic problems of the day. There was a belief that 'something had to be done' (apart from removing digits).

This is central to an understanding of the relationships amongst, and policies towards, the external account, devaluation and domest-ic economic strategies; exchange rate policy was being determined neither according to the logic of Bretton Woods nor according to the logic of an unfolding Keynesian strategy (discussed below). Rather, it was an attempt by the Treasury and others to construct a mech-anism external to the state which would impose a discipline upon governments. In this respect, it was hoped that such an exchange rate policy would provide the same automatic stabilizers as the gold standard had in the past. Quite why it was felt that such a discipline had to be looked for, and why the domestic economy failed to play its part in this scenario, are central questions.

Whilst the Bank–Treasury axis supported fixed exchange rates for the discipline they provided, Governments perhaps interpreted devaluation in a different way. As the Conservative response to the 1952 proposal to float exchange rates makes clear, they believed that falling exchange rates would simply have encouraged more expensive imports and rising unemployment (presumably amongst the firms which used a high proportion of imported raw materials) without any guarantee that the rising price of imports would decrease the quantity of imports (therefore worsening the balance of payments) (see Morgan, 1990, pp. 119–22). Therefore, whilst the politicians understood the arguments primarily in terms of the electoral consequences of devaluation, both the politicians and the Bank agreed that the crucial weak link in the argument for devaluation was that the British economy would not respond to a devaluation with improved productivity and greater competitiveness. They believed that the opportunities created by a devaluation would be squandered. Below, we argue that this pessimism was well founded because neither the state nor the private sector was capable of securing appropriate investment, managerial innovation and productivity improvement. It is this, and not the immediate power of the Bank over particular policy-makers, which is crucial. Indeed, careful consideration of the Bank's role can point to only a few occasions where it was able to bulldoze a reluctant government into a policy (see Thompson, 1995, pp. 1105–6).

The Domestic Economy

The external pressures on domestic economic policy-making were considerable. The British state, however, did not afford successive governments the sorts of institutional arrangements which would have facilitated a coherent strategic response to these pressures, or to the pressures arising from the domestic economy. To explore the reasons for and implications of this, we are going to consider two particular aspects of economic policy-making: first, the more general problem of central strategic planning, and second the more particular problem of training policy.

The weakness of the state 1: central planning

As mentioned earlier, by 1950 Harold Wilson, President of the Board of Trade, could say 'this problem of the relationship between Government and Private industry is almost a vacuum in Socialist thought' (CAB 124/1200, 4 May 1950; quoted in Mercer, 1991, p. 71). The idea that Keynesian aggregate demand management was enough, that there was no need to establish some institutional mechanisms with which to influence investment, wages, labour mobility and so forth was not seriously entertained. But neither was the idea that the post-war Labour government should build on the wartime controls to create a state capable of providing some steerage in these vital economic areas. Indeed their dismantling was symbolically celebrated in Wilson's 'bonfire of controls' in 1948. Peter Hennessy is struck by this.

> But the mystery that remains for me . . . of the Attlee governments, is why the first British government devoted to planning, that proclaimed planning and used planning to distinguish itself from all other competitors in the political field, did so little to implement real planning of almost any kind that you can notice in those early post-war years, despite having a remarkable apparatus of control at its disposal under the wartime legislation. (Hennessy, 1993b, p. 8)

If the Labour Party after the war was uncertain about its attitude to delivering planning, during the 1950s both the Labour and Conservative parties moved towards a certain, limited acceptance of economic planning. This was a gradual, and never completed, process within the Conservative Party. In a way, it involved a return to pre-war Conservative policies of industrial intervention but it was also informed by a new rhetoric of planning, much of it drawn from the influential French example. Even the Federation of British Industry at its 1960 conference on 'The Next Five Years' broadly supported the principles of such 'indicative planning'. Undoubtedly there were disputes within the Conservative Cabinet in 1961 but the logic of their commitment to full employment and welfarism drove them towards an acceptance of some element of *dirigisme*. Furthermore, Chancellor Selwyn Lloyd's 1961 White Paper 'Incomes Policy; the Next Step' insisted that wages should be linked to productivity and not to price rises. For this to be delivered, the existing voluntaristic system of wage negotiation in the country would have had to have been modified and replaced.

By the 1960s, it was, therefore, not a question of whether to have planning but of what sort of planning might be suitable. In 1964, the Conservative Party general election manifesto could boast 'NEDC gives reality to the democratic concept of planning by partnership. In contemporary politics the argument is not for or against planning. All human activity involves planning. The question is: how is the planning to be done? By consent or by compulsion?' In comparison, the Labour manifesto promised 'Labour will set up a Ministry of Economic Affairs with the duty of formulating, with both sides of industry, a national economic plan. This Ministry will frame the broad strategy for increasing investment, expanding exports and replacing inessential imports' (see Madgwick *et al.*, 1982, pp. 99–100).

Wilson's success in the general election of 1964 was not so much based on his ability to persuade others of the wisdom of planning as on his ability to present himself as the most convincing exponent of an approach upon which both main parties were agreed. It was widely accepted that modernization was necessary and that the state was a suitable vehicle for driving modernization forward.

Despite this, few serious commentators would argue that what emerged under the Tories in the period 1961–4, or later under the Wilson governments of 1964–70, provided the institutional basis for such planning. The National Economic Development Council lay at the heart of the proposed new institutional structures. However, as Zysman notes, '(T)he questions for the Conservatives in 1961 were what kind of planning apparatus should the NEDC be, whom should it involve, where should it be located, and what should it do? The choices they made produced a debating society and an internal lobbyist, a new hand at the table who was not dealt any cards or provided any chips' (Zysman, 1983, p. 211).

There are clear parallels with the case of training examined below; the process assumed that a consensus could be found amongst the key organized interests, and that out of this consensus actions would result capable of securing the interests of all. Indicative planning, the preferred way forward, involved establishing an optimal, or at least desirable, agreed outcome which would be achieved if all participants acted according to the targets given to them in the plan. The self-interest of particular organizations would thus be realised by acting in a way which coincidentally secured collective interests. In principle, it provided a mechanism for linking particular and national decisions.

However, it required a degree of consensus within each of the participating bodies (TUC, FBI and BEC) and between these bodies, as well as each having a degree of trust in the other. And above all it depended on a high level of faith in the capacity of the government to deliver. If 'planning' after the war had been little more than the administrative allocation of scarce resources, in its new form it amounted to little more than consensus-building and moral suasion.

The reasons for this are complex, important and not always fully understood. In the first place, NEDC was established outside the civil service framework. It was grafted onto the existing administrative structures rather than used as an opportunity to restructure the central institutions. Therefore the dominant discourse within the Treasury (including the protection of sterling and the dangers of economic intervention), and the absence of an administrative cadre equipped for systematic interventions, were two problems which were never challenged. It is significant that both the creation of the Department of Economic Affairs and the development of the National Plan left NEDC outside the decision-making process.

In the second place, the NEDC was never able to mobilize financial interests in the pursuit of national objectives. There was never a 'little neddy' (the name given to sectorally based committees working under the auspices of the NEDC) for the financial sector, and it was not until 1965 that the City was first formally represented on the Council (see Moran, 1983, p. 61). Attempts were made to involve the City in the administrative structures of the NEDC but by the end of the 1970s, when the NEDC had developed a committee structure which addressed the question of finance for industry, the arrival of new players in an increasingly globalized financial marketplace had diminished the significance of purely domestic collaboration between finance, manufacturing and the state.

Further proof of the recognition of a need to create a new institutional basis for securing industrial restructuring can be found in the establishment of the Department of Economic Affairs following the election victory of the Labour Party in 1964. The theme of a productivist strategy, with the state harnessing the powerful forces of the scientific revolution, was laid out at Harold Wilson's speech to the Labour Party annual conference in 1963 and reiterated throughout the ensuing year leading up to the 1964 general election. The analysis of the problem was widely shared by the media and by economic commentators: an outdated industrial structure made up of excessively small firms which lacked the capacity to apply the latest technology in a state-sponsored growth project.

On coming to office, Wilson announced the creation of the Department of Economic Affairs (DEA) responsible for constructing a National Plan capable of addressing these problems and thereby bypassing the Treasury. At the same time, the lack of City involvement in the NEDC was to be compensated for with the creation of the Industrial Reorganization Corporation, which would find the financial resources needed to facilitate the reorganization of industry into larger units capable of securing the application of new technologies.

Rather like the NEDC, the creation of the DEA implicitly presumed a level of consensus amongst key economic players which, ironically, might have rendered a body like the DEA redundant. The detailed story of the failure of the DEA successfully to challenge the Treasury, the political marginalization and eventual departure of its minister, George Brown, and the later abolition of the DEA in 1969 are not central to our interests here. What is important is that indicative planning required the creation of a link between the decisions taken by capitalist enterprises and the objectives of the National Plan. The example of training policy below suggests that few such mechanisms existed in manufacturing industry. We also know that the City's autonomy remained largely undisturbed. For this reason, the DEA was scuttled neither by the Treasury nor by its own (increasingly erratic) minister but by the inevitable logic of a state which lacked the mechanisms necessary to convince all the participants in the plan that the declared objectives would indeed be secured.

There are many leftist and rightist searches for the 'guilty politicians' of the post-war period. Elevating Harold Wilson high on this list (at least for leftist commentators) is his 'failure' to devalue prior to 1967 and this is directly linked, it is alleged, to the failure of the National Plan. However, the case against devaluation was never understood at the time as a simple privileging of financial interests over those of manufacturing. Indeed, there remains little merit in the (implicit) argument that a 1964 devaluation on its own would have rescued the DEA or the National Plan (although devaluation could certainly have played a positive part in an overall rescue package for Keynesianism). A devaluation can only have economic benefits if the opportunity it creates for greater profitability is used to increase investment (rather than dividends and wages) in a continuing process of economic adaptation and restructuring. It would have been perfectly respectable to believe that a devaluation would not achieve this outcome. According to this approach, the best protection for sterling lay in the growth project embodied in the National Plan.

Not surprisingly, therefore, initial failure of the National Plan prompted a response from the Labour government (although Callaghan appears to have been particularly content to downgrade the National Plan's importance and, by January 1966, he was already telling the

TUC that the Plan was 'more a hope than a scientific instrument') (Middlemas, 1990, p. 138). However, the claim that the state could be used to modernize the economy in the collective interests of the whole nation lay at the heart of Labour's claim to the right to govern. The reformist, social democratic electoral strategy then, as in more recent times, was to counterpose the chaos and instability of the free market with a planned, consensual and efficient social market.

The Industrial Reorganization Committee (IRC) was therefore given powers and resources to intervene in pursuit of industrial restructuring. Its main way of acting was to intervene in take-over battles, often deliberately siding with players from outside the British Establishment in the belief that they would better serve the interests of industry. The IRC therefore went beyond simply seeking a consensus and towards deliberate attempts to influence market outcomes. However, with a budget of just £150m and the requirement to make a profit on its overall activities within two years, its ability to do so was limited. Of 3,400 mergers which took place during its existence, the IRC intervened in only 50 (Coopey, 1995, pp. 105–6). Furthermore, its chosen form of intervention (intervening in take-overs) facilitated neither industrial restructuring nor changes in the production process itself, since it mainly influenced winners and losers within the existing structure. In this context of a failure to match the more extravagant rhetoric about planned growth, both incomes policies and trade union reform were seen by unions and the left in general as attempts to make unions and the low-paid carry the burden of wider policy failures.

If the IRC was a small step towards a more interventionist state, a further step was taken with the 1968 Industry Expansion Act. This explicitly recognized the need to shape market outcomes more directly. Its background lay in the expansion of the Ministry of Technology from its more narrow origins as a support for technological innovation stuck somewhere between the DEA and the Treasury, to a wider brief relating to industry as a whole which was confirmed in October 1969 when it was merged with the Board of Trade to form the Department of Industry. Under the terms of the Industrial Expansion Act the new department had powers to intervene in pursuit of national objectives, even where the particular intervention was itself unprofitable. By 1969, Mintech could point to a record of some success, and Coopey is right to argue that it 'represented the major initiative on both science and technology and industrial policy of the Wilson years' (Coopey, 1995, p. 120). The comment made by Mintech's permanent secretary, Sir Richard Clarke, might also have been made of the National Plan and the IRC: 'the problem for Mintech was elusive, for neither Mintech nor anyone else had any levers to press' (Clarke, 1973; quoted in Coopey, 1995, p. 116). Before the wider brief given to the Department of Industry had the opportunity to prove itself Labour lost power to a Conservative Party which had spent much of its time in opposition thinking about both managing and limiting the state. Based on the belief that British *dirigisme* was fundamentally flawed, the Conservative Party sought to solve the problem of this administrative deficit by pursuing policies which required less administration.

Consequently, the Heath government set about dismantling or restricting what they took to be the institutions of economic planning. In order that the 'chill winds of competition' might blow more freely, the trades unions were to be 'reformed' and their capacity to shape labour-market outcomes curtailed. Furthermore, to give these winds a more international dimension, Britain re-applied to join the EEC in 1971 (and finally entered it in 1973) whilst simultaneously abandoning fixed exchange rates (also in 1971) and thereby eroding still further sterling's role as an international reserve currency. Finally, markets require incentives, and these were created by shifting the burden of taxation dramatically away from companies and the better off and onto the bottom end of income earners; some £2bn was shifted in this way (Leys, 1989, p. 90).

The outcomes of these 'Selsdon Man' policies are well known. The trades union movement was largely united in its opposition to the 1971 Industrial Relations Act and this eventually made it unworkable. Furthermore, in the context of the 'Barber boom', the weakness of British manufacturing industry in the international marketplace combined with the end of the long boom in export markets to create a massive deficit of £2.4bn on the visible balance by 1973. This effectively ended the prospect of any immediate further growth. Thirdly, and equally dramatically, the refusal to intervene in industry was reversed when (for different reasons) both Rolls Royce and Upper Clyde Shipbuilders were salvaged by state interventions. This was completed in 1972 with the establishment of the Industrial Development Executive and the reintroduction of a system of investment grants.

The period 1972–6 can be seen as the last attempt to make Keynesianism work in Britain. The Conservative attempt was terminated in 1974 due to their inability to construct an effective basis for the participation of organized labour, and the Labour effort ended in 1976 when it became clear that British capital could not sustain a fully employed work-force whilst simultaneously avoiding massive deficits. This impasse provided the context within which what was to be called Thatcherism emerged in the years after 1976, first as an apologetic weakening of full employment and past welfare commitments and later, after 1979, as a more forceful rejection of the post-war settlement as a new-found touchstone of political rectitude. The issues raised by the rise of Thatcherism are discussed in later chapters.

Heath's about-turn in 1972 was dramatic; the Industry Act of that year gave the government wide and sweeping powers. It contained the seeds of a possible conservative collectivism, based upon a productivist alliance of employers and state with trades unions playing an active (if subordinate) role. This is what was created with the Manpower Services Commission, for example (see below). Whether or not it could have succeeded we discuss later in this chapter but before it could be tested conjunctural factors took the lead in dictating political action. The quadrupling of oil prices following the Egypt–Israel war combined with a poorly managed miners' strike to lead to the three-day week and electoral defeat in February 1974.

The Labour Party came to office with its most radical programme since 1945. Its manifesto had promised a 'fundamental' shift of power and wealth. To achieve this a National Enterprise Board was to be set up with powers to intervene in the expanding sectors and provided with £1000m funding. With these resources it could strike planning agreements with the private sector in pursuit of national economic objectives. In association with this, the 'Social Contract' promised the repeal of the 1971 Industrial Relations Act, a degree of industrial democracy and welfare improvements.

In keeping with these changes, institutional change followed within the state. In the Ministry of Industry an Industrial Development Unit was established, whilst at the Treasury a new Industrial Policy Department was created. New staff with private sector backgrounds were recruited and the use of contacts created through the NEDC working parties became more extensive. These changes certainly did not assuage the doubts and fears of the private sector but, in the end, the anticipated confrontation took place only by proxy in the form of the terms imposed by the IMF loan.

The steps on the road to this dismantling of Labour's programme (before it was ever implemented) are easily identified. First, the balance of payments crisis worsened towards the middle of 1975. Second, inflation threatened to erode this situation still further. The only significant short-term lever available to the government was wage restraint, and in 1975 the TUC accepted the first of a series of wage restraints which were systematically to erode trades unionists' living standards in real terms for the following two years. The third step was the sacking of Tony Benn as Secretary of State for Industry in June 1975 with the clear message that the powers of the National Enterprise Board would be limited. None of these measures altered the fundamental balance of payments crisis and by September 1976 it was clear that applying for an IMF loan had become unavoidable. 'From this point onwards,' as Leys puts it, 'the Callaghan government's policy was almost entirely subordinated to the deflationary goals set by the IMF' (1989, p. 98).

The weakness of the state 2: the case of training

As far back as the Royal Commission on Technical Instruction in 1884, the failings of the British training system were both well known within the British state and a matter of concern. Despite this, no coherent national training system was established after the Second World War. The Manpower Services Commission (MSC) was later to characterize British training in the 1950s in terms of the following five features (see MSC, 1980):

1 Training was almost solely the responsibility of industry and commerce.
2 Some vocational training was the responsibility of further education and the Ministry of Labour Training Centres.
3 The state provided some instructors and trainers through the 'Training within Industry' service.
4 Training decisions taken by firms were subject to a very wide range of influences from trades unions, professional institutions, Joint Apprenticeship Councils, the British Association for Commercial and Industrial Education and so on.
5 Craft apprenticeships attracted most of the available money and most of these were for school-leavers only.

In terms of providing preconditions for industrial restructuring, this system clearly conflicted with the expressed interests of the state. The TUC also expressed a strong preference for a national system of training (although, arguably, member unions regarded the extension of the apprenticeship system as an opportunity to exert further influence over the flow of workers into the labour market). Employers, however, continued to express hostility to anything resembling the state direction of training, and consequently, despite widespread concern about skill shortages and the link this had to the stop-go cycle, the Carr Report rejected a stronger role for the state (National Joint Advisory Council, 1958). Instead, it led to the creation of the Industrial Training Council with inputs from the TUC, the British Employers Federation and the nationalized industries. Some public funding was available but the system was inherently incapable of addressing underlying structural problems. Where employers exercise a veto over training policy they tend to reject both training workers to use new technologies which employers do not intend to introduce, and training which is intended to encourage workers to move out of declining sectors and into expanding industries. It would be perverse for employers to do otherwise; it is equally perverse for those concerned with economic efficiency as a whole to allow employers to exercise such a veto.

However, the existing system came under increasing criticism as even employers began to suffer from skill shortages and consequently the White Paper on Industrial Training was published. This was yet further evidence of the will to create new institutions to secure economic restructuring. In 1964 the Industrial Training Act led to the creation of twenty-seven Industrial Training Boards (ITBs) which were in place by 1969. This covered fifteen million out of a total work-force of twenty-five million. Its framework was industrial rather than skill-related with a Central Training Council responsible for overall coordination. This was a corporatist body with representatives from both unions and employers and, predictably, it was most successful in those industries where the preconditions for corporatism were most advanced (clearly identifiable industrial needs, an agreed area of mutual interests, a small number of employers and a small number of well-supported unions).

One limitation to this system was the weakness of sanctions against non-cooperating employers. The ITB levy rarely exceeded 1 per cent of the wages bill and, whilst employers who failed to provide training would lose this, many regarded this as a price worth paying to avoid the need to provide effective training. Perhaps an even more important limitation to this system is that an industry-based system providing training primarily for male school-leavers is an inappropriate mechanism for pursuing either industrial restructuring or a regional economic strategy (or, indeed, for creating opportunities for women and older workers). The perception of the extent of this problem was reflected in the 1972 White Paper 'Training for the Future'.

It is significant that an avowedly free-market Conservative Government should produce a White Paper which so strongly challenged the ability of market forces to secure the public interest. It advocated a movement away from an industry-by-industry approach and towards the creation of a National Training Agency. This was the very minimum required if training policy was to play a part in actively facilitating industrial restructuring. Yet once again, British employers refused to finance a scheme which would not protect their immediate and particular interests, and significant concessions had to be made before the 1973 Employment and Training Act was framed.

The 1973 Act symbolized the problems associated with government intervention in the processes of economic change. In the Act the government rejected both the proposal to phase out the levy and the creation of a national system of training under a National Training Agency. Instead, it created the Manpower Services Commission, a hived-off agency supposed to coordinate, supervise and stimulate the work of the ITBs (who were to remain the main providers of training). It was to influence training policy through the Training Services Agency, and the Central Training Council was abolished. The proposed mandatory powers of the ITBs were to be only enabling powers and a maximum limit of 1 per cent of the pay roll was established for the levy. Places of employment which were either small or already had adequate training facilities were exempt from the levy. Finally, employers were no longer to be responsible for funding the administrative costs of the ITBs which were to become the responsibility of the Exchequer.

The structure of the MSC was typically tripartite with both trades unionists and employers represented. It sought to establish a dialogue between itself and the ITBs which focused on the individual ITB operating and strategic plans. However, not only was this a remote and imprecise instrument for influencing ITB policy but also the willingness of employers to contribute to the levy diminished and consequently Treasury funding expanded (see MSC, 1980, p. 11).

With central funding becoming more important, the ITBs were placed in an ambivalent position; they were being funded as part of a national programme but were themselves only responsible to sectoral interests. It is characteristic of this compromised approach to industrial intervention that the most detailed controls imposed by the centre were over ITB staff terms and conditions (this was to cause considerable resentment as pay restraints imposed on the public sector inhibited the ability of ITB to attract satisfactory staff).

Training policy highlights the inability of the British state to secure its own objectives. 'Training for the Future' indicated an intention to strengthen the centre in order to overcome sectional interests but there existed an evident gap between these intentions and the reality of power relationships. These relationships were complex but we can capture at least some of their characteristics. By the end of the 1950s, as the Annual Reports of the British Employers' Federation make clear, employers were becoming increasingly concerned about the lack of available skilled labour. In their contribution to the Carr Committee this concern was reiterated and they supported the principle of a centrally coordinated system of training. However, they also insisted upon voluntarism (i.e. no compulsion) and individual employers were to use this to avoid participating in a system of training based upon national objectives and priorities. This inability to orchestrate collective interests out of individual actions characterized employers' participation in the ITBs following the 1964 Act and their reaction to 'Training for the Future'. It is hard to disagree with Vickerstaff's conclusion that '(I)ndustrial capital, in the guise of the CBI, could not agree on the neo-corporatist option; it wanted the pay-offs but not the costs . . .' (Vickerstaff, 1985, p. 57).

Amongst the central state, the TUC and employers' representatives, there was a broad agreement about the need for a nationally coordinated training policy and the content of such a programme. In this sense it was a relatively solidaristic network at the societal level. However, there were no adequate organizational forms capable of linking these agreements to decisions taken by individual employers in particular industries. The proposed procedure was too easy to evade and carried with it too few incentives to bring local and national decisions into line.

The government lacked the instruments which would have allowed it to intervene in the training system in a coherent way. It was therefore forced to look for new forms of participation in, and new partnerships with, non-state interests. Their inclusion in the implementation of public policy fundamentally weakened the conditions required by a dynamic Keynesian strategy in the face of the sectoral, regional and labour-market problems which existed in the Britain of the post-war settlement.

The State in a Changing Political Economy

With the dismantling of the Labour programme in 1976 went the last attempt to create a state able to secure a vibrant and politically acceptable Keynesian strategy. It is clear that throughout the post-war period, Britain did not have a public sector capable of maximizing an expansive and mutually beneficial relationship between the state and the major economic players. Attempts to fill the organizational vacuum between the central state and the actions of capitalist enterprises through moral suasion, exhortation (including the inevitable appeals to the Dunkirk spirit) and a rather half-baked attempt at indicative planning do not appear credible from the vantage point of hindsight. Nor did the state have in place a cadre of officials with the culture and practices needed to do this. A state-focused account will obviously pick up on these shortcomings. However, we have also seen that the state was not the only weak link in post-war British political economy: the financial system was damaging to domestic manufacturing interests; the institutions of the trades union movement were often inappropriate for securing and policing tripartite agreements; and British employers remained culturally (and sometimes perversely) hostile to a more positive role for the state and, like their trades union counterparts, their organization and structure did not help to overcome such hostility.

In seeking to unravel the processes at work we find that certain problems present themselves. In particular, the post-war British political economy within which the state was located was rapidly evolving. There were important drivers for change in the economy which are shared across a wide variety of post-war capitalist regimes and which are not dependent upon particular varieties of the liberal democratic state. During this period the capitalist economies changed in significant ways which we should be aware of here. Lash and Urry (1987, pp. 5–7) have produced a list of the factors associated with the shift which they describe as a change from organized to disorganized capitalism. This is a useful checklist which might be paraphrased as follows:

1 an increasing internationalization of economies, restricting the capacity of governments to control their domestic economies through aggregate demand and other nationally controlled interventions;
2 the weakening of traditional class politics and the rise of parties associated with the growing proportion of workers employed in the new administrative and technologically based sectors;
3 a decreasing relative size of the traditional working class as a consequence of the decline in manufacturing and extractive industries;
4 the decline in national-level bargaining and the growth of plant-level negotiation as production-line technology gives way to

flexible specialization in the organization of the work-force (typically this includes more female and part-time workers employed in
smaller work-places);
5 as the representatives of capital become more internationalized,
corporatist methods of shaping their choices become less effective;
6 the new international division of labour reinforces the importance
of service industries in the advanced capitalist economies;
7 the deconstruction of class identities leads to changes in leisure
activities and new cultural forms;
8 following the spatial reorganization of capital, regional economies
become less exclusively associated with single industries;
9 economic restructuring and shifting power relations leads to the
decline of the industrial city and of the dominance of such cities
within their regions. This is also associated with the decline of the
inner city.

These are, of course, general statements about a variety of capitalist
economies. Such a transition implies that the sorts of economic strategies associated with the problems of 1930s and 1940s would need to
be supplemented with new institutional forms during the 1950s and
1960s. For example, the problems associated with the decline of
manufacturing and extractive industries cannot adequately be addressed through aggregate demand policies, whilst the sorts of factors
associated with successful economic regions in the 1970s and 1980s
also implied a new role for state agencies.

We can develop this argument still further with particular reference
to the British case. An overriding element associated with the political
economy of post-war Britain is the persistent inability of manufacturing capital to compete in the international market. This decline can be
seen in the reduction of the balance of trade (as a percentage of GDP)
from a surplus of 8.8 per cent in 1951–5 to one of just 3.2 per cent in
1976–80 (Harris, 1988, p. 17). To some extent this reflects the fact
that British industry was located in declining world markets but to a
far greater extent it is Britain's performance in expanding world
markets which provides the key to British post-war economic failures.
The British car industry in the 1950s and the British high-technology
consumer electronics industry in the 1970s were both well placed to
ride on a surge of global demand. Neither did.

A further (and not unrelated) peculiarity of the British case is the
role of financial capital. Unbound by the need to ensure the success of
manufacturing in its economic hinterland, the City of London was
free to enter into global markets with enthusiasm. However, the

model of 'Keynesianism in one country' assumes that increase in demand will be associated with an increase in output and (once under-utilized plant is brought into production) this requires investment in new plant and machinery. If the flexibility required to adapt to the changing circumstances outlined by Lash and Urry is not provided by readily available and appropriate finance, then the dependence upon aggregate demand management is unlikely to be sufficient to maintain growth and full employment.

Thirdly, the deep-seated commitment to voluntarism displayed especially by employers (and also, to a lesser extent, by trades unionists) created an environment within which the sense of solidarity and trust needed if tripartite arrangements are to succeed was hard to build. This was very evident in our example of the fate of a national training strategy.

This leads us to the question of the extent to which we see in the architecture and management of the British state the causes of Britain's relatively poor economic performance. Whilst we will consider the wider aspects of this question in the following chapters, certain interim conclusions are nevertheless possible.

Some Interim Conclusions on the British Post-war State and the British Economy

Britain was amongst a small number of countries to emerge from the Second World War explicitly committed to a Keynesian strategy. This involved 'an acceptance that budgetary measures are to be judged by their impact on aggregate demand rather than on the financial balance of the government itself (i.e. the rejection of the balanced budget as a policy objective), and a willingness to use such measures in order to attain the desired level of effective demand' (Bleaney, 1985, p. 117). Viewed more broadly, Keynesianism implied, indeed required, an economic order which largely regulated itself through competition, one which could be regulated by the light hand of experts at the core of the state giving the economy a nudge here and a tweak there. At a fundamental level, it was a conscious effort to sustain the separation of state and economy and especially the autonomy of the latter. However, the logic of Keynesianism's very success was to create constant pressure for more localized, more particular interventions. As a result of this pressure, post-war British governments engaged in constant, but *ad hoc* interventions. For these to have worked, however, would have required an altogether more radical recomposition of the core of the state.

We know, for example, from the Employment White Paper outline (amongst many other places) produced for Churchill and quoted in chapter 1 that the commitment to a high and stable level of employment necessitated powers to shape the decisions of private corporations on training, investment, location and wages. During the second half of the 1950s and the 1960s, first under the Conservatives and then under Labour, successive attempts were made to develop the institutional capacity to influence these. This was in a political environment which was broadly sympathetic to the proposition that the state should have a role to play in actively restructuring and modernizing the economy. Indeed, a variety of new agencies was created, particularly under Labour. We have also suggested that the conventional explanation of the weakness of these institutions – the failure to devalue and the dominance of the City – is not convincing.

With the exception of the years 1970–2, governments were prepared to create new institutions of economic intervention intended to overcome the structural weaknesses in both the manufacturing and financial sectors. Even the 1970–2 period saw a significant willingness to re-examine the core institutions of the state, to introduce new laws and to manage the nationalized industries in new ways. There does not appear to be any systematic evidence to support the picture presented by Barnett (1986) or Wiener (1981) of a British political establishment who were unconcerned for Britain's manufacturing future. However, the examples of both training and the NEDC display a reluctance or inability to create new agencies with the resources needed to impose wider interests against sectional and particular resistance. There was no confidence in the capacity of the central state to impose its own conception of the national interest through, if necessary, statutory powers supported by a skilled cadre of officials.

Under Labour after 1964 a raft of new agencies was created. The operation of each of these was, however, subordinated to a different political agenda which, in times of crisis and political choice, always came to the fore. This was once again the case in the crisis of 1975–6. It arose from the fact that the British state was forced to act not as a forum within which collective interests could be established and agreements acted upon, but as a sporadic player intervening with a merger here, a confrontation with the Governor of the Bank of England there and the introduction of a new tax elsewhere. This was far short of the economic strategies required if relative economic decline was to have been arrested.

Planning – the purposive use of an organization's resources to secure preferred medium- and long-term goals – was never pursued by the post-war British state. For the decade following Wilson's 'bonfire' in 1948, planning in practice involved not even the allocation of scarce resources (see Middlemas, 1990, p. 4). If 'Butskellism' had any real economic meaning, it involved a political commitment to full employment (a point reinforced in 1958 when the Cabinet came out in favour of full employment and against monetary prudence in the arguments which led to the resignation of Thorneycroft and Powell from the Treasury) without the institutional means to deliver it. As noted above, both the Conservative and Labour Party manifestos in 1964 committed themselves to economic planning. However, it was couched in the language of consent and agreement; it was not a commitment to a purposive state.

We have, then, a financial sector which was reluctant to invest in domestic industry, manufacturers who resisted any attempted strategic restructuring and a trades union movement which was organizationally divided and defensive. Under such conditions, why did the central state pursue a strategy of consensus and incorporation? When national interests were identified, as in the case of training, why were these interests compromised in the search for agreement with the key economic agencies? In future chapters, we will argue that the organization and management of the state itself is a primary cause and that the core agencies provide the key to understanding why. All the institutional innovations of the 1960s left the core of the state (and its capacity to direct peripheral agencies) unchanged. Instead, we saw short-term, *ad hoc* and pragmatic responses which, it was hoped, would modernize the state. This is true only in the sense that, with sufficient adaptation and innovation, pigs might fly.

As Hirst points out, Keynesianism 'was a change of *policy* – not of the constitution, not the relation of the citizen to the state, and not of the basic forms of property ownership' (Hirst, 1994, p. 86). This came to matter when the limits of aggregate demand management called for new ways of organizing a coherent response to problems such as poor training, regional decline, a high marginal propensity to consume imports and an under-capitalized manufacturing base. The need to evolve new relationships between the state and the economy as Keynesian policies unfolded was more satisfactorily resolved elsewhere but nowhere with complete success. To do so would have required a radical rethinking of the form and purpose of the state capable of avoiding the failures of both state socialism and free-market economics. However, the *relative* decline of the British economy had less to do with the constraints of the liberal form of state and more to do with its failure to develop a coherent institutional response to the changing requirements of the British economy. The core of the British state was both literally and metaphorically constitutionally incapable of providing the terrain upon which conflicts of economic interests could be satisfactorily resolved and collectively shared interests actively pursued.

Summary

Economic policy requires a level of intra-state organization which at least matches the complexities of the tasks being pursued. The complexity of tasks required of the British state in pursuit of full employment, price stability, a balance on external payments and growth was understood but this understanding was inadequately acted upon. Even so, from the late 1950s, a variety of new agencies of economic intervention were established. However, these were grafted onto the existing core of the state and, cut off from the resources of a purposive central state, they were required to reach particular agreements as a basis of action. This gave all the players in a defensively minded game every opportunity to exercise a veto. In the absence of any alternative instruments for securing economic discipline, the Treasury resorted to the only controls available to it – hence its continuing resistance to devaluation. Given the character and organization of the key economic players, securing the organizational support of these agencies for governmental priorities met with widespread failure. In answer to the two questions posed near the start of this chapter, we can argue that the agencies created by the state were not sufficient to secure the outcomes of national economic policy, and, more tentatively, suggest that at least part of the reason for this was the inability of the core to restructure itself and impose a direction on the peripheral parts of the state system.

3
Managing the British Welfare State

The purpose of this chapter is to explore the general issues around the central direction of welfare agencies from the Second World War to the mid-1970s. We do this by:

- outlining the overall trends in managing welfare and examining their relevance for the state;
- illustrating and exploring these trends through a focus on one particular set of welfare agencies – the Community Development Projects;
- establishing the context within which we examine interests and state power in the following chapter.

In particular, we will see how the welfare state became a site upon which old interests and identities were transformed and new ones constituted; how the management of these new interests and coalitions created fundamental problems for the further development of the post-war settlement; and how the language of welfarism was detached from the logic of economic growth only to have the realities of a capitalist economy sporadically reimposed on the practice of welfare but with limited mechanisms for managing such interventions.

Post-war Welfare States

Throughout North America and Western Europe relationships between states and citizens were reconstructed around a number of axes after the Second World War. One of these was the formal acceptance that citizens not only had legal and political rights but also social rights to which all members of society were entitled. It was sufficient to be a member of that society to secure such entitlements (but note that in all cases being 'a member of that society' carried with it social expectations and assumptions). Such welfare regimes typically exhibited similar features (and these were to become globally shared aspirations).

1 Mass education was extended to cover more children for more years of their lives and further and higher education were extended to meet the perceived needs of specialization and fragmentation of social functions. This often focused on the issues around the expansion of the professions and implications of new technologies. Responsibility for managing schools was increasingly claimed by the state (as against the claims of churches, for example) and these responsibilities were largely discharged by a growing cadre of education experts. Pre-war education systems, in remarkably similar ways, reflected the nationalist priorities of their respective states. Typically they focused upon the creation of a single, shared linguistic community, able to locate the nation in space (geography) and time (history) and sufficiently numerate to function in a quantified society (money, weights and measures, product standardization etc). After 1945 these characteristics were elaborated but not fundamentally changed, reflecting the concern that all classes should have the resources necessary to participate in the cultural, economic and political life of 'the nation'. This belief was supported by two parallel claims: the first that education was a good thing because it benefited those being educated, the second, that because an uneducated population was inefficient and unruly, education was good for the whole of society. Securing these ambiguous objectives became a primary concern of the new education professionals.

2 Despite a variety of contexts and forms there is a remarkable convergence amongst Western states towards a system of social security which is 'nationwide, compulsory and collective' (see De Swann, 1988, *passim*). The principles that all workers should participate in insurance schemes (whether they wanted to or not), that employers should also contribute to this scheme and that the central government should ensure such a system were all widely adopted (with the US being amongst the least enthusiastic in this respect). The post-war period sees the extension of the range of circumstances to be insured against and the increase in the cost of the whole social insurance system.

3 The post-war period also saw the extension of public health care. The nineteenth century had seen the battle for public health policy won overwhelmingly by the collectivists, where few could defend the proposition that individual market choices could create the sewerage and clean water supply systems which were believed to be vital to the futures of the major industrialized cities. Improving the sewerage of the slum areas also created evident benefits for the middle classes. Less obvious was the claim that there were benefits to be gained for the better off and more powerful members of society (along with an improved equity of outcome) if the state was to ensure the provision of a mass system of health care. However, most Western states accepted at least a minimal version of this responsibility.

4 Whilst the idea that the state had particular responsibility for ensuring the welfare of children, the elderly and adolescents became institutionally entrenched, the diversity of forms amongst Western nation states through which these services were delivered was considerable.

5 The fact that housing is a commodity the outright purchase of which is both essential and beyond the reach of working-class wages has led to both private renting and public management. In a variety of institutional ways, the public sectors of liberal capitalist regimes became increasingly involved in the provision of mass housing but, as with social work, the forms of this involvement vary greatly.

Supporting the burgeoning cost of this array of institutions was economic growth. Furthermore, full employment was supposed to allow most people to meet most of their needs most of the time by spending their earned income. Resourced by the engine of global economic growth, the post-war nations of the West built their various 'people's homes' according to their own conditions and architectural preferences, but once built these homes shared many of the same strengths and weaknesses.

The British Case

An important starting-point in considering the impact of welfare is to consider the levels of expenditure associated with it. The expenditure consequences in the UK of the sorts of welfare commitments indicated above are outlined in table 3.1. We can see from this that welfare spending ('social services') increases through the period 1910–75 both as a percentage of Gross National Product and as a percentage

Table 3.1 The relative growth of different categories of public expenditure, United Kingdom, 1910–1975

	As percentage of gross national product						
	Social services	Economic services	Environmental services	Defence	Debt service	Other services	Total
1910	4.2	1.8	0.7	3.5	0.9	1.7	12.7
1938	11.3	2.9	1.0	8.9	4.0	1.9	30.0
1955	16.3	3.2	1.1	9.6	4.2	2.1	36.6
1970	23.2	6.1	4.0	5.6	4.6	3.7	47.1
1975	28.0	8.2	4.2	5.6	4.5	4.3	54.7

	As percentage of total public expenditure					
	Social services	Economic services	Environmental services	Defence	Debt service	Other services
1910	33.1	14.2	5.5	27.6	7.1	13.4
1938	37.7	9.7	3.3	29.7	13.3	6.3
1955	44.5	8.7	3.0	26.2	11.5	5.7
1970	49.1	12.9	8.4	11.9	9.8	7.8
1975	51.2	15.0	7.7	10.2	8.2	7.8

Source: Extracted from Sleeman, 1979, Table 3.1; quoted in Clarke and Langan (1993 p. 32)

of total public expenditure. Indeed it significantly outstrips increases in all other categories of public expenditure.

It is a constant theme of right-wing critics that Britain could not 'afford' such a rapid increase in welfare spending. In important ways, this misses the point. It is not self-evident that Britain could afford to increase expenditure on leisure, alcohol, tourism and so forth and yet could not afford to increase expenditure on schools or houses. As was shown in the previous chapter, the priority given to consumption over long-term investment was a problem associated with private, as well as public, choices. The real problem associated with the growth of public expenditure is better understood as a problem of the articulation of the state to the capitalist economy than as a problem of what 'the country' could afford. We will address this issue first before going on to consider the wider issues associated with managing the consensus welfare regime in Britain.

Managing Social Expenditure in Post-war Britain

The relationship between welfare spending and capitalism has been argued over since the 1970s when works such as Offe (1984), Gough (1979) and O'Connor (1973) all in their own ways explored it. These, and other, theorizations of the so-called 'crisis' of the 1970s are well summarized and evaluated in Hay (1996, part III). Each recognized that welfare spending both stabilized capitalist economic and social relationships and yet simultaneously threatened to undermine them.

On the one hand, welfare helped to maintain a high and relatively stable level of demand and it legitimized capitalism by ameliorating its worst features. It helped to create a mobile and sufficiently educated work-force. It stimulated a massive expansion of private sector activity around the periphery of the welfare state in the pharmaceuticals industry, the building industry and so forth. On the other hand, it also established a range of entitlements which exist independently of participation in the labour market and this undermined the disciplining power of the labour contract. It was funded out of taxation at least part of which undermines profits. And it potentially reduces the proportion of total investment which is available to the private sector.

From the perspective of state management, what is interesting is not simply that the logic of social expenditure becomes distanced from calculations concerning the requirements of the private enterprise, but how this distancing is managed within the state system, and with what consequences for that state system. Furthermore, the calculations of social spending departments may have been distanced from the agencies charged with controlling public expenditure (above all the Treasury) but they were not completely divorced from each other. Months of mutual indifference would be followed by a torrid round of liaisons during the annual public expenditure review process. If there exists an ambivalence between social expenditures and the requirements of capital, it will be expressed within the systems of financial management. The form which these systems take conditions and shapes the outcomes for both welfare agencies and the private sector.

Many aspects of the financial control systems with which social expenditure was to be managed had to be created after the Second World War. Despite the level of debt, downward pressure on current expenditure was not especially great. This was because reductions in military expenditure provided a substantial saving at a time when it was feared that comparable tax reductions would be inflationary. As shown in table 3.2, public expenditure as a percentage of GDP was to plummet in the years immediately after the war.

Table 3.2 Estimates of public expenditure on goods and services, 1945–1951, as a percentage of GDP

1945	46.5
1946	25.7
1947	18.6
1948	17.3
1949	19.7
1950	18.9
1951	19.9

Note: These figures do not include government transfers (which probably accounted for 15 per cent of GDP in 1951). Furthermore, whilst statisticians agree that this was indeed the trend, some sources place spending on goods and services in 1951 a little higher (see, for example, Flynn, 1993, p. 34).
Source: Feinstein (1972 table 2) ; quoted in Hill (1993 p. 26),

This created a situation in which, typically, more concern was expressed about the availability of physical resources (e.g. for house- and school-building programmes) than about the availability of finance. The Treasury had re-established itself at the centre of the core but it had not yet managed to break the wartime habit that the purpose of financial systems was to facilitate, rather than constrain, political action. Even where the Treasury pushed very persistently, as with NHS expenditure, it often found few allies.[*]

By July 1959, however, the Plowden Committee was set up to consider the overall question of coordinating public expenditure, and this provided another forum within which the Treasury and its allies could encourage the adoption of new financial management systems. The main thrust of the Plowden Report was that senior civil servants

---

[*] In the case of the NHS, Treasury concerns prompted the Guillebaud Committee to be set up in 1953 charged with examining NHS costs. However, the conclusion of the Committee, published in 1956, was that no significant new financial arrangements were necessary. Apparently, the Treasury was unimpressed by these conclusions, and in 1957 Chancellor Peter Thorneycroft announced new measures to control NHS spending, along with other social spending cuts. Following Cabinet's rejection of the Chancellor's proposals, he resigned along with two treasury colleagues.

should spend more time on managing and less on offering policy advice. The subsequent creation of the Public Expenditure Survey Committee (PESC) enhanced the capacity of the Treasury to monitor and control departmental expenditures. As Lord Bridges put it in 1964:

> One of the main tasks of the Treasury ... is to examine the stream of proposals submitted to it so as to provide material for a judgement of their comparative merits. Given that there can never be enough money ... which was the most deserving? And as between approved objects of expenditure, how much should be spent on each to retain the right priorities? (Bridges, 1964, p. 41; quoted in Greenwood and Wilson, 1984, p. 44)

That this view of the Treasury role clearly involved it in making political decisions about priorities and value-laden judgements over the 'right' priorities does not concern Bridges. As ministers in spending departments were often to complain, the Treasury, and the PESC in particular, was to be the graveyard of many projects.

From the Treasury point of view, there were two significant faults in the existing system: (a) it assessed each expenditure item in turn and not against the backdrop of overall resource availability and, (b) its planning horizon was limited to one year. The sixth report of the Expenditure Committee of the Commons had already criticized these elements of the system in 1958. In place of this, the Public Expenditure Survey (PES) was to review forthcoming expenditure targets for each department over the following five years in the light of the availability of physical resources. Conflicts between PESC and the spending department would be resolved, where necessary, by Cabinet. The apparent rationality of this system, however, was increasingly called into question as it become dominated by the objective of limiting public expenditure. It therefore led to the pursuit of the 'softest' expenditure items rather than allocating resources on the basis of a wider economic or social set of priorities (see Barnett, 1982; Heclo and Wildavsky, 1981; and Wright, 1977).

Before considering the consequences of PES, it is worthwhile reflecting on the nature of the Plowden Report which sought to enhance both the managerial and coordinating capacities of the Treasury. The value of this report for our purposes is that it is an accurate indicator of thinking about state management within the core of the British state at this time; indeed Plowden himself was the classic 'great and good' establishment figure. The 1958 Select Committee on Estimates

Report had called for an outside committee to review the principles and practice which govern the control by the executive of public expenditure. We know, however, that support for the view that expenditure decisions should be taken within the context of the civil estimates as a whole had been a position minuted by Brook as far back as 1950 (see Hennessy, 1990, p. 152). Not only did the origins of this desire lie in the civil service but also, the Treasury succeeded in dominating the contributions to the committee.

The opening of the Plowden Report notes that 'our proceedings and recommendations would be confidential . . . [it would be] an internal enquiry under the authority of the Chancellor of the Exchequer . . . our review was primarily concerned with the inner working of the Treasury and the Departments . . .' (pp. 1–3). Not only was the report to be confidential but the committee were satisfied that they did not need to interview people from outside this privileged circle because they had enough expertise from amongst the committee membership (p. 3). The process of examination consisted of 'a continuous consultation with the Permanent Secretaries and other officials of the major Departments over a period of two years' (p. 3). The report as published is therefore a consolidation of the thinking of the senior civil service, and the Treasury in particular. Alternative perspectives were rarely sought or raised. Small wonder, therefore, that the committee identified the key issue as follows: 'The central problem is that of how to bring the growth of public expenditure under better control, and how to contain it within such limits as the Government may think desirable' (HMSO, 1961, p. 6).

The 'central problem' was therefore one of controlling public expenditure but it was also about finding a more 'rational' way of allocating available resources. This required (according to the committee) surveys of public expenditure, a stable long-term planning environment, improvements in the statistical and accountancy techniques available to government and more effective machinery with which to secure the collective responsibility of ministers. In all of this, not surprisingly given the procedures of the committee, the Treasury was to have the lead role. The Treasury was held to be responsible:

(a) for allocating the amount of money and economic resources to be made available for each purpose to each department;
(b) for advising the departments on economic and financial matters, and for assisting them to maintain proper practice in the expenditure of public money;
(c) for the overall efficiency of the public service, and thus for seeing

that departments are staffed, particularly at the top levels, with the best available officers drawn from the service as a whole;

(d) for the development of management services throughout the public service; for taking the initiative in the introduction of new management techniques; and for keeping an oversight over the management practice of all departments;

(e) for the settlement of pay and conditions of service, and grading of staff throughout the service. (HMSO 1961, p. 13)

The committee placed great stress on the importance of management and, in a way which prefigured the Fulton Report, they called for improved techniques, organizations and methods with which to manage the state more effectively. This process, they believed, should be led by the Treasury. Given that the Treasury was clearly pushing for such responsibilities, there is something faintly farcical about the report's apologetic tone concerning the 'heavy additional load' which this would impose on the Treasury (p. 20).

The Treasury intended to get a close grip on the social expenditure of the agencies of the welfare state. Neither committees influenced by outside experts such as the Guillebaud Committee on expenditure on the health service, nor the 1958 ministerial resignations had delivered the sorts of financial and managerial disciplines which the Treasury wanted. The procedures of the Plowden Report were altogether more amenable.

This, of course, is to cast the Treasury in its familiar role as the monster in Britain's post-war Gothic horror – the creature, created by politicians which then evades their control and runs amuck amongst their most treasured policies. Whilst this is convenient (especially to those politicians who failed to secure certain policies) the history of the Treasury is more ambiguous. If we consider the counterfactual situation in which the Treasury had no such controls, then the outcome would have been that the core executive would have inevitably created another set of controls in another agency. No state can survive without the capacity to maintain its financial integrity. At one level, the Treasury communicated, rather than caused, the fiscal pressures of the state. However, as we can see in the Plowden Report, it did so with a distinctive inflexion and with particular objectives.

PES was therefore to be a mechanism for both controlling overall expenditure and more rationally allocating that expenditure but in practice it was the former function which quickly swamped the latter. During the 1964–70 Labour governments, the Conservative Party had used its experience of opposition to reflect upon the problems of managing an increasingly cumbersome state. They concluded that existing controls were inadequate and these concerns were stated very soon after coming to office in the White Paper 'The Reorganization of Central Government'. Three consequences flowed from these concerns: first, the creation of giant departments (the Department of the Environment and the Department of Trade and Industry); second, the creation of the Central Policy Review Staff (CPRS); third, the introduction of Programme Analysis and Review (PAR).

The intention behind PAR was to subject existing policies to the same (hopefully) rational process of scrutiny as PES gave to proposed policies. It was a further attempt to strengthen the core of the state at a time of expanding state activities. Gray and Jenkins show that Conservative policy-makers 'were not simply concerned with management techniques or governmental efficiency but rather a more extensive control of state activities which, in part, was seen to demand a much stronger central capacity' (1982, p. 432). In this we can see the beginnings of the process which was to turn a party traditionally hostile to the central state into 'the most centralist since the Stuart monarchs of the seventeenth century' (Bogdanor, 1988, p. 7).

PAR's original ambitious aspirations were soon scaled down but by 1973 twenty PARs had been completed. These were unpopular amongst those being reviewed and they could only have been expected to succeed with strong political support from the centre. However, by this stage the Heath government was immersed in the problems of industrial relations and industrial intervention and PARs struggled on towards the end of decade with only limited results.

Whilst PARs were intended to enhance the efficiency of existing programmes within departments, the Central Policy Review Staff (CPRS or 'Think Tank') was intended to coordinate the long-term activities of government as a whole. It comprised some thirteen to twenty members, with around half of them coming from outside the civil service. The Think Tank's own view of its function was:

'Sabotaging' the over-smooth functioning of the machinery of government.

Providing a Central Department which has no departmental axe to grind but does have overt policy status and which can attempt a synoptic view of policy.

Providing a central reinforcement for those civil servants in Whitehall who are trying to retain their creativity and not be totally submerged in the bureaucracy.

Trying to devise a more rational system of decision making between competing programmes.

> Advising the cabinet collectively, and the Prime Minister, on major issues of policy relating to the Government's Strategy.
>
> Focussing the attention of Ministers on the right questions to ask about their own colleagues' business.
>
> Bringing in ideas from the outside world. (Hennessy, Morrison and Townsend, 1985; quoted in Jordan and Richardson, 1987, pp. 130–1)

The language of the entrepreneurial, creative, risk-taking state, which was to resonate yet more loudly through the corridors of Whitehall in the 1980s and 1990s, was (then as later) but one of a variety of discourses. There was also the language of financial conservatism from the Treasury; of rational target-setting associated with Management by Objectives (M by O), Planning Programming Budgeting Systems (PPBS), Programme Evaluation and Review Technique (PERT), and so forth; of judicial public accountability as found in the Franks Report; and of democratic accountability. The idea that the question of how best to manage the public sector was never considered until the arrival of the realists in 1979 is palpable nonsense. Alongside this was the language of welfarism; partly this was about professionalism, partly a broad orientation towards meeting needs (however defined), and partly about the electoral consequences of welfare spending. The welfare state was therefore traversed with a variety of managerial, professional, electoral and ethical calculations. This was capable of producing strange, even bizarre outcomes. It would be hard in a book of this sort to describe the variety of ways in which these conflicting systems and cultures traversed each agency of the welfare state, so in order to get a clearer sense of what this implied for managing welfarism we examine one particular case before locating this within the wider context of interests and state power in chapter 4.

Case Study: the Community Development Projects

When looking at the post-war British welfare state, one would expect to be able to study examples of managerial competence, at least, given that so much attention was paid to the need to coordinate the work of the public sector. There was both the importation of American private sector management techniques and the stimulus of reports such as Plowden and Fulton which stressed the need for improved management. Certainly, the working lives of individual civil servants changed significantly during the 1960s. Delafons, a senior civil servant, comments: 'In the 1960s, having had not a day's training in my first ten years, I (with many others) attended courses on cost-benefit analysis, investment appraisal, discounted cash flows, PPBS, M by O, the use of computers, operational research and related techniques' (Delafons, 1982, p. 261).

It is in this context of hightened sensitivity to the issues of management and coordination that we consider one of the more interesting social interventions of this period: the Community Development Projects. As a case study, it provides insights into crucial aspects of managing social policy in the 1960s and 1970s. It was an attempt to establish central government initiatives which could be sensitive to local conditions and which could address the perceived problems of the inner urban areas. It demonstrated the extent to which many of the intra-state arrangements of the post-war settlement depended upon consensus and shared assumptions and how, when the consensus weakened, the administrative structures were unable to contain the tensions. It can also be seen as a test for the limits to, and nature of, the so-called struggle 'in and against the state'. However, whilst it helps us to gain a clearer sense of these issues we should note that, compared with many other social interventions of the post-war period, this case study is atypical in having neither a powerful professional nor bureaucratic interest involved, both of which will be considered in the following chapter.

The Community Development Projects were part of a wider policy response to what was defined as 'the urban problem'. Throughout the modern age nations, have periodically enjoyed 'official panics' (an altogether more restrained, but equally significant version of its populist relative the 'moral panic'). A host of official reports reinforced these concerns, including the Millner Holland Report *Housing in Greater London*, 1965; the Plowden Report *Children and their Primary Schools*, 1966; and the Seebohm Report, *Local Authority and Allied Personal Social Services*, 1968. 1968 was also the year of Enoch Powell's infamous 'rivers of blood' speech.

It is significant that it was the Home Office (with its brief for securing law and order) which was charged with the first legislative response to the perceived 'urban problem'. The urban aid programme was introduced in December and this involved the central government in approving and supporting specific local initiatives (and not increasing the less specific rate support grant the spending of which could be controlled locally). That the centre did so when it evidently lacked the capacities either to evaluate or to monitor this programme is a separate issue.

During the period 1968–74 there was a continuing and high political (if not financial) priority given to the urban question. In response to problems of coordination a new department was created in the Home Office: the Community Programmes Department. Meanwhile, the Department of the Environment involved itself in the locally based Six Towns Studies in 1972, and the Department of Education and Science set up and ran five Educational Priority Areas in the years 1968–71. Nor was this a concern associated with the centre and left of British politics. In Keith Joseph's 1972 speech to the Pre-School Playgroups Association he emphasized the danger of poverty being culturally transmitted from one generation to the next and the need to intervene in this process.

In the face of these various initiatives it is not surprising that voices at the core of the central state started to express concerns about the coordination of urban policy. By the end of 1972, the Treasury (but also the Central Policy Review Staff) wanted a Policy Analysis Review (PAR) on urban deprivation. The Urban Deprivation Unit was set up at the Home Office and produced an interim report by the middle of 1974 which advocated the Comprehensive Community Programmes.

The period which concerns us here draws towards an end when, following the Labour victory of February 1974, the incoming Labour government challenged the leading role of the Home Office in urban policy with the creation of a Minister of State for Urban Affairs in the DoE. Whilst the manoeuvrings over the location of urban policy in general and the CDPs in particular were going on within the state, the 'urban question' was also being located within the context of the so-called 'rediscovery of poverty'. The defeat of poverty, from the Beveridge Report onwards, had become a major task which the British state set for itself, and both Labour and Conservative parties were locked into the rhetorical promise to secure its abolition and evading the political consequences of failing to do so. Encouraging politicians in their efforts was a growing number of pressure groups, including the Child Poverty Action Group (1965–), the Disablement Income Group (1966–), Shelter (1966–), the National Old People's Welfare Council (which became Age Concern in 1970) and Gingerbread (1970–). The Child Poverty Action Group (CPAG) was to make the (probably inflated) claim that they had made poverty a crucial issue in the 1970 election campaign, and this view is supported by the journalist Alan Watkins's comment that no Ted Heath election speech was complete without a reference to the CPAG (see Field, 1982, p. 39).

Whilst the CDPs were to be spatially specific anti-poverty policies, they were also to be based upon the idea of participation. At the time it was accepted that securing and maintaining the consensus depended upon the participation of those sections of society who were potentially excluded from economic change (and those burned by the white heat of the technological revolution in particular). This view was officially sanctioned in a variety of places, including the Skeffington Report on the Town and Country Planning Act, 1971; the Bains Report (*The New Local Authorities: Management and Structure*, 1972); and the Dobry circular (Department of the Environment Circular 113/75, 1975). In its proposals for Neighbourhood Councils in 1974, the Government went beyond simply calling for greater responsiveness to existing groups and called for their creation where residents had failed to set them up for themselves.

This should be considered alongside a significant redeployment of state employees from the central to the local state. Between 1959 and 1974 the local authority work-force increased by 60 per cent to form some 11.2 per cent of the work-force. Central government (civilian) staff, in contrast, increased by just over 6 per cent, public corporations decreased by 2 per cent and the private sector work-force increased by just 3 per cent during the same period (Klein *et al.*, 1976, Table 13). Local authority spending as a percentage of GNP similarly rose from 9.8 per cent in 1951 to 18.6 per cent in 1975 (Gough, 1979, p. 97), reinforcing the impression of staff and financial resources being 'pushed' towards the local state.

The expansion of the local state linked to the pursuit of increased levels of participation in the hope of solving entrenched social problems should be directly compared with the pursuit of corporatist arrangements in the hope of solving entrenched economic problems. In each case, participation was sought in order to mobilize the resources of non-state organizations in pursuit of major objectives of state policy. In both cases this need arose from the weakness of the organizational capacities of the state in relation to these publicly defined objectives. And in both cases the capacity of these organizations to deliver these outcomes (let alone their willingness to do so) was seriously exaggerated by state officials.

It is significant that the origin of the CDPs lay not in local communities demanding that such agencies be established. The drive towards it came from within the central state. Indeed, the origins of the CDPs are associated with one civil servant: Derek Morrell. Writing in *The*

Times Educational Supplement (19 Dec. 1969) after Morrell's death, John Banks emphasized that for Morrell the role of the state and of social policy was to encourage the 'growth of whole persons ... through the formation of creative relationships'. Morrell's deep attachment to the Christian ethic was (according to Crossman) welcomed by Home Secretary Callaghan with the words 'stop all this bloody religious nonsense' – although it adds to the pleasure of reading political diaries and memoirs when Callaghan recollects things rather differently, describing Morrell as 'a brilliant and strong minded [sic] Home Office Official ... whose strong moral sense derived from religious conviction' (Callaghan, 1987, p. 238). Whatever the reality of Callaghan's attitude towards Morrell, in 1969 he announced the launch of the Community Development Projects.

The CDPs were planned to run for at least five years. They were to combine social intervention with researching ways of attacking particularly entrenched pockets of poverty. According to *CDP A General Outline*, produced by the Home Office in 1969, the projects were to have research workers to assess needs and evaluate interventions, and action teams which would stimulate local residents to participate in the assessment of need and in the development of policy responses (see CDP, undated, 1976?, p. 2). The basic structure, reflecting the division between research and action is outlined in figures 3.1 and 3.2. A total of twelve projects were eventually established at a total cost of some £5m. The research aspect was to be coordinated centrally through a research director based at the Home Office, whilst the action teams were to be coordinated through the Central Steering Group, also based in the Home Office. Inter-group coordination did not formally exist until the establishment of the Consultative Council in 1972, which also took over much of the research function of the research director's Central Research Unit. In 1973 a central Infor-

Figure 3.1 Outline of the national structure of the CDPs

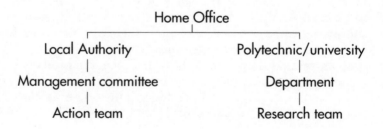

Figure 3.2 Outline of the local structure of the CDPs

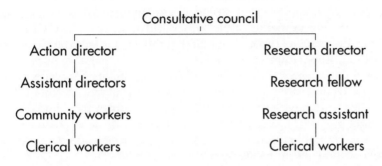

mation and Intelligence Unit was also established. These latter two developments both arose out of pressure from the projects. Alongside this structure, in 1974 the Political Economy Collective and the CDP Workers' Organization were established by project workers. These were the basic players in what was to prove to be a fascinating example of British state management in the consensus welfare regime.

Conflicting Calculations: In or Against the State?

An important feature of state management concerns the capacity of core agents to shape the calculations and priorities of agencies 'in the field'. In this case study it was almost entirely absent. In contrast to what the CDPs claimed was the Home Office's 'social pathology' explanation of deprivation, by 1974 the projects had mostly (the Oldham and Liverpool teams were exceptions) adopted a marxist interpretation emphasizing structural factors associated with the process of capital accumulation over cultural explanations which perceived a cycle of poverty (see, for example, CDP, 1975; North Shields CDP Final Report (vol. 3), undated; and the Benwell CDP Final Report Series no. 6 (5)).

On the subject of the causes of poverty, CDP publications were especially critical of the Home Office position. 'The slick theories that lay behind the establishment of the CDP', they asserted, 'seemed inadequate in the face of real situations and real people' (CDP, 1981, p. 3). Of the urban programme as a whole they wrote '(A)s we watched the development of these policies – hailed as major initiative to combat poverty and deprivation – it became increasingly clear to us that they were totally inadequate to the problems they aimed to overcome' (ibid.). The 'pathological' explanation of poverty (that poverty is the consequence of the values and attitudes of poor people) was roundly attacked throughout CDP publications (see the Coventry CDP's Final Report part 1, undated, p. 2; and CDP 1977, p. 5).

Indeed, borrowing Callaghan's alleged comment, Morrell's more Christian Democratic arguments for the ethical role of the state would probably have been regarded by most within the central state as 'bloody religious nonsense'. Even so, given Keith Joseph's speeches of 1972–3 (to the Pre-School Playgroups Association, his 1973 'cycle of deprivation speech' to the seminar of the Association of Directors of Social Services, and his 1973 speech to the National Association for Maternal and Child Welfare) it is clear that, at that time at least, he held onto something approaching the 'pathological view' so roundly condemned by the CDPs. However, it would be an exaggeration to claim that the central state (and the Home Office in particular) had anything as rigid (or as coherent) as a single view of the causes of deprivation.

But what Home Office officials certainly lacked was a neo-marxist desire to overthrow the capitalist system. So how was it possible for a Home Office-funded project to develop a position so radically opposed to the position of the central state (and the publication of which views the central state funded)? The answer lies partly in the remarkable weakness of bureaucratic controls. There are a number of possible reasons for this weakness.

At the most practical level, there was limited continuity of personnel at the central level (even by the standards of the British civil service which advocates inter-departmental movements of senior staff). Morrell died in December 1969 and was not replaced until April. John Greve was appointed to the post of Research Director in May 1969 but he was secured by Crossman at the DHSS for several days a week. Meanwhile the Home Office was heavily concerned with steering through the Children and Young Persons Act and preparing for the forthcoming general election. Morrell's replacement was himself replaced in January 1971 by Isserlis who in turn left in March 1972. At the political level there was also discontinuity. In July of 1972 Maudling was replaced by Carr, and Sharples and Lord Windlesham ceased to be ministers of state in April and March respectively. In addition to these personnel changes, of course, the Labour government had been defeated in June 1970.

By the time of Isserlis's departure in March 1972 there was considerable confusion over the purpose of the CDPs. Projects complained that their reports were not reacted to by the Home Office, and Cockburn (1977, p. 127) believes this to be deliberate ('it didn't want to know its child'). However, it was equally likely that no one at the centre knew what to do with the reports or to whom they should be sent. Before the departure of Isserlis, a Consultative Council was established, comprising Home Office advisers, officials and the project directors, and this probably marked the point at which the centre tried to get a firmer grip on the administrative structures. However, the creation of the Information and Intelligence Unit in 1973, and its subsequent critical reports, coupled with the creation of a separate Workers Organization only eroded still further effective central controls.

In June 1974, the Home Office announced a management review and it recommended that a central committee and a national coordinator be established and that forward plans be prepared. The projects resisted the first two proposals, and the Home Office finally moved to close the projects down. All new appointments were frozen, funds were cut and the Information and Intelligence Unit was closed down in September 1976. Home Office officials also tried to secure the formal objective of the whole project: the final project reports.

The CDPs and State Management

The administration of the CDPs was little short of a disaster. Was this due to something endemic within the British state or was it simply that an unusual chain of events led to the mismanagement of one small part of the British state? Many, including James Callaghan, blame the untimely death of Derek Morrell (see Callaghan, 1987, p. 238). John Greve on the other hand, who resigned as Research Director in April 1972, blamed it on a civil service culture which encouraged the 'talented amateur' and militated against effective administration (see the *Community Development Journal*, vol. 8, no. 3, 1973). Without denying the relevance of these two factors, there are other factors which are perhaps both deeper and more pertinent to the specific problems associated with managing an expansive social democratic regime.

The first factor is associated with the attempt to secure more localized and particularistic (as opposed to universal and generalized) interventions. As the Beveridge objective of providing welfare and security for all led policy towards more particular interventions (e.g. based on deprived areas or especially needy population groups such as elderly people), then this generated the need for new kinds of information about localities upon which to base policy.

Amongst other things, the development of the British welfare policy into such particularistic interventions created the need for indicators according to which resources could be allocated and through which the activities of welfare agencies could be monitored. In the case of the CDPs the need was for area-based indicators. If such interventions were to be locally based but nationally coordinated, there were certain practical requirements. Indicators must be locally relevant but nationally applicable and comparable, the cost of their collection should not be disproportionate and evidence should be up to date.

None of these conditions was met, but even if these practical problems were overcome, there were deeper methodological issues at stake. We should ask what the indicator is measuring. Commonly area-based indicators will be based on such things as housing conditions or educational achievement. Variations in such indicators, however, may tell us more about the variable impact of national policies on different communities and less about the variations amongst local communities themselves (in other words they tell us about national issues and not local characteristics). Local variations in indices may also be a consequence of the allocation of resources in society as a whole. They therefore only have a random chance of being 'right' if they give rise to locally based policies which do nothing about the impact of national policies or the wider disposition of social power. The often-repeated expression 'pockets of deprivation' demonstrated the attachment of politicians, at least, to the belief that real improvements could be achieved in deprived areas without addressing the wider context.

Whilst the CDPs were an extreme example of a localized intervention, the problem of constructing indicators as a tool to reinforce management was endemic throughout more particularistic welfare interventions. In other welfare agencies, the problem was managed through the extension of professional accountability according to which the professional body itself established and policed the criteria of good practice. As we shall see, this brought with it problems of a different kind. In the case of community work, there was a developing debate about the relationship between social and community work, and about the implications of 'community action' in particular (see the second Gulbenkian Report from the Calouste Gulbenkian Foundation in 1973, which commits a whole chapter and much of the chairman's preface to community action). However, this debate fell a long way short of a consensus around the proper practices of a community work profession.

In the absence of any professional body of community workers with which a government could negotiate, the CDPs were based on an assumed consensus; they presupposed that the research teams would identify mutually agreed problems and objectives and that the action teams would be working in harmony with local governments and the local community. From within the CDPs this assumption of consensus was challenged in largely neo-marxist terms but there is little evidence that the CDPs were ignoring an otherwise self-evident consensus about the best way forward for the communities in which they operated. As Dearlove expressed it in the then influential *Community Work One*: 'The state desires subjects, clients, supporters, and helpers, not masters, customers, demanders and disruptors' (Dearlove, 1974, p. 24). The problem was how so to manage local interventions that local communities could be mobilized as supporters and helpers and not as demanders and disruptors.

If the management of the CDPs failed, it could also be seen as a failure of the CDPs (in the projects' and not the Home Office's terms) that they did not build a consensus around a radical alternative to existing policies. Attempts to link with trades unions and local Labour Parties were largely unsuccessful. Benwell CDP collaborated with the Tyne Conference of Shop Stewards in the production of *Multinationals in Tyne and Wear*, and in opposition to the closure of the Adamsez factory (see *Adamsez: The Story of a Factory Closure*, Benwell CDP, Final Report Series no. 8). Benwell CDP also claimed to have become increasingly involved in the local Labour Party after 1974. At the national level, moral support was provided in publishing *Back Street Factory* (CDP, 1980).

In overall terms, the CDPs built up few secure alliances. Senior levels of the Labour Party were antipathetic. For example, Callaghan was later to recollect that 'I still recall watching a group of experienced local councillors and residents almost visibly wincing as they listened to the jargon of "social pathology" and "the culture of poverty" employed [by CDP workers] to describe their neighbourhood' (Callaghan, 1987, p. 238). Given that the most cursory knowledge of the CDP position would have shown that it completely rejected the use of such terms, it is clear that, even with the benefit of hindsight, Callaghan's hostility towards the CDP position was exceeded only by his ignorance of it. The example of the CDPs suggests that whilst there were serious managerial problems associated with developing the welfare consensus, there was no immediately available rallying-point around which to recruit a radical opposition.

In this chapter we have juxtaposed the managerial ideas of the central state, typified by the Plowden Report, against the operation of one (relatively minor) function of the British welfare regime. The 'official' hope of community action was expressed by Lord Boyle in his Preface to the second Gulbenkian Report published in 1973 (pp. 16–17):

> Community Work is concerned to give practical expression, in a great many different ways, to a philosophy that puts people at the centre of things . . . A society should give the maximum opportunity for the active participation of people in every aspect of the environment, social, economic and political . . . the sharing and redistribution of power in any given society or community in pursuit of the search for greater equality and social justice.

Expressed in these terms, community work is a powerful expression of the social democratic impulse to ensure the full participation of all, based on principles of equality and justice. However, could these objectives be secured through the post-Plowden procedures of public sector management?

The dominant discourse of the Plowden Report is one of controlling public expenditure, creating long-term stability within which financial choices can be made, improving the techniques of management and the statistical techniques of policy assessment, and generally strengthening the ability of the core of the state to coordinate the operations of the state system as a whole. The later developments of PES, Managing by Objectives and so forth, and much of the avowedly radical arguments of the Fulton Report, all belong to this discourse. The discourse of community action, on the other hand, is one of empowerment, responsiveness, participation and equality. For Cockburn, this apparent gulf is bridged by the evolution of corporate management techniques in the local state which ensured that, under the guise of empowerment, responsiveness, participation and equality, the state developed new mechanisms for managing the local community (Cockburn, 1977). For Cockburn, the CDPs demonstrated three things: first, 'the purposeful intrusion of government into local affairs', reflecting the growing need of the central state to generate local information; second, the growing importance of 'the management of unrest' in the wake of urban discontent; third, 'CDP is an example of the high-risk approach of the state being put to good use by collective action of its workers' (see pp. 125–6).

The problem with this analysis is that it assumes much of what needs to be explained; that the state can be so managed that it will act in the interests of reproducing capitalism. Leaving to one side the economic reductionism involved in this claim, from a state management perspective we can see that the 'local state' was in fact neither monolithic in itself and nor was it fully controlled by the centre. The fact that the CDPs were also a site of resistance to the capitalist state appears to be handled in Cockburn's account by the definitional convenience that they were somehow outside of the state.

However, despite these substantial reservations, Cockburn is surely right to identify a relationship between the development of corporate management techniques at the local level and the perceived need to manage the community (and the family) in new ways. The error was to homogenize such management techniques throughout the state and to assume that this new management unproblematically served the interests of capital.

The Maud Report on the Management of Local Government had in 1969 advocated the introduction of a more coordinated and centralized policy-making process with a 'management board' of some five to ten members to coordinate the overall activities of the local authority (HMSO, 1969). Maud was widely opposed at the local level and the same issues were returned to in the Bains Report (1972) in England and Wales and the parallel Paterson Report (1973) in Scotland. Both recommended a more corporate approach to managing local government, with the creation of a policy and resources committee on the councillor side and the appointment of a chief executive on the officer side. This basic approach was widely influential in local authorities.

Despite this introduction of corporate management structures, it did not lead to the sort of rational planning which informs the discourse of the Plowden Report. At the immediate level, there remained powerful councillors, entrenched committees and departmental interests (see Greenwood and Wilson, 1984, pp. 131–2). At a more deep-rooted level, the elected local state was placed in an ambivalent position, simultaneously responsible for implementing policies intended to reinforce the weaknesses in community and family life, whilst also meeting tighter financial targets associated with the growing fiscal crisis of the state. And this was to be done with some degree of local participation and responsiveness to the local electorate. For these reasons, corporate planning was but one amongst competing discourses within the local state. As we shall see, where alternative discourses came to the fore, and where there was a strategic interest so to do, the centre was to initiate new policies and agencies which bypassed local government in the implementation of family- and community-based policies. That these looked nothing like the CDPs demonstrates how much was learnt from the CDP experience, and there was a direct route from CDPs towards the new forms of urban intervention found in the 1980s.

The CDPs and Managing the Welfare Consensus: Concluding Remarks

The CDPs were not a 'typical' welfare intervention of the 1960s and 1970s. The case study is included here because the fact that they could be established, the fact that they were so remarkably mismanaged and the fact that it proved so difficult to mobilize 'in and against' the state all tell us a great deal about the British welfare regime. If we ask ourselves 'under what circumstances could this have happened?' we may gain fresh insights to the nature of state management at this time.

These circumstances are fluid and, at times, arbitrary rather than revealing. Nevertheless they are suggestive. In the first place, the social democratic commitment to create a society which was inclusive and participatory was genuine and was an inspiration to key policy-makers such as Morrell. However, such aspirations had to compete for resources with other, perhaps more politically immediate, objectives. Furthermore, there appeared to be absolutely no conception of how such an aspiration could be institutionalized within the British state. Many official reports emphasize the desirability of greater participation at the local level (central government was rarely treated in the same way) but adequately funded and administered schemes are entirely absent; the CDP initiative was as far as the central state ever went in this direction. In pursuit of these social democratic commitments, CDP is interesting because it tested the capacity of the British state to the limit. All urban policies after CDP learned from this 'failure' and all were to be much more tightly directed from the centre. As we shall see, however, this did not displace the need to find new participants at the local level.

The CDPs were also concerned with meeting the Beveridge aspiration to eradicate poverty and deprivation. We saw from the case study how dependent anti-poverty policy is upon the discursive construction of 'poverty' as an entity. How was 'poverty' defined? Was it caused by the culture of the poor or was it a consequence of the uneven development of capital accumulation? How were data collected and transformed into meaningful guides for policy? What role was to be given to the poor in defining their own conditions and in identifying solutions? It was not just because of the early death of Morrell and the subsequent weakness of leadership that these questions were so inadequately addressed. It reflected the broader culture and understanding of the central British state.

Above all, the CDP case study shows us the problems the British state had in bridging the administrative deficit between central and local levels. The objectives of the state led it to pursue more particularistic and locally based policies but the implementation of such programmes depended upon a high level of consensus amongst the main agencies to compensate for the lack of effective administrative controls. The CDP case shows this tested to destruction with a rapidly growing gulf opening up between an increasingly trenchant neo-marxist position in the projects and a central state conception of the 'cycle of deprivation' and 'pockets of poverty' in an otherwise well-ordered society. Whilst examples from elsewhere are less spectacular (particularly where they involve professional and bureaucratic interests) we will see in the following chapter that the fundamental problem of an administrative deficit is similar.

Summary

In this chapter we have explored the emergence of a changed managerial style at the core of the British welfare regime drawing upon a particular case study. In the following chapter we locate this within the broader pattern of agencies and interests relevant to the management of the British welfare consensus. The key issues were:

- The development of the post-war welfare state led to a greatly extended state operating at the local level. Within the various welfare agencies there were a variety of information bases, organizational capacities and cultures. There were successive attempts to recompose the capacities of core agencies to give them some purchase over the local state.
- These moves worsened the tensions within the state. The case study

demonstrates that, at least for the CDP, mechanisms for handling these tensions were poor. The absence of a consensus within the state worsened this still further.

- We have begun to identify tensions and conflicts within the post-war British welfare regime. How these are shaped by wider interests, and their implications for the question of state power, is considered in the following chapter.

4
Professional Interests and the British Welfare State

● ● ● ● ● ● ● ● ● ● ● ● ● ● ●

The purpose of the chapter is:

- to examine how professional and other interests interact with the development of an extended welfare regime;
- to consider the relationship between these interests and the wider social base of the post-war British state;
- to outline the implications of this in the context of each of the major areas of welfare intervention.

Managing the Professionals

In the previous chapter we looked both at some of the post-Plowden changes in management strategies in the central state and at a case study of welfare intervention at the local level. We noted the tensions between the core and local agencies and the inadequacy of the mechanisms designed to manage these. In contrast to the CDP case, one crucial mechanism through which these tensions and ambiguities were often managed elsewhere in the welfare state was the professionalization of agencies of intervention. We begin this chapter with some considerations of this.

Professionalization of welfare agencies provided an apparent solution to a number of managerial problems. In particular it obviated the need to create elaborate, hierarchical and bureaucratic controls in order to manage welfare interventions. The management of local interventions could be left up to professionals under the overall direction of the relevant professional organization. Similarly, change over time could be secured through negotiation and agreement with representatives of the professions.

In pursuit of the strategy of state-sponsored professionalization British post-war governments, in common with governments elsewhere, found ready allies amongst the professions themselves. Administrative structures were devised within which professional autonomy could be protected but which gave the state at least a degree of financial and managerial oversight. These varied in detail from country to country and from agency to agency, the particular history of each contributing, often significantly, to variations in the circumstances under which professionals operated.

For this alliance to succeed, however, not only was it necessary for the government of the day and the professional body to work out their areas of mutual interest, but also they had to project professionalism as a form of intervention capable of recruiting active support from amongst the population as a whole. Popular faith in professionals was initially induced but ultimately freely given. The belief that 'doctor knows best', for example, was the outcome of a complex social process in which the state is deeply implicated. It was fundamental to all post-war welfare states that they actively promoted the state-employed expert as the solution to a wide range of social problems. This is why the more recent challenge to 'expert knowledge' so easily spills over into becoming a challenge to the legitimacy of state interventions.

Professional truth requires its evangelists who 'go before' to prepare the way for the expert and a priesthood who celebrate the qualities of professional intervention. It also requires a mythological history of the profession according to which the profession's founders fought against ignorance and cruelty with the sword of science and the shield of altruism. This active promotion of professional knowledge and altruism coincided with a range of legal and other sanctions through which the power of the professional as a state employee was bolstered.

The consequence of this, from a state management point of view, is fairly obvious. Within the state there emerged professional discourses within areas such as health, education, planning and (to a lesser extent) social work which were quite distinct from the logic of financial management and political priorities to be found in the Treasury. As a result, the success of the British welfare consensus depended, amongst other things, upon the success of the state–professional alliance. However, the success of this alliance began to be eroded in at least two different ways.

In the first place, professionals became increasingly troublesome within the state and they came to be seen as a barrier to important strategic objectives. For example, by the mid-1970s, the teaching profession's control over the curriculum and teaching methods was challenged by national politicians who claimed that 'progressive' teaching methods, and a failure to attend to the 'basics' (however defined), were threatening the whole transition from youth to adulthood. Callaghan announced a 'Great Debate' about the nature and purpose of education in Oxford in 1976 and this in turn led to yet more calls to limit the professional autonomy of teachers. Evidence that the alliance between national strategists and the teaching profession was crumbling can be seen in a number of places but it was not until the 1980s that this produced significant institutional restructuring. Similarly, the independence of the medical profession began to be questioned, particularly where this inhibited the Treasury from controlling public expenditure, or where it prevented wider political objectives such as the pursuit of a more equitable distribution of health resources through the Resource Allocation Working Party.

However, the alliance was not only challenged from within the state. The position of professionals within wider social relationships was being challenged. Their claim to possess a privileged position in relation to health care, education, family breakdown, town planning or whatever was challenged from all points on the political spectrum. For historic reasons certain professional and semi-professional groups were easier to attack than others; tabloid attacks on social workers, teachers, architects and even doctors were not entirely new in the 1970s but they developed a new and more sustained ferocity.

However, as the legitimacy of professional knowledge declined so too did the contribution of professionals to the management of the state. By the 1980s the question that this posed, but did not answer, was 'how should those parts of the state which had previously been managed through the mediation of professional groups now be managed?' We consider this question in future chapters.

The Social Base of the Welfare Consensus

By 'social base', in this context, is meant those sections of society through whose active or passive support resources were made available to welfare agencies.* 'Resources' include taxation, legitimacy, electoral and organizational support (e.g. in helping in the administration of policies or in the generation of information). In this case, the social base includes the organized working class, representatives of British capital and state employees (especially welfare professionals and bureaucrats).

Undoubtedly, this social base was weakening by the 1970s. Amongst the working class, a male worker on average earnings who was married with two children would have been below the tax threshold for most of the 1950s. By the 1970s he would be paying tax on a quarter of his income whilst at the same time the rate of tax was tending to rise. At the same time, the end of the long boom had put additional downward pressure on profits and upward pressure on welfare expenditure. The latter trend was exacerbated by the changing age profile of the population. Consequently representatives of capital, as well as sections of the working class, were both responsive to the call for tighter controls over welfare expenditure.

Nor could the welfare consensus easily recruit supporters from amongst new and politically active groups. Certainly, the women's movement had little incentive to support it in its existing form (for the reasons why this should be the case see Williams, 1989 and Pascall, 1986). The welfare state was premised on the family (in practice, women) fulfilling most caring functions (see Green, 1985); the family as the instrument through which welfare policies could be made to work; and the family which should be reinforced through supportive and, if necessary, coercive, measures. In addition to this more general criticism of the relationship between welfare and the patriarchal family, there were more specific criticisms of the relationships between gender and issues such as education, the medicalization of childbirth, medical power in general and social work interventions. Consequently, whilst women were represented disproportionately as welfare workers and welfare recipients, the most politically active women were in the vanguard of criticisms of welfare provision.

Similarly, the complex relationships between welfare and race ensured that the anti-racist movement could not be unequivocal in its support for the consensus welfare state. From the welcome given by the

* Arguably, we should have spent more time in previous chapters focusing on the question of the social base of the post-war British state. This was not done largely for the sake of keeping the narrative moving forward and not overcomplicating an already complex and dense argument. However, it will play an important part of the arguments developed in the following chapters and you might like to revisit the Introduction and chapter 1 in the light of this section.

Minister of Labour in 1948 to the first group of Jamaican immigrants ('I hope no encouragement is given to others to follow their example') to Powell's lament that white people had become 'strangers in their own country' because 'they found their wives unable to obtain hospital beds in childbirth, their children unable to obtain school places, their homes and neighbourhoods changed beyond recognition, their plans and prospects for the future defeated', black people were encouraged to know their place in relation to British welfare (both quotations from Jacobs, 1985, pp. 11–19). Their presence as a supply of cheap labour was welcome but their rights to welfare were circumscribed by racism (see, also, Joshi and Carter, 1985).

In relation to both gender and race it should be clear that the 'universalism' associated with the Beveridge Report was always of a particular character. 'Universalism' in welfare means that all people who meet certain criteria will be treated in the same way. It did not and cannot mean that everyone is treated in identical ways. Once these criteria are unpacked it becomes clear that the consequences of the 'universalism' associated with the welfare consensus were very different for men and for women, for black people and for white people and for secure skilled workers and insecure unskilled workers. Citizenship, as Marshall explicitly recognized, requires that citizens should express loyalty to a particular set of social and cultural values and to act accordingly (Marshall, 1950, p. 18). In this sense the 'universal' rights of social citizenship were, paradoxically, only conditionally available.

Therefore it should not be difficult to understand that the widespread, almost passionate, support which was associated with the Beveridge Report and the creation of the National Health Service had lost some of its vigour by the 1970s. However, it is not the case that this, in itself, constituted a crisis for the welfare state. There are two reasons for this. First, it is not true that the welfare state was universally lauded from 1945 to 1976 (only to be reviled thereafter). For example, *The Times*, in February 1952, published two articles on 'Crisis in the Welfare State' not long before Iain Macleod and Enoch Powell published a pamphlet advocating the means test for health care and social security. Secondly, as with concerns expressed in the 1950s and 1960s, the demand was for the restructuring or re-orientation of welfare and not for its abolition. Representatives of capital may have been lobbying for a cap on welfare expenditure but they were not advocating the abolition of public education, health care, social services departments, council housing or social security. Particular proposals, such as arguing that education should be more vocational in orientation, were more concerned with the form and process of welfare than with the cost. Much the same could be said for feminist and anti-racist arguments.

There is no substantial evidence that the welfare state had become a focus of widespread hostility or even apathy, despite particular questions concerning 'progressive' teachers, discrimination in council housing, amoral social workers, high-rise public housing and so forth. Indeed, the levels of expenditure on welfare in the 1980s remained sufficiently high and constant to prompt observers such as Hills (1990) to question the claim that there is a crisis of the welfare state. In the conclusion of this chapter I argue that, although there was a crisis of a particular form of welfarism, there was not a crisis of the public provision of welfare in a general sense.

However, the crisis of the Beveridge/Marshall model provoked a deepening of the problems of the state management of welfare agencies. In the sense that these agencies were increasingly 'out of control' from the core and disconnected from their social bases, however, they were always likely to be the target of what in chapter 6 we call 'new technologies of state control'. Many of the policies of the 1980s are better understood in relation to this rather than as a manifestation of a wider crisis; it was more a crisis of state management than a crisis of the welfare state. Before examining the consequences of this for welfare agencies in the 1980s, it might be useful at this stage to briefly review the key problems for management in each area of the post-war British welfare state.

Managing Social Security

As suggested above, the universalism at the core of the Beveridge Report was inevitably linked to a certain conception of what social life would and should be like in post-war Britain. At its simplest, there would be full employment, and all employed men would would pay a National Insurance contribution. During short periods of frictional unemployment, working men would receive unemployment benefit which would be sufficient to maintain them and their families above the poverty level. Their National Insurance contributions would also entitle them to pensions in their old age. Most women would be married to men who worked, and their children would be protected primarily through the male wage but also through the family allowance scheme. In the rare circumstances where individuals slipped through this net of full (male) employment and unemployment benefit, there would be National Assistance which would be means tested but, given the small numbers envisaged, could be handled with both compassion and administrative ease.

This scenario made assumptions about the labour market and social relationships more widely (especially those between men and women) which were never based simply upon empirical evidence but which became progressively less fitting as the post-war years passed by (see Ling, 1994, pp. 43–52). In response to these changes, and to lobbying from pressure groups and researchers, the range of both insured benefits (based on contributions) and uninsured benefits increased dramatically (see Clarke and Langan, 1993, p. 38)

The administration of such universal insured benefits is not especially complex. However, administering means-tested benefits is much more complex. During the same period (1950–80) the total number of persons benefiting from National Assistance and (as it later became) Supplementary Benefit increased from just under 2.3 million to just under 5 million (Clarke and Langan, 1993, table 2.5). In 1938, the equivalent figure was 1.3 million (ibid.).

The increase in the number of persons receiving a means-tested benefit is a manifestation of a deeper problem. The scenario presupposed by Beveridge and outlined above not only implies a certain relationship between the social security system and the rest of society (the explicit content of the Beveridge Report) but it also implicitly presupposes a certain type of society and a particular organization of the labour market. As the nature of society and the organization of the labour market changed, governments sought to adapt the social security system to these new circumstances but change was neither sufficiently quick nor fundamental.

The relevant social and labour market changes, as suggested by Lash and Urry, were outlined in chapter 2. The implications of these changes for social security are:

1 As full-time, largely male employment is replaced with part-time, insecure and more frequently female employment a contributory insurance scheme provides less security for all workers.
2 As women participate more fully in the labour market, and as women become more independent of men outside the labour market, then male employment plus insurance-based benefits become a less effective way of ensuring the security of both women and children.
3 As employers are looking for employees to work flexibly and for

variable hours, the benefit system becomes uncoupled from the labour market as unpredictable weekly incomes require a constant process of re-assessment for benefit. Furthermore, since earned income may be offset by loss of benefit, the incentive for employees to collude with such employment practices is reduced.

4 The social security system will always shape the pay and conditions under which low-paid workers are prepared to enter the labour market. As the economy becomes more globalized, and as governments seek to attract inward investment, social security policy will become increasingly influenced by what is available in other nations competing for the same investment (this may or may not interpret accurately the factors influencing the decisions of trans-national corporations). It will create a tendency for all governments to compete for economic advantage through restructuring the social security system. It will also be shaped by attempts to regulate this form of competition through the European Union.

By the mid-1970s the implications of these trends for the social security system were still being widely resisted. David Donnison, recollecting his feelings on being appointed to chair the Supplementary Benefits Commission in 1975 was to comment that 'I had seen enough to know that the scheme [supplementary benefits] was growing increasingly unmanageable' (Donnison, 1982, p. 25). Both Conservative and Labour governments settled for applying downward pressure on individual benefits but this was not enough to prevent overall social security expenditure increases. Whether the changes which have taken place since the 1970s suggest a tendential paradigm shift in the nature of the welfare state, as suggested by Jessop (1994), will be considered in future chapters.* For our present purposes, however, it is enough to note the pressures on the Beveridge social security system which such trends created.

---

* There are significant questions to be raised about the relationships amongst: corporate management techniques such as those considered in chapter 3; large-scale, centralized structures for delivering welfare; relatively unified working-class movements; and a 'Fordist' pattern of economic growth. Tempting though it is to address these here, we will have to wait until chapter 8 before we have sufficient evidence and conceptual range to discuss them usefully.

Managing Health-care Delivery

The National Health Service Act was passed in 1946. It imposed a duty on the Minister of Health to promote the establishment of a comprehensive health service to be free at the point of delivery. The introduction of the Health Service was delayed until the summer of 1948 in order to give time in which to create the necessary administrative machinery. During this time the medical profession was to secure for itself the most privileged position of all welfare professionals in post-war Britain. As Hill (1993, p. 35) puts it, 'from the outset the National Health Service proposal was exceptionally deferential to medical interests and could only be implemented by a further concession to medical power.' Consequently, in Ham's words, '(A)s volumes of research into NHS decision making have demonstrated, doctors have traditionally exerted a great deal of influence over the allocation of resources and the delivery of care' (Ham, 1996, p. 13).

Hospitals were to be managed through thirteen Regional Hospital Boards (RHBs) apart from the major teaching hospitals which were to be managed by boards of governors accountable to the Minister. Consultants in the hospitals were free to negotiate contracts allowing them to treat private patients in NHS or private hospitals. General practices were answerable to local executive Councils with a national Medical Practices Committee responsible for the overall distribution of medical practices. Pollitt has summarized the main developments in the management of hospitals up to the 1989 White Paper *'Working for Patients'*:

1 1948–89: Hospitals loosely supervised by the RHBs but mainly run by their own local Hospital Management Committees (HMCs). Little new hospital spending. Treasury kept a fairly tight lid on NHS spending.
2 1962: The then Minister of Health announced a *Hospital Plan for England and Wales*. This proposed a centrally coordinated building programme for ninety new hospitals, and a progressive standardisation around the concept of a district general hospital with a full range of medical specialities. During the implementation this plan turned out to take much longer than had been anticipated, and to cost much more.
3 1974: Major modification of the administrative structure of the NHS (DHSS, 1972). Henceforth there were to be, in effect, five

tiers – individual hospitals, Districts, Area Health Authorities, Regional Health Authorities and the Department of Health and Social Security. The hope was that the various services of the NHS would henceforth be better co-ordinated within a framework of long-term plans (DHSS, 1976).

4 1982: One of the middle tiers (Area Health Authorities) was abolished. This move represented a growing impatience with the cumbersomeness of the machinery created by the 1974 reform.

5 1983: The Conservative government announced that it was going to introduce a general manager into each unit, District and Region. Previously the mode had been one of governance by 'consensus teams' of administrators, consultants, nurses etc. (Schultz and Harrison, 1983). Now a single manager was to assume overall responsibility at each level (National Health Service Management Inquiry, 1983).

6 1983: A series of experiments with new budgeting systems was begun. These attempted to make groups of doctors and nurses more conscious of the costs of their activities and more active in seeking ways of improving the efficiency and effectiveness of expenditures. In 1986 some pilot schemes for a new system called Resource Management (RM) were begun. (Pollitt, 1993a, pp. 189–90)

The structures for managing hospitals – and health more generally – were left intact by the Conservative governments of 1951–64. As we have mentioned, the Guillebaud Committee had weakened the Treasury's attack on NHS expenditure and control over this remained largely in the hands of the medical profession. By the end of the 1950s, the combination of producer dominance and weak democratic and consumer control created what Klein describes as 'a bias towards inertia' (Klein, 1989, p. 58). Pollitt describes the hospital system of the 1950s as 'an administrative hierarchy perched on top of a series of individual institutions which were themselves dominated by an unusually powerful collegiate medical network' (Pollitt, 1992, p. 19). He goes on to comment:

> we can now begin to see why the ramshackle hospital system of the inter-war period was *not* quickly transformed into a rational, modern system. . . . it was starved of resources by a suspicious Treasury, dismayed by the extent to which the initial cost of the service had exceeded the original estimates. The expenditure squeeze was particularly tight on capital spending – so no new hospitals. Second, the administrative

hierarchy lacked the clout to ensure that any plans for the rationalization of existing current spending were actually carried through at ground
level. (Pollitt, 1992, pp. 19–20)

Attempts to establish more central control over the NHS were
generally undermined by an effective professional veto over any reforms which did not ensure representation for the medical profession.
So too were attempts more closely to coordinate the management of
hospitals, general practices and local authority community services.
This power was used not only on pay and conditions – Castle wrote
in her diaries that she and her team 'agreed that no TUC union would
behave with such intransigence. You just couldn't negotiate with this
lot' (Castle, 1980, p. 556) but – also to matters of policy (including
Barbara Castle's attempts to abolish private pay-beds in NHS hospitals in the 1974–9 Labour government).

This privileged position began to be eroded following the Report of
the 1982 National Health Service Management Inquiry (the Griffiths
Report) and then again following the 1989 White Paper 'Working
For Patients'. The implications and consequences of this will be
considered in later chapters.

Managing Education

If health is an example of a bargained compromise in which the
medical profession was the dominant force, education comes closer to
what Rhodes describes as a policy network. For Rhodes a policy
network involves the representatives of separate organizations in
relatively stable relationships based upon a perceived mutuality of
interests. Furthermore, this operates to the exclusion of other interests
which are organized outside the network (such as Parliament or
members of the public) (see Rhodes, 1991a, p. 120).

Following the 1944 Act, the Local Education Authorities (LEAs)
were responsible for ensuring the provision of education under the
direction of the Minister for Education. However, the network-like
relationships identified by Rhodes saw the emergence of a number of
key players alongside the LEAs: the Department of Education and
Science (as it was later called), Her Majesty's Inspectorate of Schools
and the teaching unions. In Scotland and Wales a similar pattern
emerged. Between them, these groups were able to negotiate a highly
stable settlement in which, with the partial exception of the move

towards comprehensive secondary education, policy developed in a largely consensual manner which reflected the values and calculations of the constituent members of the network.

Underpinning this emphasis upon change through agreement was a statutory and administrative framework which left the centre unable to push through change where this was resisted by the other main players. The capacity of the centre was reduced still further in 1958 when local government finance moved over to a system of block grants (which LAs would then spend according to local priorities) rather than categorical grants (which were earmarked but which rose automatically with increasing local expenditure). The effect of this was to push power downwards to the LEA and to remove the sort of financial leverage which might have allowed the DES to make finances available only on condition that certain changes were made. Later, in 1972, when corporate management strengthened the power of the chief executive and the central committee of the council, some power was taken away from the education committee and into the core of the LA where decision-makers were even more immune to influence from the DES. Of the 1970s, Ranson comments that 'The centre, bereft of funds and the necessary statutory instruments, had become manifestly unable to secure policy implementation through persuasion alone' (Ranson, 1980, p. 110; in Levacic, 1992, p. 110).

It was not until the 1970s that pressure from outside this network began to impact upon education itself. We noted above the launching of the so-called 'Great Debate' on education by James Callaghan in 1976 and the growing influence of the schools–industry movement. For rather different reasons, the inertia which Klein associated with the National Health Service, was also apparent in education. Indeed, when it came to the inter-departmental competition for who should secure control over youth training, this very inertia was probably the reason why the DES lost out and the Department of Employment (DE) won. According to a Labour MP, '(I)t was authoritatively rumoured at the time that a battle raged in cabinet before the decision was made between the Department of Education and Science (DES) and the DE about which of them should be given the money to provide for the young unemployed. We are told that the DE won because it could guarantee places very quickly on the ground' (Short, 1986, p. 42).

This view was echoed by a DES under-secretary who argued that the Treasury was convinced that the rate support grant (RSG) – the main mechanism for financing education – was not a mechanism which allowed the centre to have much control over how money earmarked for education was spent:

> the Treasury is very critical: education has promised and not delivered. If you give £50m to MSC (Manpower Services Commission) it will buy you a hard edged [sic] reduction in youth unemployment, whereas if you put the money in RSG . . . That is why we lose out. The Treasury–Cabinet line is pay money into an organization which will get things done very quickly. The Treasury has been a strong controlling influence. The Treasury/MSC link has been a key one. (DES under-secretary, cited in Ranson, 1982, p. 124; quoted in Rhodes, 1988, p. 263)

According to this interpretation, the fact that the Treasury and the Manpower Service Commission (MSC) lay outside the network, while it may have preserved the autonomy of the main players in the short run, led to measures intended to bypass them in the longer term. To confuse a metaphor, the bypassing was eventually to undermine the integrity of the network as a whole.

The pressures on the education policy network which built up during the 1980s were similar to those to reform the Beveridge social security system outlined above. The vision of the social world implicit in the 1944 Act was one in which the (male) world of work required a university-trained elite, a school-educated managerial class and a technically proficient working class whose access to the world of work would be through an apprenticeship. Furthermore, the different characteristics associated with each could be tested for in the so-called eleven-plus examination. Girls would not require the same preparation for the world of work.

The two things which required a response from the education policy network were, therefore, the changing nature of the labour market and the changing relationship between education and citizenship. Most reports of the 1950s and 1960s sought to conflate these by insisting that preparation for the world of work was also preparation for the role of a citizen. Thus the Crowther Report of 1959 advocated improved technological education and more relevant examinations in secondary modern schools whilst also advocating the teaching of literacy to scientists and numeracy to arts specialists. Similarly, the Newsom Report *Half our Future* expressed concerns about the 'bottom' half of the school system for both economic and moral reasons. The 1968 Plowden Report's call for Educational Priority Areas demonstrated a commitment to pursue greater equity through the education system. The 'glue' holding the network together was therefore the belief that more spending on education could create a society which was not only fairer but also more efficient, and improving efficiency could provide the additional resources needed to fund the expansion. This argument could only work if increased spending on the existing system could be assumed to produce such a desirable outcome. This came to be increasingly challenged.

By the 1970s it became less easy to build a consensus on this basis. For the authors of the various right-wing Black Papers (1968–77) egalitarianism and child-centred learning were responsible for declining standards of discipline in schools and in society as a whole. These concerns were fully amplified throughout the media. In the face of these, and other, attacks the response of the policy network was not to build alliances with other 'progressive' movements, or with local communities and parents. The curriculum, the teaching and learning process and the training of teachers were all put out of bounds for parliamentary and popular influence. Being detached from such wider support was eventually to facilitate government attempts to weaken the autonomy of the educational policy network.

Managing Housing

One study of corporate and professional influence over policy and the marginalizing of democratic processes is Dunleavy's *The Politics of Mass Housing in Britain* (Dunleavy, 1981). This book supports the claim that the adoption of high-rise designs owed more to the professional and corporate interests of welfare providers than to any persuasive conception of the interests of council house tenants or the public more widely.

The context of high-rise development was the defeat of Bevan's determination that council housing should be of a quality which would make it attractive to the vast bulk of British citizens; he did not intend it to be a residual service for the poor. Once both major political parties from the 1940s started to compete electorally on the basis of the number of dwellings completed, and once public housing became detached from direct middle-class interests, it never enjoyed the sort of popular support given to, say, the National Health Service. Indeed, related to their exclusion from the policy process, tenants often experienced council house management as generally oppressive, bureaucratic and insensitive (see Ward, 1985) or more specifically racist (Jacobs, 1985).

The impulse behind the origins of housing policy in the nineteenth

century is not dissimilar to the impulse behind the missionary movement. Even in the early 1980s, the Labour MP Frank Field could still
write that

> Council tenants all too often live under a form of serfdom which takes
> on a number of forms. It limits a tenant's ability to move from one area
> to another, and it hems their lives with petty rules and restrictions. It has
> always puzzled me why owners on a Wimpey-type estate need no-one to
> tell them how to live, while the lives of council tenants are hedged
> around with rules and regulations which would hardly make sense even
> if the whole population was mentally handicapped. (Field, 1983; quoted
> in Ward, 1985, p. 25)

Throughout the period under consideration, alternative approaches
were proposed and often successful when implemented but these were
marginalized by the housing policy process (see, for example, Campbell,
1959; Gibson, 1984). The sense of frustration created by this is well
captured by Ward: 'The whole coalition of politicians, experts and
administrators had a vested interest in not enabling people to find
their own solutions' (Ward, 1985, p. 39).

Beyond council housing management, there was a vast array of
public organizations and policies relevant to housing. Public health,
mortgage tax relief, slum clearance, labour mobility and urban renewal all touched on the housing question in a variety of (sometimes
conflicting) ways. In this sense the field as a whole does not constitute
a policy network as defined above since a large variety of (not always
mutual) interests are represented within a shifting and unstable set of
relationships. Faced with this, the core's 'power remains limited and
many of the current trends and problems in housing are barely
understood let alone directed and controlled as part of a clear housing
policy' (Brown, 1985, p. 120).

Such circumstances called for a coordinated and comprehensive
policy initiative which cut across traditional institutional boundaries.
Thus in *Gilding the Ghetto* (CDP, 1977) the authors note the similarity amongst a variety of official reports in the 1960s:

> areas in which bad housing is concentrated should be designated as
> areas of special control in which bad living conditions would be at-
> tacked comprehensively, assisted by an enlargement of powers. (The
> Milner Holland Report: Housing in Greater London, 1965)
>
> positive discrimination . . . should favour schools in neighbourhoods
> where children are most severely handicapped by home conditions. The

programme should be phased to make schools in the most deprived areas as good as the best in the country . . .

Some of these neighbourhoods have for generations been starved of new schools, new houses and new investment of every kind. Everyone knows this; but for year after year priority has been given to the New Towns and new suburbs. (The Plowden Report: Children and their Primary Schools, 1966)

We are convinced that designated areas of special need should receive extra resources, comprehensively planned. (The Seebohm Report: Local Authority and Allied Personal Social Services, 1988)

This call for comprehensive measures and inter-agency co-operation continued like a swan-song for dying urban areas during the following twenty years. The understanding of the need for such an approach is reiterated time and again. Echoing the under-secretary quoted above explaining why the nature of the rate support grant inhibited central initiatives, one member of the inter-departmental working party on the grant system told researchers in 1974 that, on the subject of urban policy:

We fairly quickly came to the idea of a specific grant system so that we had a sanction over individual projects. The alternative would have been to put money into the general rate support grant. I felt strongly that this would not have been the way because of our concept of geographical areas, that is, areas of geographical concentration of need, I would not myself have thought of a general grant which the local authority could spend at its own discretion, not so much because of distrust of local authorities as because this is not what we were told to do. We had been told to get a central government programme going. (Quoted in Higgins *et al.* 1983, p. 57)

This understanding that delivering the promise of the welfare consensus required new instruments led both to alternative funding mechanisms being introduced (e.g. urban aid) and to the centre acquiring new capacities to coordinate, monitor and evaluate activities at the local level (e.g. the creation in 1971 of the Community Programmes Department within the Home Office). The example of the CDPs is an indication of how successful these institutional innovations were.

Personal Social Services

After the Second World War there was no assumption that the various activities which came to be described as 'social work' had a generic unity. Often work with children, older people, 'at risk' families and so forth was each carried out by a different agency. It was not until the Younghusband Report (1959) that the idea of a generic, university-trained profession of social workers gained ground. 'The Social Worker', Younghusband had told the Mackintosh Committee in 1951, 'is concerned with remedying certain deficiencies which may exist in the relation between the individual and his environment, and for this purpose is concerned with the total individual in relation to the whole of his environment, in so far as this is relative to righting such deficiencies' (HMSO, 1951, p. 8). This is a statement whose operational implications are completely obscure. It may be that the impulse created by an inclusive, universal welfare consensus leads to a need to remedy 'certain deficiencies which may exist between the individual and his environment' but clarification of what this might mean for practice was needed.

The Seebohm Report of 1968 starts with the statement: 'We recommend a new local authority department providing a community based and family oriented service which will be available to all. This new department will we believe reach far beyond the discovery and rescue of social casualties: it will enable the greatest possible number of individuals to act reciprocally giving and receiving service for the well being of the whole community' (HMSO, 1968). As the report continues, it is becomes clear that underpinning the report is the idea that welfare should not only be family-oriented but also community-oriented. The questions which we posed in relation to the CDPs concerning community-based strategies therefore re-emerged. The promise of a professionally trained, locally employed work-force working to create stable communities and secure families was always belied by the wider allocation of resources in society and by the relative paucity of resources made available to social services departments.

In many ways, social workers were at the point of impact between the expectations of an inclusive and stable social life generated by the welfare consensus, and the reality of life for some of the most socially marginal in post-war Britain. This perceived role as defenders of the poor, troubled and troublesome also attracted various campaigns against social workers in the media. The 1980s tightening of managerial direction over social workers, and a re-orientation of their work, was to reflect a shift away from an inclusive, egalitarian ethos to a more disciplinarian ethos based upon the perceived need for order and sound morals.

The management of social work since the war is a tale of three parts. The first phase involved the construction of the claim that there is such a thing as generic social work (comparable to the general practitioner in medicine) and that a common form of training could be devised which would prepare social workers for their future roles. This argument was led by Eileen Younghusband and finds its expression in the Seebohm Report of 1968. The consequential creation of unified social services departments in 1970 ushered in the second phase.

The new departments were very consciously based upon the latest developments in management theory. According to Brown, 'attempts were made to ensure decentralization of provision, to allow flexibility and discretion at field level, to facilitate the flow of communication throughout the organization and to create a truly generic social work service. There was also a concern to create the potential for effective planning and involvement in local corporate management' (Brown, 1985, p. 163).

The third phase began almost immediately and involved attempts both to constrain the professional autonomy of social work within a more managerial structure and to break up the unity of the fledgling profession. However, these attempts did not come to fruition until the Children Act of 1989 and the NHS and Community Care Act of 1990. As Langan and Clarke comment, '(T)he prolonged survival of personal social services as an unreconstructed "monopoly provider" despite years of public vilification heaped upon social workers during the 1980s is testimony to the complexities of legal, organizational and professional structures associated with service delivery' (Langan and Clarke, 1994, p. 73).

The management of social work was unlike most other welfare interventions. Unlike the CDP experiment, the management structures had been carefully planned. Unlike health, there was no overwhelming professional presence capable of applying an effective veto to change. Unlike high-rise building policy, there were no massive corporate interests. That the machinery of government in post-war Britain could not be used to secure the outcomes established in the post-war welfare consensus should by now be apparent. Yet the case of social work is an extreme example of this general problem; the objectives articulated by Younghusband in her statement to the Mackintosh Committee and the values espoused in the Seebohm Report, would have required a far more radical redisposition of social and economic power than could ever have been secured through a social services department, no matter how well managed.

Concluding Remarks

The welfare consensus in post-war Britain incorporated a wide variety of interests and discourses. It brought with it unprecedented levels of security for large sections of society. Access to health care, education, housing and income maintenance were all extended to a degree which would have made the troops returning from the First World War gasp.

In the years since the 1970s there has not been a massive collapse of electoral or other support for welfare. Indeed, even at the height of anti-welfare rhetoric in the 1980s there was not a comparable reduction in social expenditure. For these reasons, it is possible to argue that there has been no crisis of the welfare state. And yet . . .

For those who work in welfare agencies and those most dependent on their services, in particular, there is a sense that the 1970s really did mark a watershed, after which profound changes took place. As we shall see in future chapters, it is in the management of welfare agencies that the changes have been most dramatic and it is these changes which mark the 1970s as the watershed years. The factors which lie behind these changes can be viewed at three levels.

First, the core agencies of the state, and the Treasury in particular, were from the outset convinced that the relationship between producer-dominated welfare agencies and the overall financial management of the state was problematic and in need of reconsideration (and centralization). Through a series of initiatives as early as the Guillebaud Committee and Plowden, and evidenced more systematically in management tools such as PESC, PAR and Management by Objectives, they attempted to re-engineer the relationships between the core agencies and the welfare agencies. However, the core failed to develop forms of financial and managerial control which were sufficiently sophisticated to allow the twin objectives of enhanced central control coupled with responsiveness to the rapidly changing social and economic context. Under these circumstances expenditure control came to override any other management objective. The case of the CDPs outlined in chapter 3 is an extreme example of the inability to establish sophisticated indicators and targets which local management could use and by which performance could be assessed. Consequently, when the long boom finally ended and expenditure plans came to be revised and (usually) reduced, it was not possible to protect the most distinctive and progressive elements of the welfare consensus. Victorian values were contained within the Victorian institutions at the core of the state onto which the post-war welfare agencies had been grafted.

Secondly, and partly as a result of the paucity of alternative management controls, the delivery of many aspects of welfare came to be producer-dominated. In the absence of effective central control, the delegation of accountability to producers became an accepted management strategy. The content of producer-dominance varied from the powerful professional dominance of health care to the policy network of education, and to the representation of corporate interests within housing. That neither effective central direction nor effective client representation was present in any of these very different circumstances suggests that it was connected to something fundamental to the British welfare state in general rather than the particular policy field. The inertia created by these powerful producer interests combined with the poor quality of central management to further inhibit a progressive response to the financial limits of the 1970s (on producer interests in the NHS see, for example, Ham, 1996, pp. 13–14).

Thirdly, the welfare consensus led to the creation of new interests and identities; as tenants, patients, claimants, 'at risk' families and pupils. However, the experience of welfare agencies which might be patriarchal, racist, bureaucratic or otherwise over-bearing meant that potential allies for progressive change were lost. Furthermore, hostile forces gained comfort from claims that public welfare undermined the moral foundations of society and rewarded antisocial behaviour.

Together, these three forces impacted directly upon the autonomy and resources of professionals. The state no longer unconditionally sanctioned professional power. At the same time, consumer movements and an erosion of faith in professional competence further weakened the position of state-sponsored professionals. However, the implications of this for state power and for intra-state relationships were to be considerable. Professionals had not only enhanced their own power but had provided state interventions with an added legitimacy, and, without professionalism, the British state in the 1980s found itself having to legitimize its interventions in other ways (Citizens' Charters and the like). Furthermore, a mutuality of interests between the core of the British state and the expanded public sector professionals had provided a fundamental organizing principle within the post-war British state. This was being progressively eroded and in its place new mechanisms were to emerge (see chapters 5 and 6).

The British welfare regime of the 1970s was, therefore, faced with irresistible pressures to change. However, neither did such changes constitute a self-evident and general 'crisis' and nor did they have only one set of inevitable outcomes. That they culminated in the social policies of the 1980s had as much to do with the formation of the state system itself as with wider social and economic changes. The dominance of a particular discourse at the centre combined with both conservative producer interests and unrepresented welfare recipients to produce the soil in which the 'new managerialism' of the 1980s flourished.

Most accounts of the so-called 'crisis' of the 1970s are weakly specified and empirically unconstrained. We consider these towards the end of this book. However, from the evidence outlined in the previous two chapters, we can add one further (albeit more limited) conception of 'crisis'. In the sense that the state could not be managed in a way consonant with the interests, outcomes and social bases of the British welfare consensus, there was a crisis of state management. Addressing this crisis was central to the politics of the 1980s.

Summary

1 The declared goals of the post-war settlement led governments actively to build an extended state. The position of professionals within this extended state assumed a high level of importance.
2 Once entrenched, the original harmony of interests between professionals and the core progressively gave way to antagonism as professional autonomy was seen to block national objectives.
3 The welfare professionals, in particular, were to be the object of the thinking behind the 'new managerialism' which is discussed in the following chapter. This posed new problems of legitimacy for state interventions which have yet to be fully answered.

5
The Emergence of 'New Managerialist' Approaches towards the Civil Service in the Transition to Thatcherism

● ● ● ● ● ● ● ● ● ● ● ● ● ●

The purpose of this chapter is:

● to outline the nature of the so-called 'new managerialism' of the 1980s;
● to consider the origins of these ideas before 1979;
● to introduce some of the changes taking place in non-departmental governmental bodies (quangos).

The state which Mrs Thatcher inherited in 1979 was one which inhibited the further development of British social democracy. However, in many respects it was organizationally and culturally even more inconsistent with the thrust of Thatcherite policy. Despite this, there is no evidence of a systematic and long-term plan for taking on and transforming the British state. In the years to follow, politicians and managers at the centre found themselves facing a variety of problems in managing the state system and responded with a large number of usually *ad hoc* responses. We shall encounter a variety of these in the coming chapters. Nevertheless, despite this often reactive approach, the changes cohered in certain ways which fell short of 'making the British state safe for Thatcherism' but which changed the British state in certain important ways.

In the following three chapters we describe and consider this process. This chapter outlines the emergence of the new managerialism within the central state and its relationship with the so-called 'agentification' of the civil service. In chapter 6, the wider impact and implications of restructuring state management between the 1970s and the 1990s are assessed. In chapter 7 we provide an opportunity for a more detailed consideration of public sector change at this time with two case studies. Chapters 5, 6 and 7 therefore can be read very much as a piece.

The evidence presented suggests that the Thatcher governments attempted to re-engineer central control over the state system. They also became so embroiled with the problems of state management that policy choices were frequently driven by the means available (see, in particular, chapter 7). Furthermore, important and stated policy objectives (such as the creation of a rational system of local government for London) were sacrificed in pursuit of the objective of removing sites of resistance from within the state. Thus, in an article reviewing public sector management in the years 1979–92 Thomson is not unusual in listing the following 'Main themes of government policy': privatization, delegation, competition, enterprise, service quality and curtailment of trade union powers (Thomson, 1992, p. 34). These are more about the means of delivering policy than the ends. Similarly, in *Implementing Thatcherite Policies* (Marsh and Rhodes, eds, 1992), the contributors frequently identify key policy objectives in terms of the pursuit of a changed public sector.

Furthermore, these public sector restructurings took on a dynamic of their own. Creating internal markets, Charters, new agencies and so forth all had consequences which were not entirely predicted and which could not always be managed in the anticipated way. New identities and organizational interests were created whilst older organized interests regrouped and formed new alliances. Consequently reforms which claimed to be once-and-for-all measures merely became the first stage in a process of seemingly endless institutional innovation and public sector change.

However, despite the importance of these two claims, it should perhaps be repeated that a state-focused account of Thatcherism cannot tell us all that is important about the politics of these years. In the final chapter of this book we try to assess the explanatory reach of this approach in comparison with other accounts. For the moment, we consider some of the evidence relating to state management in the transition to Thatcherism.

The New Managerialism

There is no definitive list of elements which all commentators include under the category of 'new managerialism'. However, table 5.1 represents a broadly consensual position.

Table 5.1 Public administration and the new managerialism

	Public administration	The 'new managerialism'
Mission and strategy	stability and consistency	responsiveness and flexibility
External environment	unilinear trends, incremental change	unpredictable, radical change
Leadership	consensual and considered	dynamic and thrusting
Culture	inward-looking concern with standards and processes	outward-looking concern with outcomes
Structure	centralized, unified decision-making	decentralized agencies linked through contract-like relationships and performance indicators
Individual skills	conformity, rule-following and probity	proactive search for 'new' solutions
Management practices	system maintenance	outcome-oriented commitment to change
Work unit climate	an insiders' club	uncertainty
Motivation	paternalistic	enabling
Individual performance	long-term career structure rewarding loyalty and conformity	series of short-term duties in a variety of agencies rewarding dynamism and risk-taking including performance-related pay; review-based supervision and appraisal
Systems	producer-dominated	responsive
Individual needs and values	public service ethos	customer focus

Notes: For the left-hand column I have used the categories of the Burke-Litwin Model used by many management consultants. See also Kelly, 1991, p. 182.

Similarly, Hood (1991) identifies the 'new public management' as comprising:

1 a focus on efficiency, not policy, and on performance appraisal and efficiency;
2 the disaggregation of public bureaucracies into agencies which deal with each other on a user-pay basis;
3 the use of quasi-markets and contracting out to foster competition;
4 cost-cutting;
5 a style of management which emphasizes *inter alia* output targets, limited-term contracts, monetary incentives and freedom to manage. (summarized in Rhodes, 1991b, p. 548)

We can see from this that by the early 1990s it was possible to describe an emerging managerial style in the public sector which was very different from the dominant management style prior to that. Two notes of caution should be introduced here. The first is that there is an obvious methodological problem with an approach which looks only at the changes and ignores the continuities if the purpose of the study is to evaluate the extent of change. The second note of caution is that it is part of the ideology of the new managerialism that prior to 1979 there was no management in the British public sector and that public administration was little more than pin counting. Any serious study of the British state should not accept this at face value.

As early as 1918, with the Haldane Committee report on the machinery of government, improved management techniques were being called for. More recently, the Plowden Report insisted '(A)s our investigation proceeded we became increasingly conscious of the importance of management' (HMSO, 1961, p. 16). The Fulton Report also emphasized the need for more skilled managers, who should both be rewarded for innovation and be in closer contact with the wider community (Fulton, 1968, p. 12). It is part of the mythology of the new managerialism that no one had thought about state management prior to 1979. Indeed, the fact that the new managerialism was not an alien tradition forced onto the state machine can readily be seen by considering the pre-history of the new managerialism. Here we outline this pre-history in relation to the higher civil service but one could readily carry out a similar exercise in relation to other state agencies.

The Pre-history of the New Managerialism

The Plowden Report outlined the problems associated with managing the British state in the post-war consensus and suggested some responses to these. It was the Fulton Report, however, which first began to suggest that the problems could only be dealt with by radically altering the machinery of government and looked to the experience both of other governments (especially the US and Sweden) and the private sector. The tone of the whole report comes across in the opening salvo: 'The Home Civil Service today is still fundamentally the product of the nineteenth-century philosophy of the Northcote-Trevelyan Report. The tasks that it faces are those of the second half of the twentieth century. This is what we have found; it is what we seek to remedy' (HMSO 1968, p. 9). The problem which they claim to identify is one of failed modernization: '(A) century ago the tasks of government were mainly passive and regulatory. Now they amount to a much more active and positive engagement with our affairs' (*ibid*. p. 10). The processes of modernization to which the state must respond were identified as technological change, the complex intermingling of public and private, the interrelationships between central and local government, and the more international setting for the work of government.

Fulton's proposals emphasized the need for breaking up administrative structures so that individuals and units would have discrete tasks and functions for which they could be held responsible (a concept of 'accountable management' taken from General Motors). Where possible, these units should be given quantitative targets but where such targets are inappropriate Management by Objectives (MBO) was advocated. Like its more recent appraisal process (see below) this involved agreeing schedules, priorities and targets with line managers. The creation of separate agencies (so much a feature of state management in the late 1980s and early 1990s) was also proposed in the Fulton report with the idea of 'hiving off' administrative functions.

There is no evidence that the Labour government in 1968 was hostile to the broad thrust of the Fulton Report and the incoming Conservative government embraced many of the ideas with positive enthusiasm. In opposition the Conservatives under Heath had been actively planning an overhaul of the machinery of government. Influential in providing advice at this time were Richard Meyjes from Shell and Derek Rayner from Marks and Spencer. Pyper summarizes the aims of the incoming Conservative Government in 1970 as:

> – restructure the government machine by creating a smaller number of large departments of state;
> – institute a new, rational system of policy analysis and review;
> – encourage the adoption of private sector management techniques (such as the accountable management schemes favoured by Fulton) throughout the civil service. A key role was allocated to the Civil Service College in this respect. Set up in 1970, in the wake of the Fulton Report, it provided in-service training courses and developed a research facility;
> – use the Civil Service College as a "battering ram of change" which could overcome the managerial conservatism of the Treasury;
> – create a new "think tank" which would offer Cabinet Ministers strategic policy advice;
> – "hive off" blocks of work from existing departments into new agencies. (Pyper, 1991, p. 91)

The intention behind these reforms was to give the central state managerial controls over the state system which, as we have seen, were lacking (see Gray and Jenkins, 1982, p. 432) and attempts were certainly made to implement them. The 1970 White Paper *'The Reorganization of Central Government'* (HMSO, 1971) promised both the creation of a smaller number of large departments of state and the creation of small units of accountable management. Also, a number of agencies were created such as the Defence Procurement Executive, the Property Services Agency, the Employment Services Agency and the Training Services Agency (the latter two being precursors to the Manpower Services Commission discussed in chapter 7). We have also seen in previous chapters how PESC and PARs, in their different ways, were attempts to introduce a sharper approach to the evaluation of both future and existing policies.

These reforms, however, ran into the ground. The creation of large departments, such as the Department of Trade and Industry, appears to have made little difference to their operations and, in any case, they were being broken up before the end of the Heath government and this continued after 1974. Management by Objectives (MBO), and Fulton's recommendations on accountable management in general, also faced methodological difficulties (i.e. on measuring the contribution of management to the success or failure of a policy), high installation costs, staff resistance and Labour Party indifference, which taken together guaranteed their decline after 1974 (see House of Commons, 1977, para 49). The fate of the Programme Analysis and

Reviews (PARs) was similar. Despite the PAR team being led by recruits from the private sector, the Treasury chaired the PAR committees, but without strong political support the guard-dog of efficiency had increasingly crumbly teeth; it was probably a kindness when it was quietly put down by the Treasury in 1979.

No better fate awaited the Civil Service Department (CSD). Its purpose was to push through the reforms in the machinery of government but as these all began to falter its position weakened. Furthermore, whilst the Treasury appeared to have no strategy of its own for addressing the machinery of government question, it was reluctant to lend support to a department which had annexed traditional Treasury functions. After much infighting – and some ill-feeling – it was abolished in 1981 and its responsibilities reallocated to the Treasury and the Cabinet Office. The permanent secretary of the CSD and his deputy were then 'retired' with very little ceremony. That it was the Treasury/Cabinet Office nexus which was back in the driving seat of

Table 5.2 The response to Fulton by 1983

Recommendations	Situation by 1983
Encourage more specialists	Ignored
Administrators to specialize	Never implemented
Establish a Civil Service College to provide training in management	Set up (but most training done in departments)
Establish Civil Service College to be headed by Prime Minister	Abolished in 1981
Create a unified grading structure, following job evaluation	Some rationalization achieved
Inquiry into official secrecy	Franks report (1972) on Section II of the Official Secrets Act. No further action by 1983
Greater mobility between civil service and private sector	Limited progress
Miscellaneous:	
(a) hive off certain functions	(a) some progress
(b) promote 'accountable management'	(b) largely ineffective at least until the Financial Management Initiative began in 1982
(c) planning units to be created	(c) not based on Fulton model. Think Tank abolished in 1983

Source: Adapted from Drewry and Butcher 1988, table 2.2

institutional reform during the 1980s, and not a civil service department or equivalent, was to prove significant. As table 5.2 demonstrates, the institutional and practical consequences of Fulton were limited.

However, in emphasizing that concern about public sector management pre-dates 1979 (albeit with limited success), we should not lose sight of the distinctiveness of the new managerial discourse. The new managerialist discourse brought with it a new set of values and calculations, and a distinct identity for public employees. To conjure up two ideal types, in the place of the values of probity, natural justice and sound administration came the values of entrepreneurship, efficiency and flexibility. The identity of the entrepreneur was to replace that of the administrator. As we shall see, this ideal type is more applicable to some aspects of the state system than others but it characterizes a shift across the state as a whole. Like all discourses with a capacity to effect change, it included a set of institutions through which resources were allocated in support of the change process; both the financial and the status rewards for those prepared to make the shift were significant. Before examining the changes in the state system more widely, we consider those changes which occurred in the civil service.

The New Managerialism and the Civil Service under Thatcher

For many of those directly involved, the approach of the Thatcher government appeared to be, at least partly, driven by the Prime Minister's personal distaste for civil servants (see Hennessy, 1990, pp. 632–3; Ponting, 1985, p. 7; and Fry, 1986, p. 546). Added to this were the intellectual arguments going back to claims such as Niskanen's (1973) which had come to pervade the thinking of the new right and which were openly hostile to public bureaucracies. To top this off was the widespread view, expressed (amongst other places) in the Expenditure Committee Report of 1977 (House of Commons, 1977) and also in Kellner and Crowther-Hunt (1980) that the civil service had deliberately compromised previous attempted reforms and especially those associated with the Fulton Report.

For some, one of the first signs of the Thatcher government's intentions was the reduction in the number of civil servants. In 1960 there had been 643,000 civil servants and this had gradually risen to

732,000 in 1979. In the years 1979–86 the number of both industrial and non-industrial civil servants declined, as can be seen from table 5.3.

Table 5.3 Industrial and non-industrial staff in the civil service, 1979–1986 (000; full-time equivalents)

Year	Industrial	Non-industrial	Total
1979	166	566	732
1980	157	547	704
1981	150	540	690
1982	138	528	666
1983	130	519	649
1984	120	504	624
1985	101	498	599
1986	96	498	594

Source: Civil Service Statistics (1986); quoted in Drewry and Butcher 1988, p. 199.

The total reduction of 138,000, however, must be interpreted with some care. Some 100,000 are accounted for by the privatization programme, rather than from job losses and improved efficiency (Dowding, 1993, p. 238) and reductions came mainly from the industrial civil service. In fact the size of the non-industrial civil service was about the same as it had been at the end of the Second World War. Reductions in the non-industrial civil service were unevenly spread with Defence being the single largest contributor to the total and Environment achieving the highest single percentage reduction (38 per cent).

In addition to staff reductions, the government adopted a hardline approach to the civil service strike of 1981 (and this also worsened relationships with the Civil Service Department which was abolished not long after the strike). A new grading structure was introduced and, as we have seen, the functions of the Civil Service Department shifted to the Cabinet Office and the Treasury.

More important was the creation of the 'Rayner Unit' (usually referred to as the Efficiency Unit after Ibbs succeeded Rayner in 1983) headed by Derek Rayner of Marks and Spencer (who had also been a policy adviser to Heath in the 1960s). Dowding summarizes the unit's objectives as being to:

1 examine a specific policy or activity, questioning all aspects of work normally taken for granted;
2 propose solutions to problems and to make recommendations to achieve savings and increase efficiency and effectiveness;
3 implement agreed solutions, or begin their implementation within twelve months of the start of a scrutiny. (Dowding, 1993, p. 241)

Dowding then goes on to outline the stages involved in each scrutiny:

1 A strategy was created. All departments were expected to suggest areas for scrutiny.
2 The investigation which followed was usually carried out by department staff, who submitted a report to the minister within ninety working days.
3 An action plan was then created which summarized ideas for implementing savings. This had to be approved within three months of receipt of the initial report.
4 The saving had then to be implemented. This was the responsibility of the permanent secretary of each department.
5 Two years after the initial scrutiny an implementation report was drawn up to see what savings had in fact been achieved. (Dowding, 1993, p. 241)

The Rayner reviews were closely focused on particular aspects of the work of central government departments. Various savings were identified with a total savings of £950m being claimed by 1986 (how much of this figure was actually achieved in practice is unclear). Even assuming that all the savings claimed were actually achieved, these sums are still small beer in relation to total public spending (see, for example, Pliatzky, 1985, pp. 70–1).

One of the first reviews was at the Department of the Environment (DoE) and concerned the generation of management information. The proposals were designed to give the minister much more management information and with this to establish priorities, monitor achievements and secure cost-savings. It was the DoE, after all, which had secured some of the most extensive reductions in staffing in the early 1980s. The minister concerned, Michael Heseltine, considered it to be such a success that he also introduced the system (known as Management Information System for Ministers, or MINIS) to the Ministry of Defence when he moved there. According to Liekerman, writing at the time, MINIS 'incorporates major innovations in the procedures for providing information and exercising control within a central government department . . . ' (Liekerman, 1982, p. 127).

If MINIS was such an advance, why was it not adopted throughout the central departments? Liekerman suggested that behind the 'official' civil service reasons (that other departments had their own information systems; that systems which were appropriate for the DoE might not be appropriate elsewhere; and that what was wanted by Michael Heseltine might not be wanted by other ministers) lay significant 'unofficial reasons' (that it involved a lot of extra work; it was associated with cost-cutting; it reduced civil servants to the role of line managers; and it provided too much information to the public) (Liekerman, 1982). Perhaps for these reasons, when MINIS was presented to a cabinet meeting in 1982 the response was unenthusiastic (see Riddell, 1983, p. 124; Drewry and Butcher, 1988, p. 204).

Despite this lack of Cabinet enthusiasm, the 1981–2 Treasury and Civil Service Select Committee backed the sort of tight financial controls implicit in MINIS (House of Commons 1982) and in May 1982 the Financial Management Initiative was launched. Government departments were required to draw up MINIS-like arrangements and, to assist them in this task, the Financial Management Unit was set up (which later became the Joint Management Unit). Alongside this redesigning of information systems came a new package of managerial controls, training and rewards which were designed to change the civil service culture in line with the new age.

However, despite such initial optimism, in January 1985 the Financial Management Unit could still report:

> valuable progress is being made and good practice established in assessing the performances but there is scope for very considerable further improvement. In many areas:
> – policy aims or purposes, where stated, are not clearly expressed with sufficient precision to allow assessment of whether these purposes are being achieved or not;
> – assumptions about the nature of the problems or conditions with which the policy is intended to deal are not made explicit and therefore not systematically tracked to see whether assumptions remain valid; and
> – assumptions about the link between policy and and impacts are not made explicit and therefore not systematically tested. (Quoted in Hogwood, 1987, p. 243)

This statement could have been made at any time since the 1960s and could describe any moment in the history of the British state.

Three years later the Efficiency Unit published its paper known as 'Next Steps' (Efficiency Unit, 1988). This report demonstrated that 'the key FMI objective of getting top civil servants and ministers to concern themselves with routine organisational management had almost completely failed' (Dunleavy, 1990, p. 113). Two reasons for this failure were offered; the short-termism of politicians and senior civil servants, and the size and complexity of the civil service. The suggested solution was to hive off departmental work to non-departmental agencies as far as possible. These agencies, according to the report, should be given clear managerial responsibilities, leaving the centre free to concern itself with strategic choice-making. Those familiar with the arguments dating back to Fulton and beyond will recognize that this was not a radical suggestion. What made it radical was that it was acted upon.

Before going on to consider the implications and consequences of this, there is one other feature of the Thatcher governments' management of the senior civil service which should be considered; its alleged 'politicization'. Clive Ponting (himself a beneficiary of prime ministerial support following his successful participation as one of 'Rayner's Raiders') argued that '(T)he new Tory administration elected in 1979 made it clear that they appeared to despise the Civil Service and although I shared their belief that much could be done to improve Whitehall, the way in which Ministers went about the task only lowered morale' (Ponting, 1985, p. 7). He went on to claim that Mrs Thatcher was attempting to secure 'politicisation of the Civil Service by the back door' (ibid., pp. 7–8). Another civil servant who left the service under strained circumstances was Sir Ian Bancroft who described Thatcher's approach to civil service reform as 'Poujadist, populist and silly' (quoted in Fry, 1986, p. 538).

What accounts for this lack of enthusiasm for their political masters and mistresses? There is no doubt that the gentlemanly conduct of politics amongst successive Prime Ministers and senior civil servants had given civil servants a role in policy-making which constitutional propriety would not allow. It is interesting to note the shocked terms in which Ponting complains 'the Civil Service was to implement policies without argument' (1985, p. 7). This is, after all, a statement of the formal constitutional position. It is not, however, the view which senior civil servants always have of themselves (see, for example, Cooper, 1983).

What was at issue for senior civil servants, was the sense that the club-like atmosphere which had survived Plowden (indeed, Plowden was a part of the club), and had even survived Fulton was now under threat. For some, the decision to act upon the 'Next Steps' report was further confirmation of this intention.

'Next Steps' and the Fragmentation of the Civil Service

The 'Next Steps' report (Efficiency Unit, 1988) was based on extensive interviewing with ministers, civil servants, certain private sector companies and the Council of Civil Service Unions, and its first draft was handed over to Thatcher in May 1987. It made two central points. First, the existing reforms since 1979 were deemed to have largely failed (although one suspects that sense of failure may have been deliberately exaggerated to strengthen the call for action). Second, significant improvement could only be achieved through a radical constitutional and managerial break with the past.

It was claimed that a large organization carrying out diverse tasks would develop a management style which was not suited to any of the particular tasks it carried out. In place of this, it suggested the creation of independent agencies to implement policy, leaving a core which would be responsible for managing the various contract-like arrangements with the agencies. This, the authors anticipated, would remove some 95 per cent of the civil service's activities and place them with executive agencies who would have real responsibility (free of Treasury control) for budgets, staffing, pay and recruitment.

For electoral reasons the report was kept secret (a damning account of failed efficiency drives would have been welcome reading to the opposition parties in the run-up to the election) and when it finally appeared its radicalism had been qualified. In her statement in the House on the same day as its publication (18 February 1988), Thatcher ruled out both constitutional change and any significant loss of Treasury control (see Hennessy, 1990, pp. 619–21). However, a list of potential executive agencies was drawn up and the movement towards agency-governance was tentatively begun.

By the begining of 1989, however, the Next Steps initiative was building up a head of steam and 'it promised within a decade to transform the face of peacetime Whitehall on a scale not seen since the nostrums of Northcote and Trevelyan began to work their way through the departmental capillaries a century before' (Hennessy, 1990, p. 622). Some ninety-one agencies had been established by August 1993 (Next Steps Unit 1993) and further 'agency-like' arrangements had been established at both Inland Revenue and Customs and Excise. By this time some 62 per cent of home civil service staff were employed in agencies, and Peter Kemp's estimate that at least 75 per cent of all civil servants would be agency-based by the year 2000 (House of Commons, 1988a) may yet prove accurate (although we can assume that the easiest candidates were first to receive agency status).

Agencies vary considerably by size and function. They operate within the terms of a framework document which, typically, establish:

the aims and objectives;
relations with Parliament, ministers and parent department;
financial responsibilities;
performance measurement;
personnel issues. (see Greer, 1992; Harrow and Talbot, 1994, p. 77)

The document is agreed with the chief executive of the agency and it is then the CE's responsibility to ensure that the agency achieves its objectives, and up to the parent department to monitor progress. Within this context, the Next Steps initiative raises both constitutional and managerial issues.

Issues Raised by the Next Steps Initiative

Whilst the government rejected the more radical constitutional proposals of the first draft of the 'Next Steps' report (which would have finally broken with the fiction of ministerial responsibility and acknowledged that the distinction between policy and implementation is untenable) it created a highly ambiguous situation. Chief executives are simultaneously said to be free to manage their agencies, to be accountable to the parent department and to be answerable to parliament. The conditions under which one of these accountabilities operates to the exclusion of the others are unclear.

Pliatzky insists that '(I)n the absence of fresh legislation, so it seems to me, ministers cannot abrogate responsibility placed upon them by existing legislation . . . and that is what is involved in the Next Steps Agencies' (Pliatzky, 1992). Of the chief executive of the Benefits Agency, Labour MP Kaufman wrote 'Bichard keeps writing to me and I want him to stop. Whenever I have a constituency case involving a social security problem, I write about that case to the minister responsible . . . ' (Kaufman, 1992). Kaufman complained that the minister would then write to Bichard who, in turn, would write back to Kaufman saying that the case is being considered and that an explanation would be forthcoming. For Kaufman this was part of a 'creeping abnegation of ministerial responsibility' (ibid.). This matter also concerned the Treasury and Civil Service Committee whose 1991 report states 'while Next Steps may not have changed the formal position of a Chief Executive as a civil servant who appears before a Select Committee, in practice it will have a profound effect' (House of Commons, 1991, p. xxiii). In response, Bogdanor in 1993 argued that chief executives should be directly accountable to parliament, that individuals should have greater access to an ombudsman, the framework agreement should be given statutory force, and that the responsibilities of ministers and chief executives should be more specifically defined (Bogdanor, 1993).

In addition to these consitutional questions there are managerial matters which arise. At the general level of organizational culture, the agencies are supposed to combine elements of the public and private sector ethos. However, the culture of probity, attention to the principles of natural justice and the need to ensure the statutory basis of action is not only distinct from the culture of goal-directed profit maximizing but it may be incompatible with it. As Bogdanor commented in 1992 '(T)he cultures of business and the civil service are more different than the government understands' (quoted in Phillips, M., 1992).

But perhaps the key managerial question is how the relationship between the core and the agency can be organized. Where, for example, is the core? Is it the Treasury, the office of minister for the civil service, the permanent secretary or the Minister? Is the core (however defined) prepared to focus only on outcomes, leaving agencies free to take all operational decisions? If not, what aspects of (for example) personnel and accounting procedures will the core impose and will it operate any of these itself? As Metcalfe and Richards put it in 1990:

> Conspicuous by its absence is any sustained attempt to change the way that core departments do their own work. The challenge to their traditions is at least the equivalent of the challenge facing operational managers. Preparing the strategic specification of policy, and then negotiating its implementation calls for skills of a new order. No department seems to be taking a strong line on this, and the project manager's attention seems to be directed almost solely at the task of getting the agencies into shape and ticking them off on a list. (Metcalfe and Richards, 1990, p. 235)

It may indeed be that senior civil servants, despite their scepticism, saw in the Next Steps reforms the possibility of protecting the distinction between gentlemen and players. The players could be moved into the agencies, leaving the core free for the gentlemen. If they still anticipate this, they may yet be in for an unpleasant shock.

The New Managerialism and New Agencies beyond Whitehall

The new managerialism was also to have a significant impact upon the public sector beyond Whitehall. Before turning to this it is important to consider the changed type of agency into which the managerialism was being introduced. Ultimately, of course, these two elements should both be viewed as part of the same process.

Pliatzky has listed the expenditures of the top twenty non-departmental executive bodies when Thatcher came to power in 1979 (Pliatzky, 1980, p. 15). These varied from £1.7bn spent by the Regional Water Authorities to £342m spent by the Research Councils and £49m spent by the Welsh Development Agency. To these figures should be added other non-departmental expenditures which Pliatzky estimated to include nationalized industries (£24 bn), the NHS (with a turnover of £7.5bn), and the 1,561 advisory bodies (spending £13m). The actual cost to the government of non-departmental bodies is officially calculated at just under £3bn for 1979 (see table 5.4).

Pliatzky's 1980 report was part of a self-professed assault on the 'quangocracy'. At the time, the assault on unelected quangos was a visible aspect of right-wing political argument (more so than any overt attachment to what was to become the new managerialism). Assessing the impact of this 'assault' is complicated by the variety of definitions of non-departmental bodies and by changes in the official status of some organizations over time (the water authorities, for example, became a nationalized industry in 1984 and the industry was then privatized in 1989).

Despite these difficulties, it is important to consider non-departmental bodies because they provided post-war governments with an easy response to the pressure for more particularistic interventions. They therefore became part of the fabric of post-war politics, facilitating purposive interventions whilst incorporating important interests whose support held the post-war consensus together. Thus fields as diverse as industrial training, sport, medical research and New Towns all attracted non-departmental agencies. Their perceived advantages clearly included their ability to intervene flexibly compared with the

more bureaucratic departments whose ability to generate many identical interventions in response to a central direction is of limited value
when more particularistic interventions are required.

In turn, these agencies prompted pressure-group activity (indeed
they sometimes actively promoted such activity) in and around the
state as they affected perceived interests. Both bureaucrats and politicians gained credibility, legitimacy, information and organizational
capacity by linking their agencies to such pressure groups. During the
1960s and 1970s the increase in this type of intervention and incorporation was especially marked in economic interventions but it was a
pattern of intervention which was found across a wide range of
government activities. For this period, Hood estimates a 106 per cent
increase in such quangos relating to industrial and employment policy
and a 33 per cent increase in quangos relating to law and order
(Hood, 1982, p. 49).

However, non-departmental agencies are attractive to politicians
for more than just technical reasons. As *Financial Weekly* (2 July,
1987) expressed it in relation to Urban Development Corporations
(UDCs):

> It is not hard to see Government policy as the next and possibly final
> round in the battle against Labour local authorities rather than as direct
> action to relieve the inner cities. Its emphasis on UDCs, central govern-
> ment bodies that can usurp many of the basic functions of local govern-
> ment, could be taken as corroborating the view that this is a power
> battle first and a zeal for reform second.

For an incoming and avowedly radical government, fringe organizations have an obvious attraction. However, the neo-liberal claims
made on behalf of the incoming Conservative government in 1979
anticipated a 'rolling back of the state' – including a 'cull' of quangos
(see Holland, 1981). We can get a sense of what happened in the face
of these two, apparently conflicting trends, from table 5.4.

Table 5.4 shows that whilst there was a small decrease in the total
number of fringe organizations there was also an increase in expenditure overall. Furthermore, it shows that central government funding,
as a proportion of total spending, increased during this time. Whilst
these figures do not tell us about the importance or practices of
quangos, they do at least help to dispel the idea that quangos were
being 'rolled back' at this time.

Arguably, therefore, the incoming Conservative government saw
fringe organizations as mechanisms through which to extend central

Table 5.4 Summary of non-departmental bodies 1979–1986

	Executive	Advisory	Tribunals	Others	Total
1979	492	1485	70	120	2167
1982	450	1173	64	123	1810
1983	437	1074	65	121	1697
1984[a]	402	1087	71	121	1681
1985	399	1069	64	121	1653
1986	406	1062	64	126	1658

	No of staff[b]	Total expenditure ($£m^c$)	Amount funded by govt ($£m^c$)	Govt. funding as % of total	Other departmental expenditure ($£m^c$)
1979	217,000	6,150	2,970	48.3	70
1982	205,500	8,330	3,910	46.9	87
1983	196,700	9,940	5,120	51.5	94
1984[a]	141,200	7,280	5,160	70.8	115
1985	138,300	7,770	5,100	65.6	111
1986	146,300	8,240	5,330	64.7	116

[a] Staff expenditure figures from 1984 exclude the English and Welsh water authorities which were reclassified as nationalized industries. Staff numbers in 1983 were approximately 58,000 and expenditure approximately £2,600m.
[b] Figures include staff at ACAS, HSE and MSC who are civil servants.
[c] Current prices.
Source: HMSO (1987, p. 51) with penultimate column calculated from previous columns

control. If this were true, then we would expect to find non-depart-mental agencies being changed in ways which enhanced their capacity to intervene in support of the Thatcher governments' policies and diminished their links to organized interests which were hostile to those policies. These are changes which are hard to quantify and can perhaps best be assessed through more qualitative case studies. In the chapter 7 we consider two policy areas (training and urban policy) and examine whether the relevant fringe organizations have been restructured in this way.

Whilst remembering Rhodes's admonition that, on this topic at least, '(T)he only permissible generalization does seem to be that there is no uniformity' (Rhodes, 1988, p. 180), certain trends can be detected. Whilst agencies like the Manpower Services Commission were apparently being prepared for abolition in the first years of the Thatcher government, in many cases this changed. The role of employers within training was strengthened and their expressed interests privileged; in urban policy, private sector investors (especially property developers) were given more direct influence over the allocation of public funds; public research bodies were compelled to interpret and act upon market signals; and employers were encouraged to influence the allocation of public funding in education through such things as the City Technical Colleges. In each of these cases, previously established interests were, to varying extents, marginalized.

There are at least two reasons for supposing that this situation would be unstable. First, it is not always possible to exclude 'hostile' interests (especially where such interests have organizational capacities which are useful to the quango). The weakening of the trades union movement, on a variety of fronts, obviously made it easier to exclude or contain their representatives. A second factor is that even where 'hostile' interests can be excluded, it is not the case that employers share clear preferences for training policy, or that property developers will all agree on the optimal urban policy, or that 'end-users' will agree upon a programme for public research bodies.

The New Managerialism, the Civil Service and Next Steps: Concluding Remarks

The channels of state power have in certain senses been re-engineered. As Sir Richard Clarke told the Civil Service College in 1971, 'I have little doubt that within the next few years, if the giant departments go well and if the PAR-PESC system really gets moving, the centre will appear as too weak and fragmented; and pressure will develop to strengthen it' (Clarke, 1971). We now know that neither the giant departments not the 'PAR-PESC system' went well, but this only worsened the sense of a state system which was resistant to central direction (see Hood, 1982, p. 67).

The new managerialism, Next Steps agencies and the continued deployment of quangos were therefore responses to a much wider change in the organization of the state system. Devolving budgets, creating units of accountable management, creating purposive, *ad hoc* agencies and so forth all had their origins prior to 1979 and were driven by an agenda which was not exclusively Thatcherite. We have seen many of the elements of the so-called 'new' managerialism going back to the Fulton Report and beyond. In this sense it is historically wrong to associate these phenomena exclusively with Thatcherism.

However, in practice, these developments were invested with a particular content which we might call 'Thatcherite'. The politics of exclusion have led to the marginalization of key players in the Keynesian welfare state. Representatives of trades unions, professional associations, local democratic organizations and pressure groups have all found themselves making way for an enhanced role for employers, business interests and (in ways which we will consider) consumer interests. In understanding what was involved in the transition to Thatcherism it is important to consider the relationships amongst the marginalization of 'hostile' interests, the construction of new interests and identities and the reorganization of the public sector. For example, how do the changes in the civil service outlined above relate to the weakening of the social base of the Keynesian welfare state? To what extent did the emerging new interests and identities provide a social base for Thatcherism? Was it possible to implement Thatcherism (whatever this means) using this new state system?

In the two case studies in chapter 7, we get a clearer picture of how these processes worked. We can also begin to derive a sense of the extent to which these changes have created a new and stable basis for managing the state. First, however, we need to look in more detail at the overall changes within the organization of the British state in the 1980s.

Summary

In this chapter we have introduced three main arguments:

the so-called 'new managerialism' introduced changes in the practice and organization of the British state which in important respects contrast with earlier approaches;

however, almost every aspect of the new managerialism has at least some pre-history prior to 1979;

not only are central departments changed by the arrival of the new managerialism but also the non-elected agencies which are accountable to these departments are recomposed.

6
The New Technologies of State Management

The purpose of this chapter is to explore two related themes. The first is the pursuit of new centralized strategic controls through devolving management and by fragmenting large-scale organizations. We came across aspects of this in relation to the civil service in the previous chapter. The second theme concerns representation within the state system. Not only have some organizations and interests been marginalized and others promoted within the state but also the basis upon which they are invited to participate has changed (from client to customer, for example). Taken together, there has been a significant change not only in who has power within the state but also how that power is deployed. This suggests that what we should be looking for is a restructuring, rather than a diminution, of state power.

A number of different ideas gave shape to these changes. In addition to the anti-statist rhetoric of the early 1980s came a body of ideas 'imported' from the private sector in the form of various official units and reports led by people from the business world. The distinctive problems of public sector management also prompted thoughts from within the state over how best to respond to the wide-ranging criticisms made of it. The outcome was the emergence of a cluster of ideas, outlined in the previous chapter, which during the 1980s came to be known as 'the new public management' or 'new managerialism'.

As a cluster of ideas these all shared certain conventions (being opposed to waste, inefficient bureaucracies and so forth) but these may conceal how distinctive each strand was. This chapter considers the extent to which these ideas are mutually reinforcing or compatible beyond a certain shared vocabulary and syntax. In the first instance, therefore, we have organized the sets of ideas around a number of shared analytical starting-points rather than organizing them solely around a chronological narrative. The sets of ideas which are considered here are: (a) the cluster of developments around markets, competition and the customer focus; (b) the state as an employer; (c) the audit and new managerialism; and (d) the politics of regulation.

Markets, Competition and the Customer Focus

The 'customer focus' which became prominent in public sector management in the late 1980s and early 1990s inevitably made certain assumptions about the nature of the consumer of public services. Because the ideas behind the customer focus also inform arguments about both quasi-markets and 'quality', it is important to be clear about the issues involved. There are at least two different conceptions of the consumer.

Two models of the consumer

The first might be called the neo-classical model. It draws its inspiration from the neo-classical economics of the late nineteenth and early twentieth centuries. These consumers have a number of characteristics:

1 they have a relatively fixed or predictable schedule of preferences (such that the shopping which they bought yesterday will broadly meet his or her preferences today);
2 they want to buy at least some of the things which are available on the market (they are not solely motivated by spiritual enlightenment or Arsenal winning the cup);
3 they can 'rank' their preferences and respond to price signals in such a way as to maximize their need-satisfaction within the financial resources available to them (thus they may recognize the equal amounts of satisfaction to be gained from one glass of vintage wine and twenty pints of Watney's);
4 this model also carries with it a normative assumption that freedom is best expressed through the market (conceived as a multitude of 'free' choices) and poorly expressed through state managed mechanisms (conceived as hierarchical, centralized and unresponsive).

It is worth noting that whilst Conservative politicians have associated the customer focus with such a consumer, such a model is less popular with many policy-makers. In health care, for example, it is clear that individual customers' preferences for health care vary significantly from those suggested by the neo-classical model. Health-care recipients find it difficult to establish a clear relationship between any given treatment and a consequent improvement in utility, far less to judge this against other treatments. Furthermore, the nature of the accident or illness requiring treatment may prevent the 'customer' from expressing any preferences at all. Given such unknown futures, the 'rational' consumer may choose to take out public or private insurance and then leave the provision of health care up to a negotiation between the insurance organization and the health care professional. This, however, would remove the neo-classical consumer from the immediate point of exchange. For the model, this would create problems of agency, given that some are expected to act in the best interest of others when their self-interest might lead them to do otherwise. Finally, even if individuals could establish their own clear preferences and priorities, there would remain normative difficulties in legitimizing a system of health care which leaves evidently vulnerable people to become ill and die in squalid conditions.

Since this has often been regarded as the only legitimate conception of the customer, defenders of the customer focus have often found themselves defending this (demonstrably inadequate) model whilst some critics of the customer focus have believed that a rejection of the neo-classical model necessarily entails a rejection of the customer focus altogether. This has produced a stunted debate which we would do well to go beyond.

Alternative approaches recognize the bounded nature of the choice-making consumer and reject the idea of a consumer sovereign under all circumstances whilst nevertheless upholding the positive benefits arising from informed choice-making by service users. In this account we would introduce the different circumstances associated with users of such different public services as prisons, accident and emergency units and the armed forces. This is what Warde (1994) describes as the 'social consumer'. As he points out, this model itself has several variants:

1 *the calculator*, perhaps associated with the Consumers Association and readers of *Which?*, where purchase is inspired by careful calculation of the usefulness, appropriateness and comparative cost of particular items;

2 *the dreamer*, Campbell's (1987) modern consumer, is one who is primarily inspired by imagining the pleasure to be obtained from the possession of certain commodities, but who, because the dreaming is all-important, can never be satisfied;

3 *the addict*, one who purchases compulsively, seduced by the very act of shopping, who is therefore more likely to buy on impulse without much prior thought or reference to need;

4 *the dupe*, who, according to critics of the advertising industry in the 1960s and 1970s, was inveigled by cunning media messages into buying exactly what producers happened to have available for sale; and

5 *the Joneses*, a much maligned couple whose irritating habit of exposing newly-acquired consumer goods to neighbours presently bereft of such items caused epidemics of envy in Britain during the long boom. (Warde, 1994, p. 227)

Whilst this model and its various subtypes help to deal with some of the problems associated with the neo-classical position, it does so at the cost of placing the customer in a more socially embedded context. Even 'the calculator' is shaped by socially constructed conceptions of 'intrinsic' worth and value for money. Social consumers are clearly motivated by a variety of factors. Such a consumer cannot function as the sole touchstone of good management. Consequently, as we shall see below, attempts to define 'quality' exclusively in terms of giving the customers what they want collapse. Even so, a persuasive case can be made for the claim that market (and market-like) mechanisms bring real benefits.

Arguments for market-like mechanisms

It might be helpful briefly to consider at this point what the proponents of market reforms hoped to achieve. They anticipated that the introduction of market and market-like mechanisms would provide efficiency without hierarchy or professional domination. Once market mechanisms were in place, it was hoped, the centre could adjust the overall availability of resources to different programmes and leave their detailed operation to market-like processes. As a co-ordinating mechanism, it was an alternative to both bureaucratic forms (following pre-established formal rules made available through a hierarchically structured bureaucracy) and professional forms (collegiately agreed standards policed by a professional association). Inevitably, therefore, it was associated with the weakening of both traditional bureaucrats and professional groups within the state system. Whether or not this weakening of bureaucrats and professionals is what drove the reform process forward (rather than the 'neutral' objective of efficiency) is a question to which we return.

Remaining with the arguments put forward in favour of market-like mechanisms, not only, was it claimed, do market mechanisms encourage the efficient *allocation* of resources but also do they stimulate their efficient *production*. One key mechanism which facilitates this is competition. Where producers compete the purchaser is free to award the contract to the most efficient producer. Competition has been stimulated (and simulated) not only by the purchaser–provider split in health care and social services but also by compulsory competitive tendering (CCT) in local government and market testing in the civil service. Analytically, it is possible to assess separately the implications of market-like relationships for the *production* of services and their *allocation*.

Questions over the allocation and production of public services are linked with the customer focus where providers are forced to compete, at least in part, on the basis of the value given to the customer. Partly for this reason we have witnessed the rise of the customer focus which is intended to reward those agencies which meet their customers' needs and penalize those who fail to do so. The customer focus was also a way of adding legitimacy to public sector changes which were often opposed by professionals who sought to mobilize support from the service users. It provides a disciplining mechanism over both professionals and management (particularly through 'charterism' which is discussed below). The 'customer focus', however, also has the effect of radically changing the terms upon which individuals may criticize or otherwise engage with the services provided. It may help to look a little more closely at the customer focus in one particular aspect of the state: the NHS where its origins (causally rather than intentionally) could be said to date back to the Griffiths Report of 1983 (DHSS, 1983).

The customer focus, quasi-markets and health reform

The Griffiths Report (DHSS, 1983) was an explicit attempt to introduce private sector management techniques into the National Health Service. Recommendations included the creation of general managers with overall responsibility for running hospitals in an attempt to contain the choices of the various health professionals within the priorities of management. However, the medical profession in particular successfully evaded the sorts of direct controls which Griffiths hoped for, and the general managers were left responsible for overall budgets without being able to manage a key determinant of expenditure – decisions taken by doctors. The next 'round' in the managerialization of the NHS started with the publication of the White Paper 'Working for Patients' (Department of Health, 1989).

'Working for Patients' (*WfP*) attempted to introduce a managerial dynamic into the NHS by introducing an internal market within which units of health providers (typically hospital trusts) would compete for patients who would be channelled through the district health authority and fund-holding general practices.

Furthermore, perhaps in the hope of avoiding a direct confrontation between managers and health professionals, the White Paper advocated giving doctors a greater managerial role and more generally pushing responsibility for financial management closer to them. Christopher Pollitt (1993a, p. 192) has summarized the implications of 'Working for Patients' for hospitals. These are as follows:

1 There is to be a clear organizational separation between the roles of providing hospital services (the job of the hospitals themselves) and purchasing hospital services for the population of a defined area (the job of the District Health Authority and of certain GPs – see point 4 below)
2 A DHA in its purchasing role will contract the services it estimates its local population will need with whichever hospital offers the most attractively priced bid, subject to also meeting quality standards. This hospital will not necessarily be located in that particular district.
3 Thus an internal provider market will be created, with hospitals competing for the revenue they will obtain through contracts with DHAs (and GPs – see point 4).
4 Some of the larger GP practices may apply for special practice budgets. With these they, too, may purchase hospital services for the patients on their list. Thus some GPs, as well as DHAs, will be looking for the best contract.
5 DHAs will be able to purchase services from private as well as NHS hospitals. Further expansion of private provision will be encouraged by tax relief for health insurance premiums for the over-60s.
6 NHS hospitals may apply to the DoH (the DHSS was renamed the Department of Health in 1989) to opt out of DHA control and become self-governing trusts. 'The government proposes to give NHS hospital trusts a range of powers and freedoms which are not,

and will not, be available to health authorities generally. Greater freedom will stimulate greater enterprise and commitment . . .'

7 A process of medical audit will be introduced in every DHA to ensure that doctors systematically monitor the quality of their work. Also consultants will be given more precise job descriptions than has hitherto been common.

8 At the centre a new NHS management executive will be created, reporting to an NHS policy board chaired by the secretary of state. The board 'will determine the strategy, objectives and finances of the NHS in the light of government policy.' The executive 'will deal with all operational matters within the strategy and objectives set by the Policy Board' (Cmnd. 555, 1989, p. 13).

9 RHAs and DHAs will be retained but slimmed down in numbers to make them more business-like. Local authorities will lose their former right to appoint some DHA members.

10 The resource management initiative (RMI) will be extended from its original six pilot sites to a total of 260 acute hospitals by 1992. This will give doctors and managers much better information about patient diagnoses, treatments and costs.

'Working for Patients' met with widespread hostility from the medical profession, the professions allied to medicine and from the general public. The BMA was particularly prominent in its opposition. However, within half a decade most of these reforms had become widely entrenched with trust status becoming typical amongst hospitals and fund-holding GP practices increasingly common. The internal market and the contract culture which this requires have also developed apace.

Professional autonomy has been qualified (although certainly not removed). It has required an elaborate and complex range of new mechanisms to achieve this. These include: the use of contracts to define the medical input which is being purchased (and this can then be monitored and managed from outside the profession); ensuring that consultants are given new, more specific contracts; through the medical audit process managers will be able to monitor aggregate choices within a unit and to question why these may vary from what is considered to be good practice (see Pollitt, 1993a, p. 205).

Alongside the increased use of market-like mechanisms and competition we have seen the development of the customer focus or consumer choice. In the Health Service, the preferred expression is often 'patient choice'. As Walby and Greenwell point out, this element provokes a positive response from some because of its connections with a concern with the rights of the consumer and the rights of clients in their relationships with professionals in particular (Walby and Greenwell, 1994, p. 68). The extent to which these more radical interests are satisfied may be gauged from a glance at the arrangements for representing patient interests in the NHS.

The proposals did not include an enhanced statutory role for community health councils. Nor did they include a greater role for the well-established representatives of patients' interests such as Age Concern. Patients were not even expected to be involved in decisions about which hospital they should be sent to (a purchasing decision and not a consumer's decision). They may be empowered as informed and rightful consumers but the conception of the 'consumer' is specific and limited.

Before the middle of 1996, the NHS's medium-term priorities included the need for 'Giving greater voice and influence to users of NHS services and their carers in their own care, the development and definition of standards set for NHS services locally and the development of NHS policy both locally and nationally' (Priorities and Planning Guidelines 1996/97 EL(95)68). In June of that year the NHS Executive published *Patient Partnership: Building a Collaborative Strategy* (NHS Executive, 1996) in which it was explained that the inclusion of this strategy was driven by at least five factors:

> – appropriate and effective services are more likely to be developed if they are planned on the basis of needs identified in conjunction with users;
> – growing social expectations of openness and accountability mean that the users of public services are increasingly seeking more say in how the NHS is developed, what services are provided and to what standards;
> – patients want more information about their health condition, treatment and care. The Patient's Charter responded to this trend by formally stating a right to such information, but it is of course integral to the whole notion of 'informed consent';
> – there is some evidence that involving patients in their own care improves health care outcomes and increases patient satisfaction;
> – as we become gradually more sophisticated in assessing clinical effectiveness and outcomes, it is important to find ways of communicating that information to patients in a form they can understand and to ensure that the information itself reflects the patient's perspective on the benefits of their treatment. (NHS Executive, 1996, p. 2)

This commitment should be qualified in at least two ways. First, resources have not followed the commitment and, indeed, the strategy has not been a significant feature of either national or local strategies. Secondly, the language of the strategy is similar to the language used by colonial powers when discussing the need to educate the locals 'in a form they can understand' before they could be allowed to exercise power on their own.

Even so, the desire for such a strategy is a genuine part of the world-view of many within the NHS Executive. In an era when the legitimacy of the NHS was a reflection of the trust widely placed in doctors, there was no need for such an approach. However, with the wider cultural challenge to professional expertise coupled with the NHS's own determination to manage professional choices, 'patient choice' provides a possible source of renewed legitimacy. Whether it becomes central to the NHS's self-legitimation, or whether, for example, 'evidence-based medicine' provides a revived scientistic legitimation, remains to be seen. We can approach this question from a slightly different angle if we consider its relationship to information technology strategy in the delivery of benefits.

Customer focus, information technology and the Benefits Agency

The issues around the introduction of information technology (IT) in the public sector may be instructive here for what they tell us about the weight given to consumer interests in the development of new forms of state management. The evidence is fairly unambiguous: the potential which IT provides to institutionalize the 'customer focus' has not been pursued (see Collingridge and Margetts, 1994). As Bellamy and Taylor argue, the information policy is not simply about creating a neutral 'electronic highway'; '(T)he real issues lie in the structure, meaning, ownership and regulation of the information flowing on the highway, and its dissemination' (Bellamy and Taylor, 1994, p. 9). Whatever the claims of the Citizen's Charter, there exists a countervailing dispersion of power within the state system over which the expressed interests of the 'customer' rarely dominate.

In the phrase favoured in the mid-1990s information technology was to 're-engineer' the relationship between the state and the citizen. Towards the end of 1995, Michael Heseltine created the Central Information Technology Unit with the objective of providing citizens with new and easier access to the state. In the Department of Social Security (DSS) alone, £371m was spent on computing systems in 1995. However, the aspiration far exceeds what has been delivered.

The computerization of the Inland Revenue and the DSS in the 1980s, for example, created two separate systems scarcely able to communicate, whilst the introduction of the Jobseeker's Allowance was delayed by the incompatibility of the systems in the Benefits Agency and the (then) Department of Employment (see Margetts, 1996, p. 179). Furthermore, costs and disagreements over which agencies should fund particular new developments, have prevented initiatives such as the Benefits Agency touch-sensitive screens. These could be placed in libraries and other public places but, so far, no agency is prepared to fund it. The fragmentation of the departmental system into a multitude of agencies, coupled with the requirement that wherever possible major public IT initiatives should be funded through private finance initiative, only makes these problems worse. As Margetts expresses it, 'information technology can only reinforce existing organizational links, it cannot be used to create them' (Margetts, 1996, p. 180).

To extend Margetts's point, IT will not create a customer focus if it is developed within an organization which does not itself share this focus. In the Benefits Agency, where apparently the customer focus has been taken especially seriously, we can see that whilst the implications are significant and by no means only rhetorical, the outcomes do not flow solely from the principles of 'charterism'. The Benefits agency was a Next Steps agency launched in April 1991. Immediately, the agency published a 'Have Your Say' leaflet to encourage 'customer' feedback. The agency also established six-monthly meetings between the chief executive and both the National Association of Citizens' Advice Bureaux and the British Association of Social Workers. The agency also liaises with the Commission for Racial Equality and claims to have established 'good working relationships' with the Royal National Institute for the Blind, Child Poverty Action Group, Campaign for the Homeless and Roofless, Age Concern and the National Council for One-Parent Families (see Benefits Agency, 1992, p. 11). In addition, all units had appointed customer service managers, and in January 1992 it launched its Customer Charter. Corporate dress and name badges were introduced and facilities used by the public improved. One of its targets for its first year of operation was an 85 per cent satisfaction rate amongst their 'customers' (Benefits Agency, 1992).

Two aspects of its framework agreement (establishing the quasi-contractual obligations of the agency and agreed by its chief executive – see chapter 5) were relevant to the customer focus. The first was to achieve progress towards the operational strategy and the second was to achieve improved levels of customer satisfaction. We will look at these in turn.

The so-called operational strategy of the Benefits Agency is relevant to the customer focus because one of its stated purposes is the improvement of the quality of services to the public (DHSS, 1982, p. 1). However, the phrase 'quality of service' requires some unpackaging. Adler (1992) shows that at least three different constructions are possible. It might mean 'cost-effectiveness', it might mean 'quality' in the context of a professional–client relationships (paternalistic, caring) or it might mean the clear articulation of legally binding rights with redress readily available where these rights are not met. The chief adjudication officer has also recognized the continuing 'tension between good adjudication and the need to clear claims quickly' (HMSO, 1991, p. 5). Adler argues that in these circumstances, with the implementation of the 'operational strategy', 'the interests of the government were put first, those of the staff next and those of claimants last' (Adler, 1992, p. 4).

In practice, therefore, not only was 'quality of service' given a narrow meaning, but administrative savings tended to be given priority. For example, the Benefits Agency commits itself to being courteous, fair, confidential, private and accessible. It sets clearance-time targets for payments, and it promises to consult with the representatives of ethnic minorities and disabled people. Arguably, however, in the wider context of addressing social needs, these are much less important than take-up rates. An improved take-up of benefits would disproportionately benefit the most vulnerable groups. This, however, is not a target of the agency. Indeed, the chief executive of the Benefits Agency told the Treasury and Civil Service Select Committee that neither were such targets set nor did he know what the take-up rates were (House of Commons, 1991, pp. 29–30). Similarly, if a claimant feels that the agency has been less than courteous, fair and so forth, the claimant must complain directly to the agency itself. Presumably, less assertive claimants would feel uncomfortable about this. Randall (1992) has suggested the need to provide alternative and more supportive procedures (for example a Benefits Ombudsman or existing agencies such as local government). Indeed, one could imagine a 'mixed economy of advocacy' (including self-advocacy) which would give the customer focus sharper teeth (see chapter 8). Addressing these problems is a prerequisite for the successful use of IT in reengineering the relationship between the state and the citizen.

In addition to the framework agreement, and partly in an effort to sharpen the customer focus, the Benefits Agency published its Customer Charter early in 1992. This followed the official launch of the Citizen's Charter in July 1991, at which the Prime Minister announced, 'I want the Citizen's Charter to be one of the central themes in public life in the 1990s' (Prime Minister, 1991, p. 2). By 1993 some thirty Charters had been published alongside the Benefits Agency's Customer Charter. Senior management at the Benefits Agency also responded with enthusiasm to the Charter Mark award scheme and in 1992 the agency submitted three applications and was successful with two. In February 1993 the Charter Mark scheme was relaunched to give (so it was hoped) a new impetus to the scheme. The intention behind this was to encourage more public organizations to apply for an award (although some managers were applying for the competitor scheme the British Standards Institute 'quality' Kitemark BS5750).

The Charter Mark scheme can be regarded as the flagship for encouraging the adoption of 'charterism' across the public sector and it is worth briefly considering its content. The Charter mark Scheme *Guide for Applicants* (Cabinet Office, 1993) includes nine criteria which might be summarized as:

1 setting and monitoring explicit standards and publishing outcomes;
2 providing full and accurate information about how services are run, what they cost, how well they perform and who is in charge;
3 consulting the public before establishing priorities and standards and providing choice wherever practicable;
4 being courteous and helpful;
5 having well-publicized and accessible complaints procedures;
6 providing value for money;
7 providing customer satisfaction;
8 providing measurable improvements on previous standards;
9 providing innovative improvements at no additional cost to the tax-payer or customer. (see Ling, 1994a, p. 53)

The questions raised by these objectives parallel those raised by the commitment to a 'customer focus' contained in the framework agreement. These concern not only the content given to targets such as 'improving standards' and 'consulting with the public' but also the relative weight given to each target and the outcomes when different targets conflict. However, 'charterism' is not simply an ideological cover concealing sinister intentions; its implications for state management are significant. These implications must first be considered before we make the common error of technological determinism in assuming that changes in IT of themselves bring changes to the relationship between a state and its citizens.

The implications of charterism

Charterism is intended to pull accountability downwards within de-centralized agencies. By establishing formal structures which empower service users and condition the activities of local management (albeit within very particular limits) it introduces a new set of calculations into the local operation of the state which has real effects. It is emphatically not only a masquerade. What are these effects?

Underlying charterism is a neo-classical model of the consumer. As we have noted, this involves a conception of the consumer as a rational, choosing individual who can identify and express his or her needs and calculate the best way to maximize need satisfaction (see Buchanan, 1968; Friedman, 1980; Hayek, 1986). Were charterism and this model of the consumer to become generalized throughout the public sector it would progressively transform the relationships which exist between the state and civil society. This relationship, in all but the most dictatorial of regimes, has been mediated by organized interests which have the capacity to bring pressure onto governments in defence of perceived collective interests. Individual, legally grounded rights have always been an important basis for such action but they have never been sufficient to provide a defence against state power. By marginalizing participatory and collective forms of political action, charterism, on its own and unlimited, would erode the very institutional basis for a democratic society. Well might Shell (1993) ask 'is not real citizenship stronger stuff than this?', and he concludes that 'a fraudulent concept of citizenship is being peddled.'

However, this argument must be qualified. It is not the case that charterism will become the sole, or even the primary, mechanism through which the relationship between the state and the people is mediated (and, indeed, in chapter 8 it is argued that where it is one of a variety of mediating mechanisms it has positive advantages). At the Benefits Agency, for instance, we saw that organized interests were being represented in regular meetings (although what power they might have is less clear). Furthermore, the pressure on management to achieve objectives other than those of satisfied customers remains great. Indeed, these pressures are often more immediate. In particular, market testing and competition have brought with them an acute need for management action which may conflict with the purposes of charterism.

Competition and market testing

Theoretically, internal markets and the customer focus are complemented by competition. Through competition, it is argued, incentives are created which will encourage innovation and managerial efficiency. Starting with local government, competition has been introduced throughout much of the private sector. Since 1989 competitive tendering has been compulsory for local government where the original list of functions which were to be put out for competitive tendering included :

- refuse collection
- cleaning of buildings and other cleaning such as street cleaning and litter collection
- catering (in schools, staff canteens and so forth)
- ground maintenance
- vehicle servicing. (see Elcock, 1993, pp. 158–9)

To these were added street lighting and the management of sport and leisure facilities.

The process involves inviting private companies to tender for the provision of these services. Each company offers to provide the service for a sum of money (and the local authority may submit an in-house bid also). The contract is then awarded to the lowest bidder unless the local authority is (legitimately) satisfied that the task requires a technical or professional input which is missing from that bid.

'Market testing' is the equivalent of compulsory competitive tendering for central government services. The official *Guide to Market Testing* states 'In market testing, an activity currently performed in-house is subjected to competition. Market testing compares with "make or buy" decisions in the private sector and exists to ensure the efficient provision of services to the public' (Efficiency Unit, 1993). Harrow and Talbot (1994, p. 88) list the twelve-point process involved in market testing: 'identifying scope and nature of service for test; establishing what level of service is necessary; identifying baseline costs; assessing the market; developing a specification document; inviting interest from potential suppliers; selecting a suitable list of bidders; calling for bids from the selected participants; evaluating competing bids from external providers and the in-house team;

awarding a contract or service-level agreement; monitoring the performance and the cost of the operation on a continuous basis; retesting.'
Market testing began in April 1992 and included activities involving something under 80,000 civil servants and over £2bn worth of activities in the following two years (see Harrow and Talbot, 1994, p. 89).

The precise impact of CCT and market testing on costs is a matter of controversy. However, together with the customer focus and the internal market, we can identify an attempted wholesale redesigning of state management. The consequences vary substantially throughout the state system. The senior civil service, for example, is not subject to market testing, it does not face CCT, and it is not about to become a Next Steps Agency. Professionals in the health service and in local government are more protected from the consequences of competition than ancillary staff and street cleaners. To some extent, at least, there appears to be a new public sector labour process emerging, in which a new division of labour, with new controls, incentives and patterns of resistance, is being created. Let us look at this a little more closely.

Managing Public Employees

All modern states employ individuals who, in return for payments, carry out tasks which establish the state as an active force in society capable of reproducing itself over time. In all modern states, the employment of individuals also brings with it certain problems. The separation of ownership and policy success from the immediate incentives facing public employees creates inevitable problems. In no particular order, we can say that these problems involve:

1 how to organize the negotiation and delivery of pay and conditions and resolve disputes concerning these;
2 how to prevent the possible embedding of state employees within non-state interests (of either a corrupt or a more politicized form);
3 how to create and maintain a public sector culture and organization through which a discourse of public responsibility and political accountability may be sustained.

The elements creating the negotiation and organization of pay and conditions for much of the post-war period are often referred to as Whitleyism. They included: the idea of comparability of public pay;

the state as a 'model employer' in the (uniform) terms and conditions which it provided (as summed up in the Priestly Report, HMSO 1955, p. 39); union recognition; and, finally, centralized bargaining (see Farnham, 1993, p. 105). Whilst most of these elements pre-date the post-war settlement, they were absorbed into it and routinized as an important aspect of the fabric of post-war politics. This was part of a wider discourse of the state acting in the common good and the pursuit of the public interest being the primary function of the state to which trades unions, professional associations and employers were all broadly committed.

The 'fair comparisons' were to be based on the findings of the Pay Research Unit and any failures to agree were to go to arbitration. The centralized nature of this was routinely taken for granted with, for example, the Plowden Report insisting '(O)n pay and conditions of service, there must be a high degree of central control; chaos would result if there were different rates of pay for the same kind of work or different rules governing conditions of service operating in different departments' (HMSO, 1961, p. 15). Within this fundamentally centralized structure, individual and local grievances would be dealt with by personnel managers who were supposed to both be a part of management and yet function as a sort of 'neutral umpire' between management and work-force (see Farnham, 1993, pp. 107–9).

The formal centralization of these structures was abated by a number of factors. First, the growth of public sector unionism was not fully absorbed into centralized negotiating bodies. Some power, at least, continued to be exercised by regionally based, (often) full-time trades union officials. In addition, public employees were often locked into the kind of sub-central relationships and interdependencies described by Rhodes (1988) where the operations, calculations and perceived interests of local agencies are shaped (or 'colonized') by their contacts with adjacent agencies. Alongside these two developments was a separate but reinforcing trend towards the growth of public sector professionals (such as accountancy, education, planning and so forth). In this way, not only the centralized nature of pay negotiation became difficult to sustain (with various well-publicized breakdowns culminating in the so-called 'winter of discontent'), but the idea of a cadre of public officials mobilized towards a shared conception of the 'public good' also lost its force.

As we have seen, efforts were made throughout the 1960s and 1970s to recompose the state officialdom. There was an increasing emphasis upon the importance of management as seen in both the Plowden and the Fulton reports on central government, and in the

Bains Report on corporate management in local government. Alongside this was an extension of the use of judicial and quasi-judicial forums within which the discretion of public officials could be challenged and checked. Despite the absence of continental-style administrative law, the efforts of Lord Denning and others to construct an enhanced legal basis for using the courts to constrain public agencies bore some fruit. At the same time, a greater willingness by governments to regulate the behaviour of public officials through statute, a wider use of both statutory inquiries and administrative tribunals, and the introduction of an 'ombudsman' for public administration and elsewhere all had the effect of 'juridifying' the working lives of state officials.

By the mid-1970s, therefore, public employees were likely to be operating within a more 'managerialist' atmosphere and to be subject to more precise and forceful legal and quasi-judicial limitations. Despite this, the principles of centralized negotiating, union recognition, comparability and so forth were largely still applied. During the following twenty years, however, much of this was to change (although there have also been significant continuities).

The sorts of changes to the organization of the state in the 1980s and 1990s which we have already outlined required significant changes in the experiences and activities of state employees. The debureaucratizing of the civil service, compulsory competitive tendering, internal markets, market testing and new approaches to personnel management have combined with cost-cutting, deprivileging public sector professionals and senior civil servants, a weakening of (public and private sector) unions and an overall questioning of the value of public services to change fundamentally the experiences of state employees. For those entering the new management positions, the direction of change is away from the public service ethos of a job-for-life, a clear career pattern and an interest in probity and rule-following and towards a managerial ethos of opportunistic career patterns with an interest in outcomes rather than rule-following (see Kelly, 1991, p. 182).

For many public employees the fear of competition and impending privatization encouraged acquiescence. However, there was also trades union resistance which was significant not only for its extent but especially for its form. In the water industry, for example, the 1983 Water Act abolished the tripartite structures which had characterized its industrial relations structures throughout the post-war period, removed local authority representation, brought in ministerial appointees from industry and commerce and cut back public expenditure. Employment in the industry collapsed from 109,000 in 1980 to 7,900 in 1989 when the industry was privatized (Foster and Taylor, 1994, p. 5). The trades union response was to campaign against all such measures but to do so effectively they were compelled to fight on the basis of the public interest and not merely in defence of members' security, pay and conditions. Alongside the 'Water Works Keep it Public!' campaign, trades unionists organizing in the water industry established campaigning links with environmentalists, local pressure groups, local councillors and others in an effort to redefine the 'public interest' in relation to the industry. Furthermore, they campaigned on the basis that a privatized industry would fail to meet the needs of the 'customer' (see Foster and Taylor, 1994, pp. 5–9). Similarly, public sector unions campaigned against CCT on the basis of not only protecting jobs but also protecting service quality. Much effort was put into contesting government definitions of 'quality' and 'value for money'.

The response of trades unionists demonstrated not only the need to challenge the attempted reconstruction of conceptions of the 'public interest' but the willingness of trades unionists to enter such a terrain of struggle. Arguably this attempt was stunted by the desire to go back to a pre-1979 conception of the state as an altruistic actor working on behalf of the whole people, but there are many examples of interventions which went beyond this. The strategic responses of trades unions and their allies demonstrated how government strategies can create (unanticipated) new alliances and new identities through the opposition which they generate. In chapter 8 it is suggested that this sort of willingness to reconsider conceptions of the public interest and the role of the state opens up new forms of political represent-ation and action.

Identities were also recomposed through direct managerial inter-ventions (rather than deliberate political action). There are two sepa-rate groups who have become subject to the power of the new managers. The first is the state-employed working class who have become more proletarianized. In the place of Whitleyism, which 'softened' the nature of class relations within the state, management (whether in new agencies or in private sector companies successfully tendering for public contracts) have been given enhanced powers to codify tasks, monitor their execution, punish failure and reward success (however defined). The role of contracts in defining tasks and outcomes has been important in establishing a basis for so redefining the state labour process (which includes a worsening in pay and conditions for many women in particular). Obviously, management's capacity to operate in this way has been enhanced by successive labour market legislation which has included the abolition of the minimum wage, the reconstruction of training policy, changes in social security legislation and successive Industrial Relations Acts intended to undermine the power of unions (on the changing class position of state employees, see Fairbrother, 1989).

The second group being more clearly brought under the direction of management is the public sector professionals. This has always been a more complex objective to secure. In particular, controlling the process of professional decision-taking through segmenting and monitoring the routine choices of, say, teachers and doctors, would involve the claim that the knowledge-base of management was at least as legitimate as the knowledge-base of professionals. In the absence of this, management have moved to redefine and narrow the contracts given to, for example, hospital consultants, but also to focus on outcomes rather than processes. Therefore medical audits will look at the overall expenditure on pharmaceuticals by a general practice, league tables will place schools in a hierarchy of examination results, the Audit Commission will compare the administrative costs of comparable local authorities and so forth.

Christopher Pollitt quotes a number of responses to this rise of management (Pollitt, 1993b, pp. 2–4). These range from Michael Heseltine's exhortatory '(E)fficient management is a key to (national) revival' to the visionary 'management is the life-giving, acting, dynamic organ of the institution it manages' to the half-crazed '(P)erhaps there is no more important area of human activity than managing.' Pollitt is right to stress the ideological nature of the new managerialism which brings with it the claim to provide objective truth, a source of values and a guide to action. The grandiose claims made on behalf of the new managerialism makes it difficult to assess soberly the extent to which it has altered the nature of state employment. As Clarke *et al.* point out it has tended to encourage academics either to view it simply as an ideological cover for the 'real' changes taking place or to accept its ideological starting-points and assess it as a purely technical exercise in pursuit of greater efficiency (Clarke *et al.*, 1994a, pp. 3–4).

However, the impact of the new managerialism on the state as an employer has had neither the extent nor the nature of change that the more zealous commentators suggest. First, it is not the case that all the features of Whitleyism outlined were eradicated by Thatcherism. Kessler (1993) argued that in the early 1990s there were two opposing views of civil service pay determination; on the one hand fair comparisons, centralized bargaining and uniform pay and conditions, and on the other hand greater pay flexibility as a means of enhancing management's capacity to secure more complete assessment, perform- ance-related pay and regional pay differences. 'The pay agreements of the late 1980s', he went on to argue, 'embraced rather than reconciled these differences, the result being that operational difficulties arose and the expectations of both sides were not fully met' (Kessler, 1993, p. 339). Similarly, whilst we have seen the emergence of a pay spine linked to flexibility in the civil service this has proved difficult to implement in practice. Equally, the Treasury has been very reluctant to hand over all responsibility for pay to the Next Steps agencies. Indeed it has proved difficult to develop performance indicators for the agencies in general (see Carter and Greer, 1993).

Studies done of the extent to which a 'cultural revolution' has transformed the public sector also suggest that change may be more limited than is sometimes imagined. A longitudinal study of managers in Britain (albeit on a limited and rather different range of issues) concluded that during the 1980s and early 1990s 'on balance our findings indicate a high degree of constancy over time in the attitudes of managers in the public and private sectors' (Poole *et al.*, 1994, p. 562). In another study of cultural change in HM Customs and Excise, it was argued that it takes more than FMI and Next Steps to change the culture of such an organization (Colville *et al.*, 1993, p. 562).

This failure to fully liberate public sector managers to direct com- pliant professionals and workers towards legitimated performance indicators results from two factors. The first is that both workers and professionals have retained certain capacities for collective and indiv- idual resistance. Indeed, for those interested in sustaining a progres- sive politics there is much that is potentially positive about the nature of this resistance. The second factor is that there are organizational limits to the new managerialism which arise from the institutional nature of the state system itself. We return to this question in the concluding chapter of this book.

Performance Indicators, Audits and Quality

Two factors lay behind the drive towards the vast expansion of audits, quality assurance and the use of performance indicators. The first and more general factor was the breakdown of consensus within the state system which we have already noted. Throughout the 1950s and 1960s it was broadly assumed that if a sum of money was allocated to, say, education or training then there would be wide-spread agreement on how that money should be spent. In practice, this meant trusting the key players in the implementation process. In the case of education, it was left to teachers' representatives, the Department of Education and Science, the local education authorities and HMI to agree amongst themselves. In training, it might be the employers, the trades unions and the officials at the Manpower Services Commission. Once this element of solidarity began to break down a process was set in motion which was to lead towards performance indicators.

The second factor was more particular to the logic of state management in the 1980s. The introduction of competition, market testing and the customer focus was intended to alter the behaviour of public officials and state agencies. As controls, however, they were significantly incomplete. In the case of training, for example, the question could always be asked, 'who is the customer?' Was it the trainees, their future employers, the department 'buying' the training, or 'society' more broadly? If training agencies were to compete for contracts on the basis of cost alone, how would it be possible to compare the outputs of each agency?

Traditional financial controls revolved around the annual budget with each budget-holder seeking to manipulate their pattern of expenditure to ensure that the actual annual expenditure came as close as possible to the budgeted expenditure. This would often lead either to end-of-year orgies of expenditure in order not to underspend or, alternatively, to moratoria on expenditure well before the end of the financial year. Both of these obviously had damaging side-effects. The purpose behind performance indicators was to link the use of resources more precisely to agreed outcomes. This obviously filled an emerging gap left between the customer focus and competition but it also created a parallel technology (although by including performance indicators which set targets for customer satisfaction they may often reinforce each other). By the early 1990s Flynn stated that the public expenditure planning process involved some 2,500 performance and output measures (Flynn, 1993, p. 111).

Performance indicators therefore became an important mechanism through which the centre could discipline the state system. However, they have always been beset by methodological problems. For example, quantified measures of a hospital's achievements, typically measured as 'through-puts' – deaths and discharges – may not tell us a great deal about the quality of the health care provided. 'Through-puts', it is often pointed out, might be increased dramatically if hospitals discharged ill patients only for them to be subsequently re-admitted. On an annual basis, therefore, we have seen calls to produce agreed and improved performance indicators (reiterated in the editorial of the NHS Executive 'house magazine' – *NHS Magazine*, in the autumn of 1996). Their importance, however, is not simply that they provide techniques with which public agencies can be directed towards certain value-laden ends, but that they simultaneously conceal these values behind a technical language of efficiency and effectiveness. In a parallel movement, the Audit Commission was to move beyond its early focus on costs and begin to look for 'objective' standards of quality with which to discipline its clients.

The Audit Commission and the Pursuit of Quality

The Audit Commission was established in 1983 under the terms of the Local Government Finance Act 1982. This Act removed a local authority's right to choose its own auditor and gave these responsibilities to the Commission. In addition to the traditional auditor's role of ensuring compliance with the legal and accounting conventions, the act also required the Commission to ensure that the local authority had made proper arrangements for securing 'economy, efficiency and effectiveness' in its use of resources. The 'value for money' audit had arrived. From that point onwards the Audit Commission's publications were to track, and very often lead, the emergence and subsequent evolution of the new managerialism.

Originally, the Audit Commission, through both its individual reports and its production of league tables which identified high and low spenders, was associated with a narrow focus on expenditure rather than the quality of the service provided. By 1989, however, it had moved away from such a narrow focus and it bemoaned the priority given to controlling expenditure over effective management (Audit Commission, 1989a). In the same year, for example, its critical report on the criminal justice system advocated new forms of inter-agency co-operation, new ways of working with difficult offenders and a reversal of the trends towards the use of custody rather than fines (Audit Commission 1989b). This clearly took the commission some distance from its 1983 position, although a continuing focus on value for money was often apparent alongside a concern with the wider questions, as in the 1989 report on sports facilities (Audit Commission, 1989c).

By 1992, the Audit Commission had moved even further towards a position which encouraged independent and vigorous management rather than a narrow focus on controlling costs. Langan and Clarke describe this new flavour in the case of community care:

> If the new mixed economy of care was advanced as the solution to the failings of local authority social services departments, the new managerialism was the decisive force in effecting the transition and implementing the new arrangements. Indeed, to pursue the metaphor self-consciously adopted by the Audit Commission, managers are the Bolsheviks of the community revolution. The commission recommended that councils appoint a full-time officer to provide 'strong, committed leadership' to the revolutionary process, while designated cadres of 'care managers' should act as the 'catalyst for change' (Audit Commission, 1992). (Langan and Clarke, 1994, pp. 78–9)

As the report recognized, in order to liberate management, the existing powers of both professionals and traditional public administrators would have to be challenged and overcome. However, once liberated, what should the managers do with their new-found freedom? Earlier in the chapter we noted various eulogies of the managerial role but whilst all of them believed that managers should be in the driving seat, none of them established where managers were driving to. Indeed, the underlying ideology of the new managerialism consistently privileged structure over strategy.

It is a commonplace that this is a particular problem for public sector managers because, unlike their private sector relatives, they have no single agreed objective towards which to work. Profit provides a ready basis upon which to calculate the desirability of alternative corporate strategies (although these may be complicated by wider concerns of corporate governance). As we have seen, neither the customer focus nor a quasi-market can fully provide a public sector equivalence to the pursuit of profit. In some parts of the state system, performance indicators were to provide targets for managers. Elsewhere (and usually earlier) following the work of mainly North American writers on management (Deal and Kennedy, 1982; Schein, 1985; Peters and Austin, 1985) the pursuit of 'quality' was suggested. By 1991 it infused key policy statements on public sector management (Audit Commission, 1991; Prime Minister, 1991; Treasury, 1991).

The dominant conception of 'quality' running through these texts identified it in terms of meeting the needs of public service users. This same objective underpins the growth of 'charterism' throughout the public sector. Consequently, the pursuit of quality often meant, in practice, monitoring and responding to the expressed needs of service users and implementing systems which ensured that policy reflected these preferences. Undoubtedly this undermined still further the role of the professional both in calculating needs and in determining the most appropriate way to meet those needs. However, it failed to resolve the problems associated with the customer focus which we identified earlier.

The late 1980s and early 1990s certainly saw a number of apparently new themes in official statements on the public sector. 'Quality' was a particularly prominent part of the new managerialism but not only was its content often unclear but also it sat alongside a number of other themes which pulled in different directions. To highlight them once more, these other themes are:

1 a greater emphasis on quasi-markets and competition;
2 the customer focus;
3 the attempted renegotiation of the pay, conditions and roles of public sector employees;
4 the extension of auditing;
5 the extension of performance indicators;
6 the growth of 'charterism';
7 the pursuit of 'quality'.

Whether these mark a clear break with the management of the 1980s is doubtful; the general distrust of professionals and bureaucrats, the preference for markets and the faith in the wisdom of the sovereign consumer are all given a new sense of energy but they are not in themselves new. More important, however, is the point, that taken together, these themes still did not amount to a coherent whole. Not only were the meanings attached to these themes slippery and unclear but, to the extent that they did have a meaning they did not always reinforce each other. On consensual areas where the choices are relatively easy it is more likely that they will mutually support each other (on avoiding waste, answering the telephone quickly or whatever). However, on the more difficult questions (such as NHS priorities, the location of community care accommodation, the closure of a school and so on) the different logics of competition, the customer focus, quality, human resources management and charterism rarely pulled unproblematically in the same direction. Many very different actions could be justified under at least one of them. As in so many revolutions, the toppling of the *ancien régime* was followed by conflict, uncertainty and instability.

Regulation

This section on regulation* is included as an aspect of the new technologies of state management because the outcome poses continuing – and interesting – problems for the boundaries and operation of the state. The term 'regulation' is used more or less widely but it generally involves at its core the idea that private economic actors can be so regulated that while they pursue their private interests (primarily maximizing profits) they will coincidentally satisfy public interests (however these are defined). By implication, therefore, it is assumed that markets would, if left to their own devices, produce outcomes which were in some way harmful to the public interest. This apparently critical view of markets must be balanced by the other use of regulation where it is used to create (or at least to simulate) competition in the face of a public or private monopoly. According to this perspective the market (or, at least, competition) is held to be an inherently good thing. This ambivalence helps to explain why both left and right are often in favour of regulation.

Following Swann (1988, pp. 16–21), we may distinguish between three types of regulation. The first is where private monopolies or oligopolies may collude against the public interest. In Britain this currently involves the Monopolies and Mergers Commission (MMC) and the Office of Fair Trading (OFT). The second case involves the regulation of natural monopolies (i.e. industries where imposing competition would introduce costs far in excess of any efficiency advantages which competition might produce – linking every house to two separate water-supply systems would create competition but at massive costs). In Britain a number of these 'natural monopolies' shifted from the public to the private sector during the 1980s and 1990s and these are regulated by bodies which were set up under the same Acts of Parliament which secured their privatization. (Confusingly, the American literature usually refers to this process as deregulation and for this reason Price, 1994, p. 81, suggests that we should call it reregulation). The third type of regulation is where it is believed that market forces will work against the public interest and this includes both ethical questions (censorship and abortion, for example) and

* This section on regulation benefited greatly from discussions and correspondence with Paul Sanderson. Any remaining errors are mine and despite his best efforts.

concerns about business ethics (the provision of personal financial advice, for example). We discuss below those aspects of regulation which are particularly related to the government's strategies in the 1980s and 1990s.

The privatization of public utilities brought with it the new problem of how these utilities should be regulated. Responsibility for this was given to single-purpose dedicated agencies created under the same Act which privatized the industry (alongside the more general functions of the MMC and OFT). By 1995 there were six such agencies:Office of Water Services (OFWAT), Office of Gas Supply (OFGAS), Office of Electricity Regulation (OFFER), Office of Telecommunications (OFTEL), Civil Aviation Authority (CAA), and Office of the Rail Regulator (ORR).

The regulatory regimes which these agencies were empowered to police originally focused primarily on regulating prices. This was unlike the approach widely adopted in the US which focused on regulating returns on capital investment (which tended to encourage over-capitalization in the regulated industries) (see Jackson and Price, 1994, p. 12). Other types of regulatory regimes available at the time included a focus on the share price (but these had been undervalued at the original flotation and in any case fluctuate for reasons other than pursuing efficiency and the public interest) and a focus on costs (but lower costs may indicate little about the quality of service).

The regime selected for electricity was therefore to allow prices to rise in line with the Retail Price Index (RPI) minus a figure to be determined by the regulator which was in line with the efficiency savings believed to be possible. This is usually known as the RPI–X approach. For water, there was a recognition that capital expenditure was necessary to meet improved standards. There was also a recognition that there might be additional costs over which the industry had no control (described as Y). So the water companies were given a formula of RPI+K+Y where K was a level of capital expenditure deemed to be necessary to achieve improved standards and Y was the cost of items such as water metering (see Price, 1994).

As with all forms of regulation, this approach is not without problems. First, controlling prices might be associated with a poor quality of service (as was seen in the low level of customer satisfaction registered for British Telecom following its privatization). Secondly, concern might be expressed over other aspects of privatized utilities, such as the high salaries paid to the senior managers or the possibility of a British utility being bought out by a foreign company. These may well put pressure on governments (if not regulators) to intervene to

Figure 6.1 The regulatory hierarchy in the financial services industry, 1996

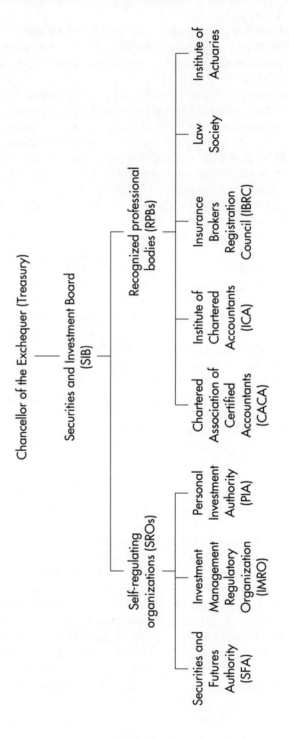

ensure that strongly supported conceptions of the public interest were being satisfied. Thirdly, there is the danger that the regulatory agency may become 'captured' by the industry which it is supposed to regulate. Failure to act on any of these could lead to a loss of legitimacy associated with the privatization exercise. Alternatively, if the political logic leads to increased regulation, the regulators would find themselves increasingly substituting the decisions of management with their own judgements. This, however, defies the whole logic underlying privatization which is that private companies, acting independently in the marketplace, are the most efficient organizations for achieving the public interest.

The major privatized utilities inevitably tend to be monopolistic and the regulatory regime reflects this. It is possible for regulation to be used as a vehicle for introducing elements of competition into what might appear to be a natural monopoly (e.g. ensuring that British Telecom's competitors should have access to parts of BT's network, or separating power generators from power distributors). However, the main concern with the regulation of utilities has been with regulating outcomes (especially price) rather than processes. In more competitive market situations the focus has been on conduct and the preferred instrument one of self-regulation.

The supposed advantages of self-regulation have been widely canvassed. According to Howells and Bain they include: (1) faster reaction times than statutory bodies; (2) practitioner involvement increases compliance; (3) practitioners understand how the system works and will therefore detect rule-breakers more readily; (4) self-regulatory bodies can be established more quickly; and (5) government is kept at arm's length (see Howells and Bain, 1994, p. 272).

Such self-regulation is typically operated through organizations established specifically for that purpose and/or through recognized professional bodies. For example, in the case of the regulatory regime for financial services which followed the Financial Services Act of 1986 the hierarchy set out in figure 6.1 was eventually to emerge. This structure of regulation involves a set of statutory obligations, overseen by the Treasury, whose more routine functions are largely given over to SROs and RPBs. The Financial Services Act of 1986 was amended in 1989 by the Companies Act to create three tiers of regulation; principles were to be laid down by the SIB; core rules (or second-tier rules) were also to be made by the SIB, and the SROs and RPBs were to provide a third tier of supporting rules and to expand upon the principles and core rules.

There are at least two potential problems associated with this style of self-regulation. First, since the costs of the regulation are largely born by the industry (and ultimately the clients) there are limits to the costliness of implementing self-regulation (at the point at which the cost of regulation drives too many firms out of business). More importantly, perhaps, self-regulation involves non-state bodies (and certainly non-judicial bodies) acting in a quasi-judicial context. Although it would be possible to take the body to court for breaches of proper conduct, conduct in the financial services industry has been juridified without the expansion of courts of law. In addition to this breach in liberal principles of jurisprudence, the capacity to generate delegated legislation under the terms of the primary legislation challenges liberal conceptions of the role of the legislature as the law-making body.

In general, then, what are we to make of the extensive use of regulation both as an alternative to public ownership and as a response to perceived market failure? What is immediately apparent is that, as Davidson points out, the idea that markets and hierarchies are mutually opposed ways of regulating economic activity, and that the 1980s witnessed a simple expansion of the former at the expense of the latter, is untenable (see Davidson, 1994, p. 171). State regulation has been used both to manage market activity and to introduce competitive markets where economic factors alone would tend to lead to the emergence of monopolies.

What changed in the 1980s, therefore, is not a shift from state control to market mechanisms. The changes lie in the content of the new regulatory regime. Both before and after privatization, the electricity and gas industries entered into market transactions to buy raw materials and labour and to sell their products. In both cases the political problem is with ensuring that adequate incentives, controls and information exist so that public interests are met. In this sense, privatization and new forms of regulation only displace the problems of state management. However, they displace them in important ways.

Through the process of displacement, state power has been used to strengthen certain interests and weaken others. The relationships between the state and key industries have been reconfigured. Certain consequences flow from this. First, the privatization of public utilities was intended to be achieved quickly and to guarantee the support of the financial markets. The extent of both competition and regulation was therefore limited. This produced immediate, short-term gains for share-holders (of which there were some nine million by 1991). It also reduced the responsibilities and problems of the state as an employer with some 650,000 workers changing from the public to the private sector, that is over half the public sector work-force in 1979 (see Marsh, 1991, p. 463). Furthermore, it empowered management who were presented with a wider range of strategic choices (including the popularly condemned strategic choice of paying themselves lots more money).

In the sphere of self-regulation, the layers of regulation may produce a dense pattern of regulations for individual practitioners. The density of such regulation is matched by its largely secretive and quasi-judicial form which may be frustrating for practitioners but is also hard for the public to have access to. Furthermore, law courts have generally been reluctant to substitute their judgement for that of the regulatory body (and if they did so on a regular basis the rationale for self-regulation would inevitably crumble). With limited public access and limited redress in the courts, fundamental liberal rights are weakened.

However, looking at the regulatory regime as a whole in the 1980s and 1990s, it is the changed form, rather than the changed extent, of the regulation which is most interesting. However, there are also continuities. Post-war regulation was also extensive. In the milk production industry, for example, regulation was orchestrated through the Milk Marketing Board and primarily reflected the interests of producers (albeit in the name of stabilizing output). The 'regulation' (if we can call it that) of nationalized industries, to take another example, was through a combination of ministerial direction over strategy and managerial control over the day-to-day affairs of the industry. The purpose of post-war regulation was to provide producers with a degree of security and influence in return for maintaining stable and high output. As such it had a certain affinity with the post-war settlement.

There is some contrast with the regulation associated with the Thatcher and Major governments. One policy was to create a new privately owned structure and, where the market was unlikely to provide spontaneous competition, then regulation was used. Another was to recognize that regulation might be needed to prevent firms from exploiting imbalances of information to the evident detriment of the client (personal financial services, for example). A third was where it was held that certain decisions should not be made solely on the basis of market calculations because of their ethical content or social content (abortion, for example). Each of these was pursued prior to 1979. There is a greater reliance on the first type of regulation during the 1980s and, within this, a greater use of price control as the key form of regulation. With the second, there was some tension with the strategic objective of liberalizing economic activities (such as personal financial services) and a preference for self-regulation. The third may have become more troublesome during the 1980s but this owed more to a growing unwillingness to trust the 'experts', an increasing diversity of ethical views in the population and a greater willingness to express these ethical concerns politically. None of these types of regulation look likely to diminish and the arguments surrounding each (for example, the desirability of price controls as a regulatory device) show no sign of diminishing. The politics of regulation, therefore, are set to continue and, if anything, to intensify. They displace, rather than solve, the problems of state management.

Concluding Remarks: a New State for Britain?

The strengths of the new technologies of state control are mostly negative: the weakening of professional power within welfare agencies; the recognition that centralized corporatist bargaining structures were becoming less and less appropriate; the erosion of an inward-looking bureaucracy concerned with rule-following and established procedures; and the break-up of large bureaucracies which had become unwieldy and distanced from the public. However, it has created a public sector which has brought into being a new set of formal rules to be followed. These are driven by contracts, framework agreements, the pursuit of Charter Marks, performance indicators and a formalized conception of 'quality'.

Imagine, if you will, a society characterized by a self-regulating economy and a society peopled by rational, egotistical utility maximizers. In such a context a charter-marked, competitive, audited and PI'ed state would, arguably, have much to recommend it. Indeed, the construction of empowered and rightful consumers of public services being well serviced by an efficient and vibrant public sector is surely something to pursue rather than to deride. However, in a context in which social efficiency depends upon a public sector entrenching economic flexibility, risk-taking and legitimacy, such a state becomes less attractive. And it became less attractive still in the context of substantial and growing inequalities in which the state reinforced the powerful, and parliamentary arithmetic ensured that the marginalized could be ignored. These questions will be reviewed at greater length in the final chapter of this book.

There are, perhaps, three important general consequences of the new managerialism. First, certain interests are included; second, other interests are excluded (or weakened); and, third, the identities and perceived interests of those included and excluded are reshaped. Those excluded or weakened are professional bodies such as those representing teachers and doctors, public sector trades unionists (who have lost much of their capacity to influence policies which directly impinge on the interests of their members) and traditional bureaucrats. These were at their most powerful where networks of professionals and officials previously exercised some direct influence over policy development. Those included are the new public sector managers, outside consultants and intra-state auditing bodies such as the Audit Commission, who have been empowered in an attempt to universalize the principles of the new managerialism.

Perhaps most importantly of all, the language and calculations which must be used in order to participate in the decision-making process have contributed to the new identities of even the old faces operating within the state. As bureaucrats became purchasers, controllers of devolved budgets, providers and contract-holders, not only did their job titles change but so too did the machinery through which they could effect change. Clearly, there are cadres of managers who wished to secure outcomes which differed from some of the objectives of central government, but they could not escape the calculations and dynamics embodied in the new managerialism. One consequence of this is the presence of the public in their calculations not as clients or citizens but as consumers. (Although, given that the public were only weakly involved as citizens under the pre-1979 arrangements and remain only weakly involved in the new customer-focused public sector, they might be forgiven for doubting the impact of this transition on their lives.)

The limit to these changes is suggested by the inability of successive governments in the 1980s and 1990s to establish a stable institutional settlement around which a new hegemony could materialize. At its heart the changes presuppose a self-regulating civil society which requires only the efficient delivery of a small number of public goods and the light regulation of certain industries to create vibrant and stable economic and social life. Even if these new technologies were not in conflict with each other, such a society would still fail to provide a public sector capable of addressing the pressing requirements of economic efficiency in a globalizing economy and the politics of including all identities and interests within a legitimate and stable state regime.

In the next chapter we use two case studies to show the complex interrelationships between the attempts to re-engineer the British state and the wider realities of public policy and private power.

Summary

The new managerialism is not simply a 'smoke-screen' to conceal questionable objectives. It was a response to very real problems within the British state and it has had equally real consequences. However, it failed to create a stable new intra-state settlement both because it contained mutually discordant strands and because it included heroic assumptions about the nature of the social and economic context within which it works.

7
Two Case Studies of the Changing British State: Youth Training and the Instruments of Urban Intervention

●　●　●　●　●　●　●　●　●　●　●　●　●　●　●

The purpose of this chapter is:

● to use two case studies to illustrate and explore in more detail some of the wider characteristics of the post-war British state identified in previous chapters;
● to begin to consider how these characteristics were changed during the 1980s;
● and so to prepare for the more general claims developed in the final chapter.

Introduction

We have already considered changes in training policy and the Community Development Projects as examples of state management under the Keynesian welfare state. In this chapter we have the opportunity to look in more depth at particular examples of institutional innovation. It should be clear from chapters 5 and 6 that the emergent forms of state management had an ambiguous relationship with Thatcherism. On the one hand, many of the key ideas pre-date Thatcherism and to some extent both were a response to the same circumstances (changing role of the state, changing economic structure and changing social relationships). On the other hand, we shall see how intimately related are the wider politics of Thatcherism and the politics of state management. In this chapter, therefore, we not only examine in some detail the processes at work within the state system but we also assess the extent to which these have a political content.

The Manpower Services Commission and Youth Training

The Manpower Services Commission (MSC) was established in early 1974 under the 1973 Employment and Training Act. As we have seen, the Act itself reflected the inability of successive governments to establish an effective national training system which was capable of simultaneously securing the expressed objectives of the state whilst also enjoying the support of both unions and employers' representatives. The 1972 White Paper 'Training for the Future' had advocated a movement away from an industry-by-industry approach and towards the creation of a National Training Agency. The intellectual core of the White Paper was the argument that the smooth restructuring of industry during a period of rapid economic change required a work-force trained in skills which they could transfer from one sector to another. Employers effectively vetoed the national and compulsory elements, and the 1973 Act therefore left the Industrial Training Boards (ITBs). Despite this, the Act still gave the MSC responsibility for coordinating training within an overall national programme.

There were at least three reasons why coordinating the ITBs in this way was problematic. First, ITBs could charge employers within their industry a levy but they could not compel them to provide training for their work-force. Since the levy did not exceed 1 per cent of the wages bill, it was insufficient to act as an inducement to provide training (see Kaufman, 1986, p. 142). Secondly, employers in declining industries had no incentive to train their employees for employment in expanding industries. Thirdly, the ITBs left out some 10 million workers. The 1973 Act removed the mandatory powers of the ITBs and replaced them with enabling powers and a maximum levy of 1 per cent of the payroll was established. The consequences for the employers' contribution can be seen in table 7.1.

By increasing the proportion of training funding coming from the Exchequer, the ITBs were placed in an ambiguous position: they were

Table 7.1 ITB levy income (net of expenditure) and exchequer support

	Levy income[a] (£000)	Exchequer support[a] (£000)	Total (£000)
1971/2	381,835	10,844	392,679
1972/3	340,874	10,372	351,246
1973/4	276,590	6,715	283,305
1974/5	194,590	5,317	199,742
1975/6	92,882	44,174	137,156
1976/7	87,185	59,069	146,254
1977/8	81,099	65,373	146,472
1978/9	71,686	64,659	136,343

Notes:
[a] 1971–9 figures are based on ITB published accounts. The accounting conventions adopted by the ITBs and the MSC differ slightly. Figures revised to reflect 1975 prices using GDP deflator.
Source: MSC 1980, p. 11

being centrally funded as part of a national programme and yet were responsible to sectoral interests. This tension was recognized by the MSC (see MSC, 1980, p. 11). In practice, the MSC sought to shape each ITB's operational and strategic planning but lacked either the inducements or the coercive capacities to secure its objectives.

This, then, was the context within which the MSC operated at the start of its institutional life. To provide a clear focus, we consider just one aspect of the MSC's work; the management of the Youth Opportunities Programme and the Youth Training Scheme.

From the Youth Opportunities Programme to the Youth Training Scheme

The MSC was responsible for coordinating the work of the ITBs. Three additional schemes were lashed onto the ITB structure: the Special Training Measures (to encourage training during a recession); Training for Skills, A Programme for Action (a failed attempt to encourage a collective response to the problems of inter-sectoral immobility); and the Unified Vocational Preparation (for young working people who were not apprenticed and who would otherwise receive no training).

Alongside these were two programmes for providing training for unemployed people. For adults there was the Training Opportunities Scheme and for young people there was the Youth Opportunities Programme (YOP). YOP arose from the report *Young People and Work* (MSC, 1977). The background of rising youth unemployment and concern about a generation of ill-disciplined school-leavers ensured widespread support for the scheme (including from the TUC). It was seen as a short-term and counter-cyclical measure which would no longer be required when unemployment fell. In 1978/9 £62.7m was spent on 162,000 trainees. By 1981/2 this had risen to £400.9m on 553,000 trainees. In 1978/9, YOP accounted for just 10 per cent of the MSC's expenditure and by 1982 this had risen to 42 per cent. Furthermore, by this stage there was evidently nothing temporary about the government's youth training strategy.

How was this to be delivered? The state lacked the resources needed to provide training and supervision for this number of young people throughout the working week. It therefore depended very heavily upon sponsors to provide Work Experience on Employers' Premises (WEEP). Most of these employers (63 per cent) were from the private sector (see table 7.2). This dependency upon employers was to exert a decisive influence over the government's youth policy; employers could exert an effective veto simply by refusing to provide placements for trainees.

Table 7.2 demonstrates YOP's heavy dependence upon private employers. Unions were not without influence, partly through their representation within the MSC structure but also because employers were reluctant to enter disputes with unions over training. Therefore growing criticisms of YOP were taken seriously by the MSC and by

Table 7.2 Composition of YOP, 1978–83

	1978/9	1979/80	1980/81	1981/2	1982/3
Work experience	128,200	182,100	304,500	461,500	393,400
(% with private employers)	(84.5%)	(76.2%)	(79.5%)	(80.4%)	(78.6%)
Work preparation	34,000	34,300	55,500	91,500	67,800
Pilot YTS places					81,900
(12 months long)					

Source: Finn, 1985, p.115

government itself. The main criticisms, according to Farley (1985), were:

- rising unemployment for YOP leavers;
- inadequacy of the training component;
- job substitution;
- lack of an equal opportunities commitment;
- lack of integration and progression between and within schemes;
- the inadequacy of the training allowance;
- the lack of a representative structure for trainees.

However, the unions' ability to address these problems was circumscribed. In the regions, YOP schemes were overseen by the area boards which comprised TUC nominees, employers and, to a more limited extent, voluntary organizations (who had placements at their work-places). Locally elected organizations were absent. Importantly, the Boards had no authority over schemes with fewer than twenty trainees, and some 65 per cent of trainees on WEEP were in such a position. Furthermore, many trainees were in work-places with no trades union representation (see Carter and Stewart, 1981, p. 6).

If the MSC represented a very constrained form of corporatism it did retain the voluntaristic element which corporatism implies; at its core was an exchange between employers and trainees which depended both upon young people volunteering and employers supporting the scheme. In return, employers got the opportunity to examine new recruits to the labour market at first hand (and receive subsidized labour whilst doing so) and young people had the opportunity to move towards a secure, full-time job.

However, rising youth unemployment threatened to undermine this transaction. In any case, employers were typically 'more concerned with the general social dispositions and characteristics of their workers than with their abilities to carry out specific technical tasks' (Finn, 1984, p. 96) and this made the technical component in YOP less useful. Combined with an increasing volume of complaints of the sort listed above (some of which, such as job substitution, the MSC was later to accept) the circumstances suggested that the days of youth training might be numbered. In addition there was in government a party which had promised to provide 'real jobs' and to roll back agencies of the corporatist state of which the MSC was a prime example.

Whilst in 1980 it appeared that the MSC faced an uncertain future, circumstances were to change significantly. In February 1981 the

Think Tank warned the Cabinet that unemployment would reach 3 million by 1983 and expressed particular concern about the young unemployed: '(T)he effect in terms of future training skills, attitudes to work and opportunities for crime and other forms of social disruption is undoubtedly a matter for justifiable concern' (quoted in Riddell, 1983, p. 49). At the same time a paper produced by the head of the Downing Street Policy Unit argued:

> We all know that there is no prospect of getting unemployment down to acceptable levels within the next few years. (Consequently) we must show that we have some political imagination, that we are willing to salvage something – albeit second-best – from the sheer waste involved. There are many people who would like to do something, even if it is of marginal economic value. (quoted in Riddell, 1983, p. 50)

That 'something' was to include the Youth Training Scheme. This was no longer a short-term scheme to meet the training needs of young unemployed people in the midst of an economic downturn. Rather, it came to be seen as a permanent route to the adult world for young school-leavers. YOP had been heavily conditioned by the need to secure sponsors, primarily private sector employers, who would provide placements. A reluctance on the part of the MSC to police the system (for fear of losing placements) combined with inadequate mechanisms through which trainees' interests could be represented (either by unions or by young people's own representatives) to create a training system which was roundly condemned. The YTS, however, was also a further step away from the consensual pursuit of the mutual interests of employers and trades unions. If YOP was employer-dependent, then YTS, as Finn has emphasized, was employer-led (see Finn, 1987, ch. 7). As David Young, chair of the MSC, revealingly expressed it:

> In short, the YTS offers a fresh start to our young, and at the same time is attractive financially to employers. You now have the opportunity to take on young men or women, train them and let them work for you almost entirely at our expense, and then decide whether or not to employ them. I know that we will soon start to have better trained, better motivated young people coming into industry and commerce, and that can only be good for us all. But it will only work if it is employer led, and I do hope that we will all be working together, for we must rely on you to be involved in the key decisions and plans to shape the scheme. (*The Director*, October 1982)

The MSC's publicity material produced for employers makes the same point (for more on Young's attitude towards YOP, see Finn, 1987, pp. 155–6). On the first page it rhetorically asks '(W)hat are the benefits of the Scheme to you?' and it states:

> The overall aim of the youth training scheme will be to produce a better motivated and more adaptable workforce, capable of developing its skills to meet changing employment needs. This will have the effect of reducing training costs as well as minimising wastage and should prove in the long term of benefit to employers and to the economy as a whole. (MSC, 1983)

By the middle of 1985, fewer than half the YTS graduates went on to find work. The number staying with the same employer fell to less than one in five (see *Guardian*, 19 June 1985). Statistically, young people stood no better chance of finding a job if they were on YTS than if they were registered unemployed. Furthermore, by October 1985, 13,000 trainees had been injured and twenty-one killed whilst participating on YTS schemes (*Guardian*, 24 October 1985).

Not only was the scheme being shockingly run but also the standards of probity normally associated with post-war British public administration were not reached. For example, an MSC document leaked to the South Eastern Region TUC (see *Labour Weekly*, 22 February 1985) showed that:

– information on YTS accidents should not normally be disclosed;
– even deaths should not be reported to the Area Manpower Boards (AMB) unless the details had already been made public;
– MSC staff were instructed not to break down the accident statistics on a constituency-by-constituency basis (allegedly this was in order to make MP's questions easier to avoid);
– staff were told not to compare YTS accident rates with Health and Safety statistics;
– AMBs were to be told that accident statistics were not available when, allegedly, they were.

The MSC was chosen as the instrument with which 'something' would be done about youth unemployment because it had an organization already 'on the ground'. By strengthening the organizational dependency on employers, weakening the representatives on the AMBs and marginalizing the role of trades unions, David Young and the MSC should 'sell' the idea of YTS to employers on the basis that it would provide them with a cheap way to get a close look at potential employees who would mean-time be working for the employer at subsidized rates. However, when it came to running a public scheme capable of securing trans-sectoral objectives the administration was clearly compromised by its dependency upon the private interests of individual firms.

The employer-led YTS was not only administratively flawed. Its employer-led characteristic also shaped the training model that was used within YTS. The preference of the Further Education Unit within the DES was for an approach which encouraged the trainees to assess their own progress and to negotiate the educational content of relevant training material (see FECDRU, 1981; Finn, 1987, ch. 7). Against this, the Institute of Manpower Studies preferred a more work-oriented approach with greater emphasis on learning specific work-related skills (both general and specific). The MSC opted for the apparently more employer-friendly Institute of Manpower Studies model.

The immediate problem with the second model was the difficulty it posed in defining 'skill'. Under the rubric of 'The World Outside Work', trainers were expected to assess the following skills:

– understanding the importance of keeping clean;
– knowing how to use a bank or a building society;
– knowing how to plan money;
– knowing about any staff discounts, the social club etc;.
– knowing how to be loyal to the workplace;
– knowing what people expect of each other away from work;
– knowing how to apply for a job;
– knowing how to use the telephone. (see MSC, 1984)

Some of these, at least, were more about attitudes than skills (keeping clean, planning money) and, in any case, it assumed that young people were unemployed because they lacked such skills. The idea that the substantial increase in youth unemployment both absolutely and as a percentage of total unemployment was in some sense caused by a widespread failure of young people to keep clean or use telephones properly is, of course, as insulting as it is misguided. These policies would not have been produced by the education sector. However, given that the British state could not trust its own educational institutions to implement its preferred policies, it was driven to a set of policies which reflected its institutional dependence upon private employers to deliver a public training programme.

Despite these shortcomings, YTS was extended to a two-year scheme (with the Chancellor stating the Treasury view that 'in the long run, we expect employers to meet the full cost, as those in other countries do' (*The Times*, 19 March 1985). There were, however, continuing problems in managing this scheme at the local level. In 1985 there were some 4,200 managing agents using over 100,000 work-places. Independent research had already concluded in 1983 that 'the MSC is in no position to police the scheme thoroughly', and that 'its staff have neither the experience nor time to monitor schemes adequately' (Incomes Data Services, 1983; quoted in Finn, 1987, p. 174). The ability of the Area Manpower Boards to police the system was also severely restricted by being unable to scrutinize schemes in large companies which were negotiated centrally, by having to provide advance warning of any visits to work-places and by having to be guided around the work-place by the employers. When the British state is described as 'weak' this is in part what is meant; the inability to achieve nationally agreed goals because of the absence of the required agencies of monitoring and control.

Youth training and corporatism

When it came to responding to the political pressure to 'do something' about rising youth unemployment, the MSC was attractive to the central government because it had organized capacities on the ground. This was despite its tripartite form which, on the face of it, would give trades unions some control over the implementation and monitoring of training policy.

However, the original tripartite structures within the MSC were increasingly sidelined, and its employer-led nature became increasingly apparent (it is also worth stressing that power lay with individual employers and not with their representative bodies). Individual employers had very little interest in the Further Education Unit model (which is more concerned with providing the skills needed to learn new skills) which was a longer-term strategy for enhanced labour mobility. Individual employers were more concerned to train the current work-force for existing jobs.

Under these circumstances, it is not immediately apparent why the trades unions should have remained loyal to the MSC. In part it was because the unions had always seen themselves at the fore-front of campaigns to improve the skills of the British work-force and therefore it was hard to attack a scheme which claimed to be doing exactly

that. Also, trades unionists' attitudes were revealed in a postal survey
carried out by the School of Advanced Urban Studies, Bristol University. Despite widespread cynicism about the MSC, the survey showed
that of the 148 who replied, 90 per cent agreed with the statement
that 'through active Trade Union involvement, improvements can be
made in schemes like YTS and CP (Community Programme) to the
benefit of unemployed people.' Only 2 per cent disagreed with this
statement (Randall, 1986, quoted in *Unemployment Bulletin*, no. 19
February 1986).

The trades union movement also faced internal disagreements over
strategy which, given the federal nature of the TUC, inhibited a united
approach. Unions representing workers in industries with ITBs had
much to lose if YTS training replaced craft unionism. These joined the
'Save Our Skills' campaign in support of the ITBs. Other unions, such
as the Civil and Public Services' Association believed that their clerical
members were vulnerable to replacement with YTS trainees. Similarly, the National Association of Teachers in Further and Higher
Education were attracted by the prospect of MSC money but worried
by its increasing use of private training agencies which offered only
short-term contracts.

With so many divergent views, the TUC decided to respond to each
programme on its merits. With no very clear policy at the centre,
opposition tended to shift to the local level. The formation of the
MSC led to the replacement of the Local Employment Committees
with 88 District Manpower Committees (DMCs). These fed information into the central decision-making process of the MSC but had
little influence over policy. In 1978 to these were added 28 Special
Programmes Area Boards (SPABS) to provide some local input to
YOP and the Special Temporary Employment Programme. However,
faced with mounting criticism about the inadequacy of monitoring of
YOP, these, in turn, were replaced by 54 Area Manpower Boards
(AMBs) in 1982. These were to have both information-gathering and
monitoring functions.

AMBs not only bypassed elected local authorities but they were
organized into areas which cut across existing local authority boundaries. The regional TUC and CBI sent representatives but these individuals were accountable to the AMB rather than to their parent
organization. Boards had the power of co-opting local representatives
but examples of this are rare.

Furthermore, the AMBs lacked the capacities which would have
been needed to carry out their monitoring responsibilities. In 1985
there were 102,000 locally approved YTS places with a high level of

work experience and 30 per cent of these involved private training agencies (see Finn, 1987, p. 174–5; TURC, 1986). A study conducted by NATFHE in Birmingham established that out of thirty agencies, only ten were long-standing companies; seven had failed to file up-to-date accounts as legally required, two had had their accounts seriously qualified and three were not registered as companies at all (see Finn, 1987, pp. 174–5; TURC, 1986). The AMBs may have enjoyed some of the corporatist trappings but they lacked the capacity to give that corporatism any teeth.

If the TUC had difficulty representing a unified trades union inter-est, the CBI faced even greater problems. The historic roots of this difficulty went deep into the Keynesian welfare state and beyond. First there was a division in the perceived interests of large and small industrialists (see Strinati, 1982, p. 100). Then there was an ambiva-lence towards corporatist training bodies. In the British Employers' Confederation submission to the Carr Committee in 1958 they sup-ported both the principle of central coordination and the practice of voluntarism. Following the 1964 Industrial Training Act there was a reluctant acquiescence to corporatist structures amongst employers but a major objective of employers was to weaken the restrictive practices associated with the apprenticeship system. Throughout this period employers preferred policies intended to free up the labour market over more collectivist responses (see CBI, 1968). This was seen again in CBI resistance to the stronger proposals contained within *Training for the Future*. As Vickerstaff has noted, the CBI wanted the benefits of corporatist strategies without the costs (Vickerstaff, 1985, p. 57).

With the abolition of the MSC in 1988, the employers largely got what they thought they wanted. In the National Training Task Force, which had been announced in the 1988 White Paper 'Employment in the 1990s', there were thirteen members. Nine of these were chairper-sons or chief executives of leading private sector companies, one was a trades unionist, one was an educationalist, one was a voluntary sector representative and one was a local authority representative. At the local level, in place of the Area Manpower Boards, the Training and Enterprise Councils are similarly packed by employers. This, according to NATFHE, at least, 'dealt a death blow to tripartism' (*NATFHE Journal*, Jan./Feb. 1989). The British Institute of Manage-ment is similarly ambiguous, insisting that schools should train stu-dents for particular jobs (employers were described as the education system's 'customers'), and that YTS should be more 'flexible', but that YTS should be seen as an educational matter and not an employment measure (see the *Manager's Manifesto*, British Institute of Management, 1987). Presumably the latter point implied that YTS should be funded out of the DES budget and not from employers' contributions.

The ninety or so Training and Enterprise Councils (TECs) were local-employer dominated groups with responsibility for running the Employment Training Programme for the long-term unemployed, YTS, the Business Training Growth Programme and small firm counselling. Each was given a budget of some £25–50m. In total some £2.7bn was given over to local employers through their representatives on the TECs.

This was the end of a tripartite training policy. But it was not simply 'corporatism without labour' which emerged. This would imply a mediating role for employers' representatives who would be responsible for arriving at a shared or collective set of interests amongst their members. In what emerged, this mediating role was missing and a training system evolved which was based upon the direct, unmediated participation of employers. The difficulties which this creates for generating a training strategy which meets the more collective needs of employers are considered below. First, however, we will briefly consider the extent to which the considerable efforts taken to undermine the corporatist element in training policy paid dividends in the form of enhanced central government control.

Enhanced central control over YTS?

An important mechanism of central control over quangos is through ministerial appointments to key positions. The first chairperson of the MSC was a career civil servant and very much an administrator, Sir Dennis Barnes. He was followed by Richard O'Brien who was proposed by the CBI and appointed by Michael Foot. Following the Conservative election success in 1979, O'Brien followed a quiet but firm opposition to proposed cuts in MSC funding. He also publicly adhered to the MSC's own (more accurate) predictions on unemployment in preference to those of the government. The MSC's Corporate Plan of 1982–6 was pessimistic about the employment situation and the prospects for the young and long-term unemployed in particular (p. 5). As early as May 1980, O'Brien readily acknowledged to the Employment Committee that he had felt obliged to make 'a series of reasoned protests' to the government (House of Commons, 1980).

The same Employment Committee asked Jim Prior, the Employment Secretary, why he did not simply abolish the MSC rather than being challenged in this way, Prior offered perhaps the last ministerial defence of corporatist practices in the 1980s: the MSC, he said, can 'bring into its consultations the various constituent parts of the TUC, the CBI and the education authorities' providing 'a forum in which the CBI and TUC can discuss with the Government the day-to-day problems' bringing a 'different angle' to the problem (House of Commons, 1980, p. 86).

However, neither Prior nor corporatist politics were to enjoy government support for long, and Richard O'Brien was also soon out of favour. Coinciding with a determination to address the problems posed by rising youth unemployment, the government moved away from a consensual model. O'Brien was sacked and in his final introduction to an MSC Corporate Plan, O'Brien welcomed both his successor and an increase in MSC funding. The two were not unrelated. His successor, David Young, was so enthusiastic in his support for government policies, that he earned himself an elevation to the House of Lords and a place in the government. In years to come the press response to Young's successor, Bryan Nicholson, would be that he was another avowed Thatcherite.

However, Nicholson perhaps had more consensual leanings than was first imagined (see his interview with Caroline St John-Brooks in *New Society*, 13 June 1986) or perhaps he recognized that the MSC without a corporatist rationale was pointless. In an exchange of letters between Norman Fowler the Employment Secretary and Nicholson following the 1987 election their differences became apparent. Fowler insisted on changes which would have pre-empted any corporatist discussion or input. The MSC's response highlighted its successes to date and went on to claim:

> None of this would have been possible without the partnership we and so many others have worked hard to forge – at national, regional and local levels, with employers, trades unions, local authorities, professional education, voluntary organizations and many others. As a result of this an organization and relationships have been established which are of very great value. (letter from Norman Fowler, MP, to Sir Bryan Nicholson, 30 June 1987 and the Manpower Services Commission's reply of 23 July 1987; reproduced in full in Ling, 1991, appendix 3)

Perhaps it is not surprising that within a year, the MSC was abolished.

Did the abolition of the MSC, the corporatist instrument which lay between the secretary of state and the implementation of policy, enhance central direction over training policy? The immediately apparent answer is 'yes' because it allowed ministers to dictate to the key policy-makers in the subsequent training system. However, the correct answer to this question is 'no', because, as we shall see in the following section, just as it left the old corporatist partners without an institutional mechanism with which to mediate their interests, so too did it remove an intermediate level of governance through which the state could play a leading role in defining and pursuing collectively agreed public interests. Greater ministerial control over the leadership of state agencies only enhanced overall central control where those agencies retained the capacity to secure the objectives set for it.

The loss of strategic control

Training policy from the 1950s to the early 1980s was characterized by the (not very successful) pursuit of a consensual, coordinated and planned response to the changing requirements of the labour market. The changes in the labour market were extensive and significant. In the twenty-five years up to 1985, full-time employment fell by two million with part-time employment rising by a similar amount and accelerating thereafter. By 1980, one in five employees was part-time. Self-employment, casualization and subcontracting were also further encouraged by the government. Between 1951 and 1981 the number of women in employment rose from 7 million to 9.2 million whilst the number of men decreased from 13.5 million to 12.9 million. In 1961, 36 per cent of the work-force was employed in manufacturing industry whilst in the 1980s this had declined to 28 per cent. To exaggerate a little, the stereotypical worker changed from full-time, skilled and male to casual, semi-skilled and female (see Massey and Meegan, 1983, p. 23; Beechey, 1985; and *Employment Gazette*, various years).

For the Conservative government of the mid-1980s, however, the best way to respond to these changes involved three things: first, to facilitate labour-market mechanisms by training workers in the skills employers wanted; second, to end the regulation of wages which 'prevented' workers from pricing themselves into a job; and, third, to have fewer regulations (see the 1985 White Paper, 'Employment: the challenge for the Nation'). Once these were identified as the solutions, then corporatist instruments became less credible. However, removing corporatism does not remove the problems which corporatism was supposed to address.

By 1981, the year of the New Training Initiative, the 'needs' of employers came to be understood within the government in terms of the removal of market rigidities. However, these 'rigidities' do not simply present themselves; they are constituted within a particular discourse. The discourse included the following assumptions and these had the following associated weaknesses (the latter printed in italics).

1 Youth unemployment (and unemployment in general) is linked to a lack of skills. *The nature of these 'skills' is unspecified. Although in a rapidly changing labour process the capacity to acquire new skills is more important than the acquisition of any particular skills, the MSC preferred a more skills-based model. Furthermore, employers' recruitment practices do not reflect an overriding concern with formal skills; rather, employers' recruitment practices reflect a preference for manageable workers (for example, workers with commitments of family and mortgage).*

2 Reflecting these preferences for manageability rather than skills, youth training therefore included an element which focused on changing attitudes and presentation rather than skills. *However, neither was there more than anecdotal evidence of a sudden catastrophic cultural change amongst young people, nor was changing youth culture clearly and causally associated with rising youth unemployment.*

3 The third 'cause' of youth unemployment within this discourse was the claim that it was caused by the narrowness of the differentials separating adult wages from youth wages. If young people were able to enter the labour force on lower wages, the argument went, then youth unemployment would fall. *However, the evidence in the British case shows that the period in which the wages of young new recruits to the labour market fell relative to those of older workers also saw youth unemployment rise proportionately more quickly. Furthermore, at a time when employers were reporting over-staffing, they would not be tempted to take on new workers irrespective of the wage rate.*

This dominant discourse posed significant problems for state strategists. Where they wish to be employer-led, clearly, any training policy must be able to satisfy at least minimally the sponsors who provide the placements. However, in the absence of a corporatist forum within which the employers' minimum requirements may be communicated and negotiated, policy-makers have to make *assumptions* about what will be acceptable. But if policy is driven by such assumptions how will it meet the wider requirements of a successful training policy? These problems were expressed by the Audit Commission in 1989:

> how will a TEC ensure consistency between its plan and the broader local economic context? If the TEC's plans do not flow from a comprehensive review of the area's economic problems . . . they run the risk of being just one more of a range of uncoordinated plans which impact on different parts of the local economy. ·
>
> how is a TEC's plan to be coordinated with the plans local education authorities must produce for work-related non-advanced further education procedures and for their further education strategic planning duties under the Education Reform Act 1988? . . .
>
> how is the TEC's responsibility for small firms support to be coordinated with services already provided by local enterprise agencies and local authorities?
>
> how will TEC's cope with the need to bring severely disadvantaged groups into the economy – the totally unskilled, illiterate etc? (Audit Commission, 1989, p. 30)

These are precisely the problems of coordination which may be worsened when the state moves towards a customer-led (or, in this case, employer-led) pattern of delivery. The paradox of training policy in the 1980s was that the moment when the intra-state obstacles to central strategic direction were removed was also the moment when the steerage capacity of public training agencies were further weakened.

Conclusions

The state direction of British youth training policy in the 1970s and 1980s highlights a number of relevant points. It shows, first of all, that the attempt to use corporatist institutions to plan and deliver training policy created a number of problems. The rigidities of the ITBs and the representation of vested interests made it hard to respond flexibly and appropriately to the changing context of youth (un)employment. This became particularly so when youth training developed into more than a temporary substitute for full employment. Nevertheless the trades unions were successfully locked into the MSC, despite its coming increasingly under central government direction. Employers, for their part, maintained an ambiguous relationship with state training, looking for public funding to further private interests. Securing agreement on those training interests which were both public and private (good for employers and good for the wider public) proved difficult for an employers' organization which was internally divided and suspicious of any state-directed element in the training system.

As we noted in chapter 2, the corporatist instruments significantly shaped the content of training policy in the 1960s and 1970s. ITBs brought with them a training methodology best described as 'sitting by Nelly' and a focus on non-transferable skills in declining sectors. It met some of the training needs of a rapidly diminishing section of male school-leavers, leaving most other sections of the work-force poorly provided for. It is important to note that successive central governments were aware of this as a problem but failed to devise alternative instruments of intervention.

On the basis of this argument, one might imagine that by successfully marginalizing and then abolishing the corporatist mechanisms through which training had been organized, the Conservative governments in the 1980s would thereby give themselves complete control over youth training. In practice, as we saw, the increased dependency upon individual employers (and not even their collective representatives) largely determined the choice of training model and the levels of scrutiny applied to the provision of training on the ground.

The gradual marginalization of the representatives of both employers and trades unions within the MSC culminated with the abolition of the MSC and the establishment of the Training and Enterprise Councils (TECs). This step is essentially a continuity of policy and not (as King, 1993, wrongly argues) a move from statism to neo-liberalism. The MSC was actively restructured to intervene to 'free up' the labour market (and especially for youth), reflecting a fundamentally neo-liberal attitude towards the market but, as Gamble shows, to do so required a strong and often forceful state (Gamble, 1988). From a state management viewpoint, the problems posed to strategists by such a neo-liberal policy objective are: how can state agencies know what the market requires, how can state agencies develop the capacity to intervene on behalf of market flexibility and how can such agencies avoid being captured by sectional or private interests? The creation of TECs led to a system of training which was led by the interests of private employers and thus became dependent upon their calculations and interests – a version of private-interest government in which public resources are utilized towards private ends.

This reminds us that states cannot be autonomous; they depend upon the resources and organizational capacities of non-state agencies. Different political strategies, however, bring with them different dependencies. If it is not possible for the state to be autonomous, it is at least possible for political strategies to make some choices over whom the state should be most dependent on. A central aspect of state management is then concerned with how the ensuing participation and/or representation should be managed. If we consider the case of urban interventions, we can develop a wider view of this changing pattern of dependency in the transitions from the Keynesian welfare state to what was popularly called 'Thatcherism'.

The Transformation of the Instruments of Urban Intervention

We examined in chapter 3 one agency of intervention – the Community Development Projects – which was very much a creature of the Keynesian welfare state. We have also looked at the MSC which began its life as a classic example of Keynesian welfare state corporatism and was subsequently transformed during the 1980s. In this section we will focus particularly upon urban interventions which were created during the 1980s and which reflect very clearly the nature of state management of that time: Enterprise Zones (EZs) and Urban Development Corporations (UDCs). We need, however, to locate these developments within their wider context.

Urban policy

In order for states to have a policy on anything, the object of that policy must be given an identity and meaning, assumptions must be made about the causal processes which produce outcomes, and value judgements must be made about the desirability of one set of outcomes over another. These state-centred activities can be as important as the object of policy itself in determining policy outcomes. Simultaneously, agencies of intervention both shape these and are in turn shaped by them. Agencies of intervention are significant in generating state assumptions about the nature and meaning of problems (the construction of 'skills' preferred by the MSC, for example), but equally shifts in state strategy prompt changes within the agencies of intervention.

'Urban policy' – and 'inner city' policy in particular – do not simply emerge as discrete aspects of public policy; they need to be constructed. Rhodes comments:

For the bulk of the post-war period, there was no inner city policy. As McKay and Cox (1979, p. 233) point out, the arrival of inner cities policy 'is evidence of the inadequacy of other urban policies'. These 'other' policies comprised new towns, regional planning, land-use planning and housing and they were directed at such problems as urban sprawl, regional decline and over-crowding. With the 'rediscovery' of poverty, race and the inner cities in the mid 1960s these policies and problems did not disappear but they were supplemented increasingly by policies directed explicitly at the inner city. (Rhodes, 1988, p. 233)

The term 'inner city' is woven into a sense of deprivation and poverty in the public mind and in official statements. Many inner urban areas continue to thrive but they are not the objects of inner city policy. (However, as is outlined below, the scale of social problems in many inner areas was considerable.)

Furthermore, the parameters around 'urban policy' exclude many of the most important public interventions and agencies from the rubric of 'urban policy'. For example, if we compare levels of regional aid with expenditure on defence procurement we can see that the sums involved in defence procurement were more significant but we know that these were never included in the decision-making process concerning regional and urban policy (see Robson, 1988, p. 173). Thus expenditure on health, education and other public administration continued to be massively geared towards the South East. In 1988 the government spent £885 per head of the population on defence, health, education and public administration in the South East. In Yorkshire and Humberside the figure was £702. If both regional aid and public administration expenditure had been equalized, Yorkshire and Humberside would have received an additional £850m a year and Sheffield City an additional £100m per year. Additionally, mortgage tax relief is a further welfare benefit for the more prosperous regions, and even the subsidy to the south-eastern railway system amounted to a further subvention to the better-off (calculated at £233m in 1985–6). On top of this, whilst the Department of Industry was spending some £700m on industry each year, regional development grants declined from £385m in 1977–8 to some £285m in 1983–4 (*Labour Research*, March 1983, p. 69). Small wonder, therefore, that Robson is prompted to comment that the rise of economic activity in the Cambridge to Bristol belt 'has been liberally larded with indirect government aid' (Robson, 1988, p. 173).

By ring-fencing one set of policies and describing them as 'urban policy', governments isolate one set of their activities, even if other policies have more significance for urban areas than 'urban policy' itself. Indeed, urban policy is often left to deal with problems which may have been exacerbated by other public policies. It is interesting to note that, far from this precipitating a rationality crisis (as it ought to, according to models of policy-making which view policy as a rational exercise in utility maximizing), it became routinized, reflecting the conflicting demands being made upon the state. As Peter Hall demonstrated in his study of French planning, there may be a degree of deliberate incoherence in policy if this is the price of maintaining a coalition of support drawn from potentially conflicting social groups (Hall, 1981). From a state-focused perspective we would expect to see evidence of this in the priorities between conflicting interests and in the respective capacities given to competing state agencies within which different interests were dominant.

These considerations may help us to understand why, when urban policy began to enjoy a distinct status during the 1960s, central resources were not simply handed over to local authorities. From early on, the central state identified problems of state management in relation to local government. They were locally accountable and thus less easy to direct from the centre; they were strongly influenced by public sector professionals with discourses often different from those at the centre; they were multi-purpose (and therefore urban regeneration would have to take its place amongst other priorities); they could not intervene secretively and single-mindedly in pursuit of regeneration (they were required to give the public adequate information, not to damage private interests unreasonably, to follow planning procedures etc.); and they tended to be more concerned with the long-term funding of services than with one-off, high-profile capital projects (these are suggested by Batley, 1989, who contrasts local government with Urban Development Corporations using these themes). Nevertheless, local authorities did enjoy some legitimacy as locally accountable bodies and they had an existing administrative structure which might potentially be used in pursuit of urban policy objectives. They also had considerable amounts of local knowledge which central departments could only have replicated at some cost. In the first instance, therefore, the centre administered urban policy through local authorities whilst simultaneously attempting to limit the perceived disadvantages of such a strategy.

The Urban Programme was launched in May 1968. Under this, central government agreed to part-fund projects put forward by local authorities in England and Wales where the local authority could demonstrate 'special social need'. As we have already seen, the following year saw the creation of a more purposive agency, the Community Development Projects. These were relatively small-scale, concerned with action research and were expected to collaborate closely with local government. The concerns implicit in the CDPs (inadequate families and underdeveloped communities) gave way during the following years to a concern with the improved management and coordination of public agencies expressed in the Comprehensive Community Programme. At the same time, the Inner Area Studies at the Department of the Environment, emphasized the economic and structural causes of decline.

These two trends (the recognition of need for public sector coordination and the importance of long-term economic restructuring) culminated with the publication of the White Paper 'Policy for the Inner Cities' (HMSO, 1977). In its first paragraph the influence of a series of interventions and studies was acknowledged; the Urban Programme, the Educational Priority Areas, the Community Development Projects, the Area Management Trials, the Comprehensive Community Programme, studies of London Docklands and 'above all the three Inner Area Studies'. In this sense, the White Paper identified an organizational learning process through which the central state's interpretation of inner-city problems, policies and agencies was transformed. Contrasting with the 'culture of deprivation' approach, it was now stressed that economic decline lay 'at the heart of the problem' (p. 2).

The report went on to consider the institutional implications of such an interpretation and its answers reflected the intent to work by consensus (or partnership) with local people and their representatives in pursuit of economic growth and mutual interests. It argued:

> Local Authorities are the natural agencies to tackle inner area problems
> . . . The Government do not, therefore propose the establishment of
> inner city corporations, on the model of those in new towns, although it
> would be willing to consider alternative arrangements should the need
> be shown . . . A unified approach to the problem of the inner areas will
> be required in which the various local policies and services within these
> areas are closely concerted. (HMSO, 1977, p. 8)

In part V of the report, the government outlined its proposals:

> (1) give a new priority in the main policies and programmes of government so that they can contribute to a better life in the inner areas . . .
> (2) strengthen the economies of the inner areas as an immediate priority . . .
> (3) secure a more unified approach to urban problems . . .

(4) recast the urban problem to cover economic and environmental projects and to increase its size . . .
(5) review and change policies on population movement . . .
(6) enter into special partnerships with the authorities – both districts and counties – of certain cities . . . (HMSO, 1977, p. 10)

Subsequently, in 1978, seven Partnership schemes were set up and these were to receive the bulk of the Urban Programme funding. They were to be run by a management group comprising council officers, local councillors, health authorities, the Manpower Service Commission, the Departments of the Environment, Industry, Trade, Education and Science, Employment, and, finally, the Home Office. The relative paucity of targets and indices reflected the belief that a broad consensus could be arrived at and that this would accurately reflect what needed to be done. When this happy state of affairs did not emerge, the incoming Conservative government quickly developed a radically alternative approach. Before examining this, it might be helpful to see why even an overtly 'non-interventionist' government felt obliged to intervene in urban regeneration.

The scale of the 'inner-city problem'

Official concern about the inner cities was based upon well-known indices of deprivation. Between 1951 and 1981 over one million manufacturing jobs were lost in the inner areas of the six largest conurbations (Audit Commission, 1989d, p. 9). Job losses were especially acute in particular areas with, for example, Wandsworth losing 25 per cent of its jobs in the 1969–73 period and Trafford Park losing over half of its 52,000 jobs in the period 1965–85 (Tym and Partners 1986). Britain lost one quarter of its manufacturing jobs during the 1971–81 period and these were, once again, concentrated in the inner areas (with inner London losing 41 per cent) (Greater London Council, 1985, p. 4). Consequently, during the 1970s the populations of cities decreased by 500,000 and this was concentrated in the most deprived areas. Inner London declined by 17.6 per cent in the period 1971–81 (Salt, 1986, p. 52).

Making this bad situation even worse, the problems of inadequate housing, low educational standards and poor health were more marked in many inner areas. Along with housing conditions, which were consistently worse than the national averages, 24,000 people were accepted as homeless in 1983 (Greater London Council, 1985,

p. 553). Infant mortality rates in inner-city hospitals were significantly worse. Crime was perceived to be rising and a generation of young people was emerging which had not experienced the discipline of a transition into the world of work (see above). It was under these circumstances that the incoming Conservative government in 1979 developed its inner-city policy. Through what agencies would such policies be pursued?

The reorganization of urban intervention in the 1980s

During the decade after the Conservatives' return to power in 1979, urban policy, and the agencies of intervention, were radically recomposed. Lawless (1988) lists ten major initiatives during the 1979–88 period and we may paraphrase these as:

1 The Urban Programme was more tightly monitored after the Urban Programme management initiative of 1985, local chambers of commerce and industry were given vetting powers over new projects, there was greater emphasis placed upon economic initiatives, and the traditional urban policy was brought to an end.
2 Urban development grants were introduced in 1982 and by 1986 this had cost £78m and secured a ratio of public/private investment of 1:4.5. This system gave local authorities some control over which applications were put forward. However, this was replaced with the Urban Regeneration Programme which bypassed local authorities.
3 The Urban Development Corporations were established (see below).
4 Enterprise zones were established (see below).
5 City action teams (CATs) and task forces were introduced. These followed the creation of the Merseyside Task Force in 1981. Their primary purpose was to coordinate the work of public agencies and to attract private investment. By 1988 there were also sixteen task forces operating on a more localized basis than CATs.
6 Land registers detailing underused public land were made available in 1981, encouraging the private acquisition and use of such pieces of land.
7 Through such agencies as the Small Firms Service, grants for local enterprise agencies, the Scottish Development Agency and others, some resources were directed towards firms in the inner areas.
8 Initiatives in training and education such as those channelled through the MSC and city technical colleges had an urban impact.

9 Housing initiatives were limited but included housing action teams and the selling-off of council houses.
10 Amongst other proposals contained in *Action for Cities* (see below) was the establishment of a British Urban Development Company (BUD). This was backed by eleven construction and engineering companies and aimed to realize profits through management fees and the sale of developed land.

Substantial interest in the inner-city question continued to be articulated at the centre of the state. Almost the first public words of Mrs Thatcher on winning the 1987 election were a promise to do something about 'those inner cities' and in the following year, in launching *Action for Inner Cities* (Department of Trade and Industry, 1988), Thatcher said:

> The Government is determined to build a new vitality in our inner cities. In partnership with the people and the private sector we intend to step up the pace of renewal and regeneration to make our inner cities much better places in which to live, work and invest. The new initiatives being undertaken by the Government and announced by the private sector show that we are releasing the talent, enterprise and energy that is at the service of our inner cities. We are embarked on a great enterprise which will leave its mark on Britain for decades and carry our towns and cities into the 21st century in much better shape. (quoted in *Municipal Journal* 20 May 1988)

Following the launch of *Action for Inner Cities*, in March 1988 Kenneth Clarke, Minister for Trade and Industry, announced twelve further initiatives which, it was claimed, would bring the level of annual expenditure on urban areas to £3,000m (Hansard, vol. 129, no. 109, cols 28–9). Briefly, these were:

1 The creation of a new Urban Development Corporation (UDC) in Sheffield with a budget of some £50m over seven years.
2 The doubling of the Merseyside UDC with a budget of between £50m and £90m over eight or nine years.
3 Two new City Action Teams for Leeds and Nottingham.
4 The replacement of the Urban Regeneration Grant with a simplified City Grant.
5 A requirement that information on all land use by the public sector be made available.
6 Two major new road projects intended to assist Docklands and the Black Country costing some £109m.

7 A new crime initiative for twenty inner-city areas.

8 A further package of assistance (including loan guarantees) to small businesses.

9 Compacts between employers and schools to encourage more vocational training in return for the promise of jobs.

10 More MSC support to bring information and training to inner areas.

11 English Estates (yet another agency of urban intervention) to provide more space in run-down areas.

12 A system for establishing meetings between businessmen and ministers was to be set up, along with a free telephone link-up for businesses interested in establishing themselves in inner areas.

By November 1989 the Government were claiming that £4b was being spent on inner-city programmes and in the following February a further £500m was announced (although most of this was created by 'bending' existing programmes and was not 'new money').

This, it need hardly be stressed, is not 'rolling back the state'. Whilst it builds on the predominant view of the 1970s that economic change lay at the heart of the inner-city problem (and not a culture of deprivation), in other respects it marks a clear shift away from the state management of the post-war era. As some parts of the state were rolled back or recomposed, other parts were being introduced or strengthened. New relationships with the private sector were regularly announced. The influence of local government was consistently downgraded. The representation of organized interests articulating a conception of sectional and collective interests was steadily replaced by the direct involvement of certain private interests combined with attempts (through the CATs, for example) to coordinate these. By looking at two particular examples we can develop a sharper sense of what this meant in practice. We turn first to the case of the enterprise zones and then to the urban development corporations.

Enterprise zones

The claim that the solution to urban problems lies in 'liberating' markets from state restrictions goes back at least to the 1960s. Peter Hall and others advocated the 'non-plan' and, in a bizarre and questionable image, exhort us to find our freedom 'in a non-plan bra' (Banham, Barker, Hall and Price, *New Society* 20 March 1969). In more restrained terms, by 1977 Hall was suggesting to the British

Royal Town Planning Institute that free-trade zones might be a last-ditch solution when other approaches have failed. In a speech to the Bow Group in June of the following year, at a meeting held in London Docklands, Geoffrey Howe committed himself to an anti-statist, free-market solution to inner-city problems and described such areas as potential 'enterprise zones' (see Anderson, 1988, pp. 20–1). Amongst other things, the proposal was to remove detailed planning, to remove legal obligations under the Employment Protection Act and incomes policies, to guarantee not to change tax law to the disadvantage of local businesses and to force local authorities which owned land to sell it. This was to be overseen by a newly created corporation which would bypass local authorities.

The scheme which was finally introduced in March 1980 was similar but with important differences. The idea of separate corporations was abandonned (but was to re-emerge in the urban development corporations). Exemption from land development tax and rates on industrial and commercial property was confirmed and accompanied by 100 per cent tax allowances for capital expenditure on commercial and industrial buildings. In addition, official requests for statistical information was to be minimized, businesses were to be exempt from the industrial training board levy and there would be accelerated processing of customs-free warehouses.

These wide-ranging and radical proposals were introduced as experimental and this helped to deflect much potential criticism. For an experimental scheme, however, the costs were substantial. The public costs of EZs were generated in two ways. First, there were direct costs to the Exchequer (including the rate relief for which the Treasury compensated local authorities). Second, public expenditures associated with infrastructural spending which would not have been committed in the absence of the EZ. According to one of the most detailed studies on EZs, the public cost in 1981/2–1985/6 was approximately £396m (at 1985/6 prices) (DoE, 1987, p. 1). Of the 63,000 jobs located in EZs, some 35,000 were there as a result of EZ policy. Of this 35,000, all but 13,000 were jobs transferred from elsewhere (and 60 per cent of transfered jobs came from areas with above average unemployment). Tym and Partners (1984) estimate that 85 per cent of firms in EZs would have been operating in the region with or without EZ status (giving them substantial uncovenanted benefits). The total cost per job created can then be estimated at around £30,000.

It is significant that if we consider the sources of public investment in the EZs (see Tym and Partners, 1983; quoted in Shutt, 1984, p. 37) then we can calculate that only 17 per cent and 16 per cent of funds are controlled by local government and central government respectively; 68 per cent is controlled by unelected quangos. This marks a clear break with the position outlined in the *Policy for the Inner Cities*, published in 1977, in which the partnership between central and local government was to be pivotal. In its place was to be a partnership between the private sector and unelected quangos. The attitude of many private investors is summed up in the comment by Nigel Broakes (then head of Trafalgar House) when he asked 'why face aggravation from Councils opposed to the profit motive and home ownership?' (*Guardian*, 3 July 1981).

Whilst we might expect trades union criticism of such a strategy (see Anderson, 1988, p. 28), other sources of criticism were perhaps more surprising. The Public Accounts Committee Report on EZs published in June 1986 (House of Commons, 1986) criticized the lack of proper targets (paras 5 and 6, p. v), the uncovenanted benefits – estimated at £70m to firms who would have been in the EZ in any case (paras 7–8), the lack of effective monitoring (paras 10–12) and the possible adverse effects of EZs on adjacent areas (para 21). Others suggested that market calculations alone would not attract major institutional investment into most inner areas and concluded that it was more important to mobilize the support of those who already had a (non-market) vested interest in the area – the existing occupiers (Cadman, 1982).

However, opposition to EZs was, for the most part, unable to mount an effective political challenge. One partial exception to this were the enterprise boards of Labour local authorities (especially the Greater London Enterprise Board and the West Midlands Enterprise Board). It is not the case that these were demonstrably less effective than EZs. Indeed, the West Midlands Development Board claimed to have secured 5,000 jobs with its first six investments at an average cost per job of £2,380 (*Labour Research*, March 1983). By 1985, the GLEB could also claim an impressive record with the creation and protection of 2,300 jobs and it elaborated a strategy which would increase employment by 48,000 from what it would otherwise have been (Greater London Council, 1985, p. 62). Even allowing for the uncertainties of such statistical claims, these figures compare favourably with the figures from the EZs. It is clear that, for the inner cities at least, there was an alternative.

Enterprise zones and state management

Enterprise zone status was supposed to solve the problem of managing state-led regeneration policies by simply allowing the unfettered energy of entrepreneurs to drive forward the process of change. However, in each of the twenty EZs established in England and Wales by 1985, there was massive involvement of a variety of other agencies and grant-giving mechanisms. We may see the resulting complexity of implementation by considering the example of Merseyside. In 1984–5 programme expenditure on the Merseyside Task Force Area amounted to some £313,000 coming from the following sources: Urban Programme (£50,723), Derelict Land Grants (£7,200), Merseyside Development Corporation (£27,846), Housing Investment Programme (£131,187 – estimate), Housing Corporation (£43,263), Historic Buildings and Conservation Grants (£2,000), Sports Council (£251), Manpower Services Commission (£41,342), and New Towns (Runcorn) (£9,900) (see House of Commons, 1986, p. xi).

This very complexity of public agencies traversing EZs led the minister responsible to establish the City Action Teams (CATs). In turn, this prompted the Chair of the House of Commons Environment Committee to write to the minister in April 1985:

> The relationships between the partners are of course the crux of the matter in the management of urban renewal. But the remit given to the City Action Teams obscures rather than clarifies these relationships, particularly in the Merseyside case. Is the Liverpool CAT the Task Force under another name or another body in addition to it? What working relationships are expected to obtain between the CAT and the bodies involved in Partnership? To what extent does the machinery of Partnership continue to function at all in Liverpool? We should appreciate your answers to these questions. (House of Commons, 1986, p. xiv)

Jenkin's reply is revealing: '(T)here has indeed been a long line of urban initiatives. I make no apology for this; the aim has been to fit solutions to problems and individual areas. UDCs, UDGs, EZs, and the MTF [Merseyside Task Force] and UP [Urban Programme] as a whole have been strikingly successful ... ' (House of Commons, 1986, p. xv). This emphasis upon diversity and tailor-made public responses is, of course, the antithesis of the view that identical EZs would liberate the market to solve the problems of urban regeneration. The view that markets require all sorts of very different public supports before they can function is alien to Howe's original concep-

tion but it more accurately reflects the realities of government policies.

Be this as it may, not long before Jenkin had made this plea for a
variety of solutions, the government had argued precisely the oppo-
site case in *Streamlining the Cities* (HMSO, 1983). This document
proposed the abolition of the metropolitan county councils claiming
that:

> The abolition of these upper tier authorities will streamline local gov-
> ernment in metropolitan areas. It will remove a source of conflict and
> tension. It will save money, after some transitional costs. It will also
> provide a system which is simpler for the public to understand, in that
> responsibility for virtually all local services will rest with a single
> authority. (HMSO, 1983, p. 5)

There is an obvious conflict between, on the one hand, Jenkin's
support for the creation of diversity and *ad hoc* interventions and, on
the other hand, the rationale behind the abolition of the metropolitan
councils. Furthermore, both positions were pursued with vigour in
their respective fields. On closer inspection we can see that both
positions were part of a broader change in the pattern of urban
intervention based upon a re-alignment of the relationship between
the state and the private sector in urban areas. The drivers for change
were to be private entrepreneurs, and the role of local state agencies
was to facilitate this. To achieve this required the re-engineering of
the public sector to bypass the power of professional and bureaucratic interests and to weaken accountability to local interests. The
enterprise zones were one of the devices intended to achieve this.

However, such a model of the relationship between the state and
society failed from the outset. EZs, as we have seen, were traversed by
a variety of public agencies each with its own priorities and calculations. Ironically, 'liberating' entrepreneurs also required the 'liber-
ation' of state agencies and giving them the capacity to intervene
forcefully on behalf of private corporations and interests. So the
question then quickly became how to calculate what the private
sector needed and how to coordinate its delivery across a range of
public sector agencies. One answer to this question was the creation
of urban development corporations.

Urban development corporations

Urban development corporations (UDCs) are quite unlike local authorities in each of the respects which, following Bately (1989, p. 183) we outlined above. Bately points out that UDCs were associated with private investment and accountable to central government (as opposed to being traversed by a variety of interests and accountable to the local electorate); they were responsive to market demand and initiatory (rather than managing existing services and being locked into base budgets); they could control their land assembly and disposals and secretively handle planning applications based on a narrow set of criteria concerned with maximizing inward investment and land values (as opposed to operating an 'even-handed' and open consideration of competing interests); statutory limitations on UDC action was weak (as opposed to extensive requirements facing local governments); and, finally, each UDC had a small staff organized into area teams with small but relatively clear targets (as opposed to large-scale organizations with a departmental structure organized into separate service with relatively fuzzy targets). Furthermore, staff recruitment and corporate culture were very different. The UDCs, therefore, appear to have provided central government with a radically different instrument for urban intervention. They were centrally created but led by the private sector with targets firmly linked to the gearing between public and private investment and to land prices.

According to Robson, of all the attempts to create a closer relationship with the private sector the UDCs were the 'most dramatic' (Robson, 1988, p. 124). For its part, the government in 1988 was to describe the UDCs as 'the most important attack ever made on urban decay' (*Action for Cities*, HMSO, 1988, p. 12). They were unquestionably an important initiative which went beyond the free-market rhetoric of the EZs towards private sector-led planning. As Harden (1988) described it:

> The practice of economic policy, particularly with the shift of emphasis to 'supply side' concerns, has more and more involved government attempting to act as a **player in the market**, rather than as a rule maker and umpire setting and monitoring a framework for autonomous economic actors. (original emphases)

This position was echoed by Bill Bradbury, then Conservative leader of Nottingham City Council, when he wrote of *Action for Cities*:

> At the heart of the plans is an attempt to bring the private sector back into the inner city. The publicity that accompanied the launch of [*Action for Cities*], was part of the attempt to ensure that industry and commerce were aware of both the need for improvements in inner cities and of the opportunities that are presented. The new urban development corporation projects are the most specific way that government is aiming to bring in the private sector. The new Sheffield UDC was seen as almost inevitable by the city council even though it was successfully working together with the local Chamber of Commerce to develop the site of the UDC in the Lower Don Valley. The city, short of money, could see that the only realistic source of extra public sector funds was from a UDC. (Bradbury, 1988, p. 1038)

The first urban development corporations were established in 1981 under the the Local Government, Planning and Land Act of 1980. The Act stated that urban regeneration was to be achieved by (1) bringing land into more effective use, (2) encouraging the development of new industry and commerce, (3) creating an attractive environment and (4) ensuring that housing and social facilities were available to encourage people to live and work in the area. Despite these broader aims, until the end of the 1980s, at least, the UDCs in both London Docklands and Merseyside were much more narrowly focused upon physical regeneration and driven by inward investment (see House of Commons, 1988b).

The first two UDCs were established in London Docklands and Merseyside. UDCs were also established during 1987 in Manchester Trafford Park, Teeside, Tyne and Wear and the Black Country. At the end of 1987, 'mini UDCs' were established in Bristol, Leeds and Manchester. This was followed by the Lower Don Valley established in 1988. By 1989–90, UDCs covered 16,000 hectares in urban areas and were budgeted to spend £270m.

The idea of a UDC had been considered and rejected in 1977 in the broadly supported *Policy for Inner Cities*. The events leading to the creation of the London Docklands Development Corporation perhaps help to explain why the idea of the Corporation came to be embraced just three years later. Put simply, the mechanisms available for achieving the renewal of London Docklands were flawed; they presupposed a consensus amongst the communities and public agencies of Docklands over its future, and the planning structures in place had been established in order to contain and manage growth rather than to stimulate investment in the face of a massive structural disinvestment.

In 1973 Travers Morgan was appointed by Peter Walker to draw up a brief for the redevelopment of Docklands. All of Travers Morgan's subsequent suggestions gave commercial and financial interests the dominant role and it was in opposition to the Travers Morgan position that the Joint Docklands Action Group (JDAG) was established. This was drawn from those borough councils which were in the redevelopment area. As a result of their pressure a new body – the Docklands Joint Committee (DJC) – was established in 1974.

The DJC was based on the borough councils and the GLC. With a different brief, the DJC's planners invited a locally based group, the Docklands Forum, to participate in the formation of the 1976 Strategy Plan. The Forum included representatives from community groups, trades unions, the CBI, the Chamber of Commerce, churches and environmental groups. Participation was wide, open and encouraged, and plans were to emerge out of negotiation and discussion with those most directly involved. Newman and Mayo, who both worked within the JDAG, regarded the Strategy Plan as 'a political compromise within market forces' (Newman and Mayo, 1981, p. 540).

It was this process and machinery which was overthrown with the creation of the LDDC which was granted powers to acquire and assemble land, to grant planning permission on land they owned, to sell land with planning permission, to manage housing, to build housing, to allow the construction of public and private sector residential units and to construct the necessary roads. As such, the creation of the LDDC involved the bypassing of existing planning structures and of local government in relation to housing and infrastructural spending. According to a House of Lords Select Committee, this loss of democratic control was 'a step not easily to be justified' (House of Lords, 1981, p. 15). Furthermore, the committee expressed 'no doubt that the opposition to the proposed transfer of development control from the boroughs to the UDC, voiced by the local organizations which have petitioned against the Order, is perfectly genuine' (ibid., p. 13). Therefore one has to search the Report with some care in order to discover why – despite these views – it finally supported the principle of the UDC. The weight of the argument appears to rest heavily upon paragraph 68.5 which states 'in any case a UDC is more likely to attract private investment into the area than the boroughs and the DJC' (p. 4). The view that the UDCs were visibly pro-capital and could attract private funding has remained the most common, indeed often the only, official justification for their creation.

In the place of locally based and democratic institutions, UDCs were created with, typically, some twelve members on the board. All three chairs of the LDDC during the 1980s were 'property men' (see Wolmar, in *Guardian* 8 April 1989). The Merseyside Development Corporation (MDC) board was chaired by a former textile magnate and it included the chairs of two local football clubs, a quango director, a banker, the right-wing economist Professor Patrick Minford, the chair of a training agency, a Mayfair surveyor and two council-lors. The make-up of the LDDC board was similar (with a slightly less populist flavour), except that the three local authorities have gener-ally refused to take up their opportunity to be represented on the board on the grounds that what was on offer was incorporation rather than representation. Of the draft code of conduct covering the relationships between the LAs and the LDDC, the judge in the Canary Wharf hearing commented that 'this document does not constitute even a promise of consultation' (House of Commons, 1988b). The Employment Committee also recommended that the LDDC should improve its communication with the LAs as a matter of urgency (ibid., para 97).

In Docklands, the LDDC was successful in attracting inward in-vestment. By 1985–6 some £2bn of private investment was being claimed and by 1989 this had risen to £4.5bn (*Docklands Magazine*, Feb. 1989, Docklands Magazine Ltd, London) and a public/private investment gearing ratio of 1:9 was claimed (although this depends upon a definition of public expenditure which is so narrow as to make it almost useless). Attractions for investors included very favourable office rent and rate comparisons, anticipated rapid capital appreci-ation, few planning permission conditions and all the other EZ benefits.

However, the scheme was not without its problems. By 1989 the *Economist* wrote of London Docklands, 'yesterday it was being hailed as the white rabbit out of a hat. Now there is talk of it being tomorrow's white elephant' (p. 18, 9 Sept. 1989). It goes on to comment that 'Docklands was born with the Thatcher era and was intended to exemplify it . . .' and that, whilst something clearly needed to be done, 'the government chose the wrong something'. At the heart of this emergent failure were problems of planning and strategy with which we are now becoming familiar.

In 1986 Reg Ward, then the LDDC chief executive proudly boasted '(W)e have no land use plan or grand design; our plans are essential marketing images. The feeling of cohesion in docklands comes only in retrospect' (*The Times*, 18 Nov. 1986). Planning did take place, of course, but it was being done by particular investors (primarily prop-erty developers). The problems with Ward's position are many and varied. First, failing adequately to plan for transport led to a crisis for the LDDC by 1989 (see *The Economist*, 5 Aug. 1989, p. 27). According to the former chair of Trafford Park Development Corporation, 'London Dockland Development Corporation did not do their homework in my view. The development is impressive but the infrastructure is badly planned in that you can hardly get in or out of Docklands' (quoted in Salveson, Tansley and Colenutt, 1990, p. 4). Such worries are widely shared and include not only road transport. The 1989 financial crisis at Thames Line, the high-speed river-bus service, the low take-up of facilities at the London Docklands Airport and the public–private arguments over the financing of the extension to the Jubilee line all contributed to an about-turn on transport planning. The LDDC's own *Dockland Business World* ran a story in the January–March edition, 1989, headlined 'We're Getting There . . . Transport Permitting' in which the 'need for transport planners and business space planners to co-ordinate their acts' was emphasized. This was, of course, one of the functions previously carried out by local government which the UDC's investor-led approach had promised to dispense with.

Neither was an investor-led approach capable of planning training in Docklands (especially important if transport problems were to be eased by training some of the people living in the area to do some of the jobs). In 1987, LDDC commissioned Peat Marwick and McLintock to undertake a review of education, training and employment initiatives undertaken by the corporation. By 1987 the LDDC was spending £2.7m a year on training and either directly or indirectly supporting between 2,500 and 3,000 people in training. The report was unequivocal, stating that the LDDC 'has initiated a substantial number of projects related to education, training and employment. But it has done so without the benefit of a clear policy and objectives against which initiatives could be evaluated.' They complained of a lack of data, inadequate appraisal and inadequate monitoring (see Employment Committee Report, 1988, para 49). The collection of data and the imposition of monitoring had both been rejected in the rhetoric of EZs and UDCs.

Land use also suffered from a lack of planning. Sir Andrew Derbyshire, previously chair of the LDDC planning committee, said 'We have learnt from Docklands that the free play of market forces is not going to produce the best results in terms of quality' (*Guardian*, 8 April 89). Furthermore, the secretive nature of UDC decision-making and the short period of time given to local authorities (who had to service new facilities) to file objections (fourteen days) drew criticism from the Audit Commission, the Public Accounts Committee and the Select Committee on Employment.

Poor planning has also created problems in relation to attracting potential workers into the area. For example, original estimates that 13,000 dwellings would be needed had to be revised upwards to 30,000. Also, original plans did not include locations of doctors' surgeries. Just as worrying for potential workers who might move into the area, by 1989 there was a claimed shortage of 130 primary school teachers, fifty specialist teachers and twenty-five nursery teachers. The teacher making these claims was quoted in the LDDC's own *Dockland News* (February, 1989) as saying, 'It's no use just slinging up housing. The Corporation has a responsibility to see that there are affordable homes available for teachers, doctors and nurses and other workers that every community needs.' The same edition of *Dockland News* goes on to emphasize that the LDDC's priority is for education and housing. Turning over the pages there is one story after another about events and organizations funded by, or organized by, LDDC; sporting events, free lectures in local history, tree planting, safety standards, computers to improve health care, the renovation of a church hall and so on. All the sorts of things, in fact, which used to be provided by elected local authorities.

The discovery made by the LDDC was one which social scientists could have told them about more cheaply and easily: it is that medium-term economic growth is embedded in a variety of institutional, cultural and social contexts which cannot be secured though a narrow attention to private sector investment. Sooner or later, even the private investors will demand more. Meanwhile in Merseyside a similar conclusion was arrived at through a rather different route. One of the more important differences was that, whilst London Docklands was adjacent to some of the most valuable real estate in the world, the same was not true for Merseyside. The whole area had witnessed massive disinvestment throughout the previous twenty years, losing 40,000 manufacturing jobs and 20,000 service sector jobs in the years 1978–84 alone. In this depressed environment, by 1989 MDC had spent £175m but secured only £40m in new investment. On their own optimistic assumptions, the MDC hoped to have created 5,500 jobs (including short-term work in the construction industry). Under such circumstances even the director of the Merseyside Chambers of Commerce rejected the belief that market forces alone could solve Merseyside's problems (see *Guardian*, 25 July 1988).

Key to the low levels of private investment was that, whilst investors in London could anticipate strong growth in capital or rental values of properties, in Merseyside the same did not apply (a view confirmed by the MDC chief executive in 1988). This brief contrast with the Merseyside example suggests that, problematic as it was, the Docklands case could have even limited success only because of the vibrancy of the surrounding property values and the desirability of its location.

Concluding remarks on the urban development corporations

The evidence presented here fits with the view, quoted above in chapter 5, that:

> It is not hard to see Government policy as the next and possibly the final round in a battle against the Labour local authorities rather than as direct action to relieve the inner cities. Its emphasis on UDCs, central appointed bodies that can usurp many of the basic functions of local government, could be taken as corroborating the view that this is a power battle first and a zeal for reform second. (*Financial Weekly* 2 July 1987)

In the same article, David Blunkett agreed that UDCs were attempts to bypass socialism and added ruefully that, in the eight years before 1987, Sheffield 'lost as much in grants and subsidies . . . as the total public investment in the London Docklands'. As the *Financial Weekly* article asked '(I)s the government's intention to eradicate urban blight or to eradicate intractable, left-wing local authorities?'

This was clearly part of a wider strategy. Urban programme funding (over which the central government had more control) increased between 1977/8 and 1987/8 from £30m to £324m. This contrasts with reductions in Rate Support Grant (over the spending of which the centre had less control). Between 1979/80 and 1983/4 designated boroughs gained £300m through urban programme funds and lost £1,530m in RSG reductions (see Robson, 1988, p. 98). Whilst the central–local relationship was being so re-engineered, the public–private relationship in urban policy was also being restructured. For example, in order to help turn the 1970s central–local government relationship into the 1980s local state agency–private sector relationship, the government announced that local chambers of commerce should be free to examine Partnership proposals and advise the DoE to reject proposals of which it disapproved. Similarly, in March 1990, David Hunt, the Minister for the Inner Cities, announced that the

£500m increase in the inner-city programme (which the central government controlled) had been achieved by 'bending' other programmes (over which, presumably, the central government had less control).

This strategy did not end the substantial engagement of the state in inner areas. Whilst it removed a troublesome need to collaborate with local authorities, many of which were politically hostile, it was quickly to create new problems of state management. First, there were problems of setting targets and measuring success (the public:private investment gearing ratio, for example, could be measured in such a variety of equally meaningful ways that its use as an index of success is very limited). Second, UDCs were embedded in complex relationships in which outcomes can often be unexpected or perverse. For example, the 'favourable' index of buoyant land prices was also responsible for forcing local manufacturers who required large amounts of land (but employed local labour) out of business. By 1987 in the LDDC area 3,355 redundancies had been reported in existing firms (compared with 7,877 jobs created, of which 5,059 were transferred from other areas, giving a net loss of 500 jobs). Third, an investor-led approach to urban regeneration cannot work because private investors cannot be expected to provide infrastructural support without which regeneration cannot succeed. In particular, an investor-led planning system cannot secure the sorts of inter-agency coordination needed in successful regeneration programmes.

Previously existing agencies have been restructured, bypassed or marginalized. New urban agencies were established (UDCs, city action teams, task forces, the British Urban Development Company and so forth). New mechanisms of private sector participation were opened up (the restructured Partnership Programme, Training and Enterprise Councils, inner-city compacts between schools and industry, breakfasts with Lord Young and so forth). And old powers of planning, labour-market regulation and so forth were similarly reconstituted. The structural selectivity of the state was being shifted.

However, such a shift operates within limits. Systematically restructuring state management in a way which fails to meet the requirements of medium-term economic expansion inevitably prompted political opposition from within the state. The Employment Committee (House of Commons, 1988), the Public Accounts Committee (House of Commons 1989), the Audit Commission (1989d) and independent consultants produced a series of assaults on the management of urban policy. A central concern of these criticisms was the absence of effective coordination. These concerns are well summed up in the Audit Commission's conclusion that:

government support programmes are seen as a patchwork quilt of complexity and idiosyncrasy. They baffle local authorities and business alike. The rules of the game seem over-complex and sometimes capricious. They encourage compartmentalised policy approaches rather than a coherent strategy; key organizational structures have fallen into disrepair. Some partnership schemes do not in practice operate. (Audit Commission, 1989d, pp. 1–2)

However, it would be quite wrong to argue that, with a different approach to state management, the state could on its own have reversed the processes of urban decline. Throughout the Western world it is evident that states have insufficient capacities for this. States therefore inevitably find themselves having to incorporate the capacities of non-state agencies and, inevitably, this means securing the participation of the private sector. In an increasingly globalized economy, this is an increasingly transnational private sector. Planning under such circumstances is very difficult to manage and in practice it is often little more than a rationalization of measures which reflect the inherent weakness of the state.

Even allowing for these general problems of urban intervention, there is more to explaining the particular difficulties associated with British urban intervention at this time. Sharpe argued that there is an 'implementation gap' between national and subnational government but that in Britain this gap is less than in, say, Germany because the central state can bargain, co-opt professional policy communities and mobilize shared sectional interests (Sharpe, 1985, *passim*). Our case study suggests that, rather, it is the central state's capacity to create new agencies and transform old ones which is crucial to this. More importantly, however, our study shows that gaining tighter control over local agencies does not of itself transform the capacities of the state; rather it shifts the nature of its dependencies. The problem therefore still arises over how these dependencies may be institutionalized and managed. It was in addressing this problem that governments in the 1980s were so inept and vindictive. Their enthusiasm for punishing political opposition was often greater than their commitment to an optimal management of urban agencies (the abolition of the GLC being only one of the more spectacular examples of this).

The complex and poorly coordinated range of institutional interventions in urban areas by the end of the 1980s could be described by Hood's term 'multi-organizational sub-optimisation' (Hood, 1976, p. 17). That is, a complex system of intervening agencies whose separate choice-making processes inhibit optimal outcomes. The legacy of problems created by this is one which governments of the 1990s have to address.

Youth Training and Urban Intervention: Summary and Conclusions

Each of these examples of new strategies of state management in the 1980s shows that we must add to our list of 'new technologies of state management' the bypassing or closing down of those state agencies which were compromised by their relationship with the politics of the Keynesian welfare state. In the initial recomposition of the MSC, trades union and local authority representation was downgraded, Ministerial appointments were used in an effort to exert even tighter central control, new targets were set and new schemes were created to be administered. However, this was not enough to satisfy ministers' desire to secure for training policy a new relationship with private employers. This, ministers hoped, would be achieved through the abolition of the MSC and the creation of TECs. Similarly, in urban policy, local authorities were gradually bypassed and new agencies created. Private investors were wooed not only to invest their own money but to assist in the spending of public money.

In each of these cases, central governments devoted considerable resources, and withstood considerable political objections, to the creation of new agencies. A long-standing Conservative tradition of hostility to increasing the powers of central government was put to one side. Judicial concern about the forced loss of planning powers by local authorities was ignored. Audit Commission concern about a loss of coordination and House of Commons worries about a loss of purpose and accountability had no effect. In all of this the justification put forward by the government (or in its defence) was primarily that the ends justified the means. Yet the evidence available to central government could never have supported the claim that employer-led training and private investor-led urban development were adequate to meet the expressed aims of the government.

It is possible that ministers were convinced that their market-based solutions were adequate but it is more likely that governments were driven by the desire to find new forms of state management. The evidence is fairly similar and systematic in both of our case studies. In each of them trades unions, local authorities, professional bodies and even the old-style 'great and good' are displaced. Invited into the decision-making processes are private sector employers and investors along with a rather motley collection such as football club chairmen and free-market economists intended, presumably, to provide some populist legitimacy. Furthermore, new targets, indices and monitoring processes are given to these new agencies. Other information, such as accident rates on YTS or advance warning of planning proposals in London Docklands, is concealed or made available at the last minute.

If such a systematic restructuring of participation and public sector calculations had produced a demonstrably improved legacy for the 1990s then there might at least be some basis for the claim that the ends have justified the means. We have selected two examples where governments throughout the capitalist world have faced enormous difficulties whatever the forms of state management deployed. For a more complete sense of the significance of state management we would need to have a comparative account which assessed the independent impact of state management on the wider capacity of states to achieve their objectives. This would be both methodologically and theoretically demanding.

However, on an interim and necessarily tentative note, we can say that the evidence presented here is that, far from facilitating desired outcomes, the new forms of state management in our two case studies prevented governments from achieving their declared objectives. A work-force trained for mobility in a rapidly changing labour market is unlikely to be provided by a training sector dominated by employers wishing to train their existing work-force to use the technology currently being used in their work-places. Similarly, the medium-term regeneration of areas like Merseyside and London Docklands requires a concern with infrastructural spending on transport, schools, housing and so forth which private investors are ill-equipped to assess or provide.

This has left us with interesting and challenging academic and practical problems concerning state management into the twenty-first century. Addressing these requires theoretical sophistication, empirical grasp and a level of imagination which could only be the product of a collective endeavour. The final chapter is intended as a contribution to this.

8
The British State:
Interpretations and Prospects

The purpose of this final chapter is to review the substantive and theoretical issues raised in this book and, in passing, to reflect on the possibilities for the coming decades.

Introduction

A core theoretical claim of this book is that the management of the state involves choices and practices which open up some circuits of power and close down others. It makes some outcomes achievable and rules others out of court. It includes some groups and interests and denies state power to others. It concerns the ways in which the enormous coercive and welfare-providing capacities of the state may be deployed. For these reasons, it is not sensible to care about the future of politics without addressing the questions of the management and organization of the embedded state. Such a state should be conceived neither in the emaciated form of much of the public sector management literature nor in the decontextualized form of most public choice literature.

At the substantive level, this is not yet another text which claims to find both the unique and sole touchstone of Britain's alleged failure and the key to its future success. This book has drawn upon accounts which claim to identify the singular cause of Britain's fall from grace variously in the City, the absence of a fully-fledged capitalist/democratic revolution, the archaism of the British ruling class and so forth. There are many competing (and sometimes conflicting) accounts of

British politics and it might help us to assess the claims made in this book if we place them alongside some of these accounts. Therefore in this final chapter I draw together the arguments put forward earlier in this book and locate these within the wider debates concerning social theory and British politics before suggesting what this might imply for the future conduct of politics in Britain. Such a tall order must inevitably be treated schematically. We start with the theoretical arguments within which this book developed before considering some of the more substantive debates.

The Theoretical Debates

Contingency and the institutional focus

In recent developments in the analysis of public sector change, there is a line of development which moves from contingency theory in the 1970s, through intergovernmental relations and government–industry relations in the 1980s through to network theory in the 1990s (see Rhodes, 1995; Gamble, 1995).* Linking these arguments is a shared concern with the variety of organizational forms associated with liberal democratic states, the range of ways in which intra-state relations are organized and the distinctiveness of the institutionalization of state–society relations in each country. Not only is there held to be a wide variety of state–society relationships but also these variations are held to have significant outcomes for economic efficiency, policy effectiveness, democracy and so forth.

Meanwhile, a converging pathway begins with marxist-influenced political economists rejecting economic reductionism (see Jessop, 1982; and his even firmer rejection in Jessop, 1990). It includes an application of structuration theory as developed by Giddens (1979 and 1985) to an understanding of the modern state. Empirical studies which sought to apply a theoretically informed but non-reductionist approach included Esping-Andersen's *The Three Worlds of Welfare Capitalism* (1990), Middlemas's three volumes on *Power, Competition and the State* (1986, 1990, 1991), and Jessop *et al.*'s work on Thatcherism (1988). In the 1990s these arguments came close to the

---

* See, for example, Grant (1993) on government–industry relations in Britain; Wilks and Wright (1987) on comparative government–industry relations; Rhodes (1986) on power dependency in inter-governmental relations; and Dowding (1995) on network theory.

institutionalist claim that there are competing models of capitalism and of state policy formation which produce very different outcomes in terms of efficiency, growth and justice (see Hutton, 1996; Krugman, 1995).

These two pathways share the important conclusion that the systematic exercise of power is made possible by, and simultaneously constrained by, organizations and by the coordination of inter-organizational relationships. Each rejects the claim that there exists one organizational form towards which all modern organizations inevitably tend (the Weberian bureaucracy, for example) and each also rejects the idea that capitalism brings with it a necessary preference for one particular political, social or economic form. Organizations such as those found within the state system, for example, must be understood in their historical context as a sedimentation of past choices and actions which in turn both circumscribe and inform future choices.

In previous chapters we have attempted to show how such choices have strengthened some state agencies in relation to others (e.g. the Treasury) and have shaped the modalities through which such power is exercised (e.g. through financial controls, denying access to certain interests or mechanisms privileging differently constructed interests). Since different calculations are dominant within different parts of the state system, privileging one agency over another has the consequence of privileging one set of calculations over another. Similarly, different ways of exercising power facilitates some outcomes whilst preventing others (for a more abstract examination of the state's 'structural selectivity' see Jessop, 1990, *passim*). In this way, a picture has been built up which shows how the organization and management of the British state contributed to the wider politics of change and stability. In the sense that this book demonstrates that the organizational form of the state is not simply a reflection of its function and has significant consequences for the wider conduct of politics, the arguments presented here are congruent with an institutionalist account.

However, this book is not intended to dispense with the need to sustain a theoretical understanding of the state as a force embedded within a wider set of power relationships. Whilst it draws upon work in the first of the routes outlined above, it remains primarily upon the pathway which starts with non-reductionist state theory. To show why we need a theoretically informed account of the state, it might help to consider a significant attempt to dispense with state theory.

Public choice theory and the state

Public choice theory is a part of the wider approach of rational choice theory (for an introduction to this, see Ward, 1995). Starting in attempts to explain voting and party competition (Downs, 1957), rational choice theory was often developed in the form of game theory which tried to provide models of different relationships which might or might not facilitate optimum outcomes. Public choice theory applies rational choice arguments to the public sector and it starts from the assumption that actors in state agencies, like actors in the private sector, will act rationally in pursuit of their own interests (see Niskanen, 1971). Its great strength lies in its aspiration to explain the actions of state agencies in ways which take account of the choices made by individuals within those agencies. This aspiration is an important shield against ill-considered notions that state agencies, or even states themselves, have essential interests or functions which they inevitably perform. Olson, for example, poses acute problems for traditions such as marxism and pluralism which may assume that it is sufficient for a group (or class) to share interests in common for it to act collectively in pursuit of that interest (Olson, 1965). Olson demonstrates that the conditions under which shared interests lead to collective action are peculiar rather than universal. However, beyond this sensible (and widely shared) concern, what does public choice theory have to offer an account of state management?

Public choice theory proceeds by applying the deductive methods normally associated with economic analysis to the study of public agencies. It then hopes to build predictive models of how agencies will behave which can then be tested against the evidence. In Niskanen (1971) these (necessarily ahistorical) models were based upon the expectation that rational and self-interested bureaucrats would be motivated by budget-maximizing rather than by the pursuit of the public interest. Dunleavy (1991) convincingly demonstrates that the variety of types of budget and of differences amongst agencies entirely undermines this model as a predictive tool. However, Dunleavy wishes to retain the deductive method and the focus upon the rational choices of individuals. He therefore develops a model of bureau-shaping which recognizes that differences of rank and type of agency produce very different types of (equally rational) action in different parts of the state system. This more sophisticated approach is helpful when considering possible reasons for the differing bureaucratic responses to, for example, the Next Steps agencies in the 1980s. Indeed, the bureau-shaping model raises the possibility of a stimulating analysis of state management.

However, there is much of relevance to the choices made by state agencies which rational choice theory does not help us with. In what sense could the Treasury model of the economy be seen as a simple reflection of the bureaucratic interests of officials? Exactly how did social pathology views of the origins of poverty maximize the interests of Home Office officials over and above other accounts? What bureaucratic interests were represented by the logic of the Enterprise Zones? More awkwardly still, the medical model clearly benefits the medical profession but is it nothing more than an expression of professional power – is the meaning of medical science exhausted by the pursuit of power by the medical profession? Dunleavy's approach adds much-needed sophistication to the public choice tradition but it fails to capture the range, subtlety and complexity of intra-state discourses and calculations. Indeed, empirical evidence for the widespread existence of the self-interested, rational utility maximizer has never been persuasive, and such evidence as there is points to a far richer variety of factors shaping action than is suggested by the bureau-shaping model (see Dunsire and Hood, 1989). As doubtlessly Dunleavy would agree, there is more to the creation of a cadre of officials than simply managing their rational choices. Public officials are locked into public sector discourses which defy analysis through the deductive methods proposed in public choice theory. The methodological individualism of public choice theory cannot explain the origins and persistence of intra-state discourses.

The construction of public sector discourses

The alternative to the view that people make rational utility-maximizing choices is not that they go around behaving in random and unpredictable ways. One approach, at least, is to examine the cultural and institutional circumstances within which identities are forged, interests perceived and choices evaluated. Understanding the fluidity of these processes in their historical context is to understand the variety of contingent factors creating a historically necessary event. Clearly this lacks the deductive rigour and the predictive claims of public choice theory but if 'rigour' is based upon false assumptions and if 'predictive claims' have not been realized, then this may be no great loss.

Following the work of Althusser (1971), Laclau and Mouffe (1981) and Foucault* (1978, *inter alia*) we can argue that identities and choices cannot be simply 'read' from the agent's social position. Just as there are no necessary links between class location and identity, there are no necessary links between bureaucratic location and identity. The employee (including the bureaucrat) has been constructed by a variety of discourses which shapes her or his identities, interests and calculations. Thus we may indeed wish to examine the historic circumstances under which bureaucrats behave according to the bureau-shaping model. When do they become immune to discourses of the public interest, to professional obligations or to a sense of solidarity with a network of overlapping interests? And when are they motivated by bureaucratic self-interest as predicted by the public choice model? It is intuitively likely that on occasions at least they will behave as the bureau-shaping model predicts, but this is no reason to privilege it by regarding it as the universal expression of public officialdom. Rational choice theory has a purchase only under particular conditions; it does not provide a general account.

The nineteenth century witnessed the construction of a cadre of officials oriented towards a shared conception of the public interest, rewarded individually and collectively with status, income and power for pursuing that 'public interest' and able to operationalize such a commitment through the routines of administrative life. For all that this constrained democracy and ignored the constitutional role given to the civil service, for all that it entrenched the power of a conservative establishment, it provided part of a solution to the problems of state management. In any case, we have seen that this administrative elite was not, as has been frequently claimed, unconcerned with Britain's industrial future, unwilling to adapt to Britain's changing role in the world or unaware of the need for new strategies to address the problems of poverty, urban decay and so forth.

However, the organization and cultures of the nineteenth-century state reflected both its own particular functions and the management trends of the private sector corporation from where it took many of its ideas. The pressures which compel private sector organizations to adapt their internal structures in pursuit of continuing profitability do not exist in the same way for the state. However, we have seen that the British state was slow to change not due to some historical oversight (as if one hundred years went by with state managers

---

* Whilst Foucauldian arguments appear in places in this book, the central arguments do not require a systematic engagement with this approach. In order to make the main story clear, a number of interesting sub-plots have had to be sacrificed.

failing to notice that the world outside had changed) but because of the complex relationships between bureaucratic interests and wider political change.

Not only do we need to look at the historical construction of such administrative identities and practices but we should also be sensitive to the variations which exist within the state system. The central civil service, through common recruitment practices and through encouraging the career civil servant to move across departments, managed to construct a strong and shared ethos at the centre of the state. However, during the post-war period the range of research and analytical skills required by new forms of economic and social interventions brought with them distinctive ways of assessing causal accounts, measuring indices of policy success and debating normative conceptions of the public interest. As these calculations were sedimented through the generations, they shaped a senior cadre of bureaucrats which, by the 1980s, was broadly antipathetic to the view of the world suggested by neo-liberal arguments and the new managerialism. In turn, this new managerialism of the 1980s and 1990s should be seen as part of an attempt to reconstruct state officials' identities, interests and functions. The public sector manager was to become a more assertive player, with a more goal-oriented culture, and the central civil service was to become less unified.

In seeking to understand and explain this process, and to identify its consequences and limits, the public choice orientation towards the micro level is important. As Gamble rightly insists: '(T)he real challenge is not to provide yet more ahistorical economic models of political behaviour, or non-deductive historical descriptions of institutions, but to develop adequate microfoundations for political economy by providing actor-centred explanations which make realistic assumptions about the structures and institutions through which agency is expressed' (Gamble, 1995, p. 528). Furthermore, Gamble rightly emphasizes that, once divorced from neo-classical assumptions that the absence of state intervention will lead to equilibrium, public choice theory is not necessarily attached to the new right political project. However, public choice theory is necessarily attached to a methodology in which the individual is causally supreme and as we have seen, adequate actor-centred explanations of, say, the reconstruction of urban intervention, require us to consider the changing definition of the 'urban problem', the changing pattern of participants in public agencies, the changing targets and reward structures for urban agencies and so forth. The relevant 'actor' in these cases, is often not the individual. Interviewing every individual involved in the management of urban intervention at this time, and then aggregating the results, would not provide an adequate actor-centred explanation. On the contrary, it would conceal the very technologies of power and programmes of normalization which constitute officials as effective actors in the public sector. For this reason alone (and there are others), we should reject the attempt to ground actor-centred accounts of state management in a methodological individualism and draw on the insights provided by discourse theory. However, drawing on such insights is not enough.

Bringing state theory back in

The points of dispute between a state theorist such as Poulantzas and a discourse theorist such as Foucault are well outlined by Jessop (1990, pp. 227–9). I do not wish to repeat these points here but, rather, to draw out their implications for this study. First, Poulantzas maintained that the state was locked into wider relations arising from the mode of production. The key organizations responsible for the productive capacities of a capitalist regime are driven by the pursuit of profits. These capitalist enterprises generate power relations in society as a whole which fundamentally shape political strategies (including strategies of state management). State strategists cannot ignore the requirement that these organizations should continue to make profits in the way that they might ignore the strategic interests of other social groups. Furthermore, 'Poulantzas criticised Foucault for arguing that power has no bases beyond the power relation itself and therefore consists purely in the modalities of its exercise' (Jessop, 1990, p. 227). Similarly, Poulantzas rejected the idea that organized resistance to power necessarily became absorbed into the exercise of that power. Indeed, he argued that resistance is possible because the exercise of power is limited by the fact that any particular mechanism of power brings with it its own limits and potentials.

These are all relevant for the concerns of this book. First, we have argued that state management should be understood as completing some circuits of social power and disrupting others. Class power, patriarchal power and so forth all depend upon state agencies being managed in appropriate ways. Circuits of power run through the state and the state is part of these wider power relationships. Thus we wish to give the state a greater degree of causal importance than do most accounts. However, we do not wish to give it a causal supremacy. From state theory, therefore, we derive a sense of the need to examine the linkages, tensions and conflicts between strategies of state management and strategies of class domination, patriarchal power, the suppression of minority groups or what not. In addition (and this is notably absent from Foucault's account) we can see the possibility of state management strategies which not only oppress and dominate but which are inclusive and empowering.

Secondly, Jessop stresses that Poulantzas was aware of the limits inherent in any particular mechanism of power. We have seen that in the management of central–local relations, for example, the choice of strategies is wide. Empowering professionals, encouraging local participation, strengthening hierarchical controls, the use of quasi-contractual relationships have all been used and all have enhanced central control in particular ways. But we have also seen that each strategy contains its own mechanisms for resistance. Appeals to professional autonomy, alliance-building with local pressure groups and working only to the formal rules of bureaucracies or contracts can all compromise central power. We therefore see a constant shift amongst a variety of mechanisms producing multiple, overlapping and often conflicting strategies of state management. Cases such as the Community Development Projects and the reconstruction of urban intervention suggest how this can work in practice. These examples also make clear that, whilst the central state cannot secure complete control, it has access to resources which tend to make it the dominant player.

However, not only is resistance possible from within the state but also strategies pursued on behalf of class, gender and regional interests are often focused on state agencies and the state necessarily becomes a site for such conflicts. Thus we saw the (largely unsuccessful) attempt by Community Development Project workers to mobilize mainly class interests on behalf of their preferred strategies in their conflicts with the Home Office. More successful attempts to mobilize alliances of resistance might include doctors using their popular support to campaign against the proposed NHS reforms in the wake of the White Paper 'Working for Patients', or trades unions mobilizing support from environmentalists, members of the public and local authorities against water privatization. More institutionalized examples might include corporatist relationships around training in the 1950s–1970s. The management of the state is therefore doubly complicated by the inherent limits of management strategies in relation to particular state agencies and also by the limits imposed by non-state interests.

State management, circuits of power and the nature of state crises

The 1970s witnessed extensive concern amongst social scientists with the so-called crisis of the state. The two most influential approaches were the marxist-influenced theory of 'legitimation crisis' associated with Habermas (1975) and Offe (1984, 1985) and the new right-associated theory of 'over-load' or 'ungovernability' linked in Britain to King (1975), Rose (1979) and others. Both approaches have been well outlined and critiqued in Hay (1996, ch. 5) and I have no wish to review them at length here.

We now know that the much-heralded crisis of the state in the 1970s was in important respects a crisis of a more modest form than was imagined at the time. It was certainly not a crisis of the liberal capitalist state as a whole but a more discrete crisis of the post-war settlement. As we have seen, the one-nation, inclusive, incorporating strategy had eventually produced a state in which fiscal pressures, administrative difficulties and central–local tensions were all increasingly apparent. The origins of this crisis did not lie in the economic level only to be displaced into the political and ultimately into the socio-cultural sphere (as suggested by Habermas). Rather the crisis concerned a particular circuit of power involving the capitalist enterprise, state agencies and socio-economic conditions. Continued profitability depended upon the inter-organizational relationships between these as much as the separate internal organization of the firm, the public agency or the social institution. It was not in a strict sense an 'economic crisis'. Output was higher than it had ever been after thirty years of unprecedented growth. Individuals had greater disposable incomes and access to more public welfare than ever before. The 'crisis' had a multiplicity of causes but the key outcome was sharp downward pressure on profitability (see Desai, 1996, p. 84).

However, whilst the decline of profitability involved the economy, the state and the socio-cultural sphere the immediate political responses focused on the state. Corporatist agencies were used to bring down real wages. This was combined with downward pressure on public expenditure to relieve the 'tax burden' amidst claims that high public expenditure was causing low levels of profitability. Later, in the 1980s, the Thatcherite restructuring of the state helped to load the costs of economic restructuring (and significant economic restructuring was inevitable) onto the poorest and weakest sections of society whilst incorporating private sector interests into the training systems, urban renewal programmes and so forth. Indeed, Conservative policy towards the corporate sector and towards the socio-cultural sphere has been more limited (in outcome, at least) than changes in the management of the state. The more general point, however, is that the crisis of profitability should not be viewed as being a peculiarly economic crisis which then had political and cultural consequences. Rather, a crisis of profitability reflected a whole circuit of power ranging across socio-cultural, state and economic institutions which are linked within a particular regime.

On this point, it is worth emphasizing Offe's observation that the form of the capitalist state necessarily problematizes its function (see Offe, 1980, *passim*; Jessop, 1982, pp. 111–12). There is, for Offe, inevitable tension between the pursuit of legitimacy and the pursuit of capital accumulation. Pursuing these in a context of a competitive party system only adds to the tensions. To some extent, these contradictions can be managed but only by 'insulating' the agencies responsible for these objectives from each other. Thus the state as a whole may find itself pursuing mutually contradictory objectives.

In this light, state management is not only about the pursuit of technically efficient outcomes, but also about managing inevitable tensions. Different regimes may be associated with different ways of managing this tension but none successfully resolve it. We have argued here for a more diverse conception of these tensions but we share Offe's sense that managing the state is not a problem to be resolved but a tension to be managed. A historically and theoretically grounded understanding of the state can guard against the dangers of identifying 'the simple fact' which can unlock the mystery of the state. As has been demonstrated too frequently in the 1990s, once we dispose of both a historical and a theoretical understanding of the state, there need be no limit to the silliness of the claims made concerning public sector reform.

Globalization and state management

To the extent that globalization introduces new agencies and processes, it poses new challenges for state management. Some economic agents have become global players. Goldblatt writes of multi-national corporations (MNCs):

> (MNCs account) for a third of world output, 70% of world trade and 80% of international investment, they also facilitate increasingly intensive patterns of technology transfer and are key players in global

financial markets. Most MNCs have 20–30% of their assets, sales and profits in foreign locations, representing enormous international commitments and great sensitivity to international changes. (Goldblatt, 1995, p. 29)

At the transnational political level, too, Goldblatt notes the extent of change. In 1909 there were thirty-seven inter-governmental organizations and 176 non-governmental organizations. By 1989 these figures were 300 and 4262 respectively (ibid., p. 28).

More extreme claims about the extent of globalization suggest it has provoked economic and cultural consequences which have combined with the so-called 'crisis of governability' to create a 'hollowed-out' state in which the state at a national level is itself under threat. Thus Crook, Pakulski and Waters suggest that:

> both the functions of the state as a tool of social and economic regulation and reconstruction, and the scope of state power and responsibility, have started to diminish. This is partly the consequence of such external factors as the globalization of politics and the increasing strength of international agencies, and partly the result of internal processes prompted by crises of 'governability', 'fiscal' security and 'legitimation'. Some of these crisis processes are ideological in character, referring to a declining faith in the effectiveness of the state. Others refer to an actual reduction in the scope of state power and responsibility. (Crook, Pakulski and Waters, 1992, pp. 79–80)

If this were true then it would clearly have implications for state management. A 'hollowed-out' state might be no less difficult to manage but it would at least be different.

However, we have already seen compelling evidence in support of the claim that state intervention is restructured during the 1980s and 1990s rather than reduced. It is not clear that globalization has contributed to a reduced state. In one of the more theoretically sophisticated and empirically grounded treatments of globalization, Hirst and Thompson (1996) question the more cavalier claims that globalization is transforming the nature of the contemporary economy. They point to the absence of a clear model of a globalized economy which is evidently different from the previous international economy. They consider empirical evidence on labour migration, trade and capital flows and degrees of financial and monetary integration and, whilst recognizing that changes have taken place, question the extent of their novelty (see Bromley, 1996, p. 130). They identify the growing importance of foreign direct investment (and this has been of particular significance for British economic strategies) but see this more as a part of a tri-polar world of Europe, North America and Japan rather than a truly globalized world. Under these circumstances, Hirst and Thompson reject the argument that, in a globalized world, governance is no longer possible at the national level.

The importance of foreign direct investment to national economic strategies does not rule out the importance of national patterns of governance. Undoubtedly the problems of state management associated with economic strategies in the 1960s and 1970s have altered in significant ways. However, we have seen that investor-led packages for urban regeneration and employer-led training schemes bring their own problems of coordination, targets and operations. The alternative response of deregulation and state disengagement rests upon the false belief that markets (global or otherwise) can function in the absence of political and socio-cultural practices. As Hutton reminds us, 'Capitalism is socially produced and politically managed' (Hutton, 1995, pp. 17–18).

The growing importance of direct foreign investment poses new challenges for national governments and the greater openness of national economies undermines certain conventional Keynesian policies. Furthermore, the impact of the free movement of capital has fundamental implications for strategists and, should it ever arrive on a global scale, the free movement of labour would be equally significant. Nevertheless, the claim that globalization will lead to a hollowed-out minimalist state which (by implication) will be relatively easy to manage has not been sustained. The question of the organization and management of the state will continue to be important.

Substantive and Prescriptive Debates

The British state and the debate on British decline

For decades, a variety of authors have sought to explain Britain's decline relative to its competitors. The chief focus of concern is typically rates of growth of GDP and GDP per head of the population. We can see in tables 8.1 and 8.2 that, whilst the UK economy continued to grow throughout the post-war period, it did so more slowly than its main competitors. There is at least something to be explained, therefore.

Table 8.1 The growth of real GDP and real GDP per capita
(average annual percentage growth)

	1950–73 GDP	1973–79 GDP per capita	1979–90 GDP	GDP per capita	GDP	GDP per capita
USA	3.7	2.3	2.4	1.4	2.6	1.6
Japan	9.4	8.2	3.6	2.5	4.1	3.5
Germany	5.1	5.0	2.3	2.5	2.0	1.7
France	3.0	4.2	2.8	2.3	2.1	1.7
UK	3.0	2.5	1.5	1.5	2.1	1.9
Italy	5.5	4.8	3.7	3.2	2.4	2.2
Total EC	–	–	2.5	2.1	2.2	1.9
Total OECD	–	–	2.7	1.9	2.7	1.9

Source: Temple (1994, p. 34); quoted in Coates (1995, p. 66)

Table 8.2 Comparative levels of GDP per head (UK=100)

	1950	1960	1973	1979	1990
USA	148	135	139	141	136
Germany	65	98	110	119	116
France	74	84	106	114	111
Japan	27	44	91	95	112
UK	100	100	100	100	100

Source: Temple (1994, p. 33); quoted in Coates (1995, p. 66)

The continuing failure of growth to match expectations was exacerbated during the 1980s (when Britain only marginally failed to grow by the EC average) by the phenomenon of 'jobless growth' in which unemployment could rise even with a growing economy. This coincided with measures which succeeded in their intention to increase inequalities with the gap between rich and poor opening to its widest for fifty years (see Jackson, 1995, p. 23) so that the visible consequences of low growth were most apparent in inner cities, public services and amongst the poor. Taken as a package, these developments prompted a continuing sequence of analyses of Britain's relatively poor performance (despite the narrowing gap between growth rates in Britain and elsewhere). We consider one of the more recent of these analyses and ask if the approach suggested in this book might have implications for an assessment of it.

During the mid-1990s Will Hutton's *The State We're In* became the single most widely read and debated text on the British condition. In a rather different political environment, Hutton's reception paralleled that given to Reich (1993) and Thurow (1992) in the US. The central explanations for Britain's decline are not new but, as Hutton commented in the preface to the 1996 edition, this does not make the argument wrong (1996, p. xv).

Hutton identified two interlocked causes of relative decline. First, '(T)he central *economic* argument is that the weakness of the British economy, particularly at the level and character of investment, originates in the financial system' (1995, p. xi). Second: 'Complementing this economic thesis is the book's *political* argument that the semi-modern nature of the British state is a fundamental cause of Britain's economic and social decline' (1995, pp. xi–xii). (For more on the claim that Britain's financial institutions are culpable, see Ingham, 1984, 1988. For the claim that it is the archaic nature of the British state and class structure see Nairn, 1981, and Wiener, 1981. Marquand, 1988 and Middlemas, 1979 also provide important critiques of the aimless, uncoordinated and generally sclerotic nature of the British state.)

These two core explanations are presented with an enthusiasm and vigour which helps to explain the book's impact. The book also marshals a wide range of evidence in support of these positions. The book is not only explanatory, however, it is also prescriptive. Through a consideration of the different growth projects associated variously with Japan, the US and the 'social market Europe' model (Germany, its EU neighbours and Scandinavia), Hutton concludes (for both normative and practical reasons) that the latter should provide a model for Britain. As Hutton says of it:

> the political, economic and social institutions hang together to form an interdependent web. Capital and labour operate in partnership; the financial system is less market-based than in the US and thus more committed to the enterprises it finances; the welfare structure is more all encompassing and inclusive and the political system has a high degree of formal power sharing. Yet this social web still vibrates to the signals sent by the price mechanism; it may be regulated, but it conforms to market imperatives. It is a social *market*. (Hutton, 1996, p. 262)

In what way does the diagnosis and prescription offered in the book you are reading differ from Hutton's position? There are three points at issue. The first is largely beyond the realms of this book: to what extent is the financial system the origin of Britain's poor economic performance? Second, is it the semi-modern nature of the British state which is at fault? Third, given what we know about the British state, to what extent is the proposed application of the social market model to the British case persuasive?

The view that the City is largely responsible for Britain's relatively poor economic performance is widely held (see, for example, Ingham, 1984; Leys, 1986; Stones, 1990). The claim made is that the Treasury–City–Bank of England nexus has poorly served Britain because, firstly, it has failed to provide manufacturing industry with the sort of long-term financial support available to the manufacturing industries of our major competitors and, secondly, that it has exerted a malign influence over economic and industrial policy and produced a political elite which is careless of its manufacturing future. For some, the 1980s witnessed the final, complete and blatant triumph of the financial interests of the south over northern manufacturing interests (see Nairn, 1981, p. 391).

Such a view has implications about states in general and the British state in particular which are not entirely supported by the arguments presented here. Interests are not directly represented within the state system in the way in which a crude version of the 'dominance of finance' thesis suggests. 'The City' was not a unified force capable of imposing itself on a reluctant state in 1945. As we have seen, the key decisions were taken at the heart of the state through the Machinery of Government Committees when it was decided to put the Treasury back at the heart of both the co-ordination of public expenditure decisions and the determination of economic policy. The decisions not to devalue in the 1950s and to accommodate a stop-go economic strategy reflected a Treasury view that any possible benefits of devaluation would be frittered away on pay rises and increased profits. When Lord Cromer sought to impose the Bank's will on the incoming Labour government in 1964, Wilson did not roll over in submission. The rise of monetarism in Britain in the 1970s may have originated in City institutions but it required a Tory Party, sensing the political benefits of a monetarist stance, to seize upon it as a politically credible alternative to the Keynesian welfare state. And the liberalization of financial institutions during the 1980s was not universally welcomed; by opening the City up to more international competition, only the interests of the most globally competitive were served. Undoubtedly, however, in the early 1980s the combination of the removal of exchange controls, sterling's petro-currency status and high interest rates wreaked havoc throughout British manufacturing, damaging not only the internationally uncompetitive but also many relatively competitive and enterprising firms.

What are we to make of this story? We know from official reports throughout the 1950s and 1960s that the need to improve relatively poor growth rates – and the poor performance of the manufacturing sector in particular – was taken seriously and given a high priority. Heath's market-oriented modernization attempts, no less than Wilson's earlier more statist attempts, saw economic concerns reflected in action. As we have seen, the evidence does not support the idea of a political elite married to financial institutions and unconcerned about manufacturing. The truth is that despite continuous attempts, successive governments failed to develop the sort of state which might be capable of working with the flow of market mechanisms to facilitate a more internationally competitive manufacturing base. Why, then, did the City thrive and manufacturing decline? The very features of the British state which allowed the City to become the major European player in global financial markets (an inability to monitor, regulate or intervene in a purposive manner) simultaneously weakened the competitiveness of British manufacturing (it is worth noting the number of corrupt financial chickens, reared on a diet of weak regulation, coming home to roost in the 1990s). Even where key problems were identified and agreed upon within the state (such as, in the 1950s, the requirement to have credit controls if full employment was not to lead to inflation, or the need to have an effective national training policy), governments systematically failed to establish effective regulations or agencies. British manufacturing was not able to succeed because with backward management, an out-dated structure, inadequate training, inadequate financing and poor quality infrastructure no agency other than the state was capable of injecting change at the pace required. To its great discredit, every attempt by successive governments to create such agencies was rebuffed by employers who, it seems, would rather have failed on their own than succeeded in a regulated framework. The problem perceived by Olson (1965), that collective interests can only give rise to effective collective action under particular conditions, was much in evidence. The only agency capable of establishing the structures within which the collective interests of manufacturing could be pursued was the state and this was not forthcoming. In part, at least, political strategies failed because the central state could not establish, monitor and direct state agencies which might be capable of securing such outcomes.

The 1980s and 1990s saw the gradual consolidation of a different strategy towards manufacturing which was based upon foreign direct investment. Indeed the willingness of foreign investors to buy companies like Rover has been presented as proof of the effectiveness of such a strategy. Meanwhile the deregulation of financial markets had enabled entrepreneurs in institutions such as Barings and Lloyds to demonstrate that deregulation does not always secure optimum outcomes.

This, of course, is not a rejection of Hutton's claim that it is the availability and nature of finance which has been so damaging. It does qualify this claim, however. The availability of external financing is but one factor which might explain Britain's poor manufacturing performance – and may reflect such a poor performance rather than cause it. The real question is not why better financing was not available but why such a widely recognized problem as manufacturing decline failed to provoke a more effective response from the state. Does this suggest that Hutton's second cause of decline – the semimodern nature of the British state – should bear a greater weight?

The archaism of the English in general and of their state in particular has long been identified as a cause of Britain's decline. Nairn (1981) Barnett (1986), Wiener (1981) and many others have largely reversed an earlier belief that the stability of British institutions and customs was a source of great strength. In either case, it is certainly true that at a superficial level Britain can point to a unique record of institutional longevity and continuity. However, it is these very institutions which are the target of much of Hutton's concerns. 'The shortcomings of Britain's constitutional arrangements', according to Hutton, defeated both Labour's attempt to build a Keynesian social democracy and the Conservatives' attempts to use market forces, and thus '(T)he parties that were its pillars have become its victims' (Hutton, 1995, p. 32).

The case presented by Hutton that democratic – and indeed moral – principles were sacrificed in a state larded with secretive and constitutionally questionable transactions is well made. Weir and Hall (1994) provide further detailed and systematic data to support this claim in relation to the so-called democratic deficit. According to Hutton, the use of the state to satisfy party and private interests at the expense of wider public interests reached new depths during the 1980s and 1990s. He therefore proposes a less centralized, more flexible, more democratic and less secretive state which would breath new life into Britain's body politic and stimulate a new economic and social creativity and sense of purpose.

These are all desirable outcomes and we have seen throughout this book examples from fields as different as training policy, anti-poverty programmes and urban renewal in which there is no democratically articulated sense of the public interest and no effective means through which such a public interest could be pursued. However, the approach suggested in this book indicates certain difficulties. Two of these are worth dwelling on.

First, 'the public' cannot be represented in an unmediated way and 'the public interest' is politically constructed. Hutton emphasizes the need to have more localized and flexible interventions which escape the top-down control of most British interventions. How are public interests to be articulated – through corporatist arrangements, 'consumer councils', republican regulators, public meetings, questionnaires or what? And what happens when different sections of the public have conflicting conceptions of that public interest? Are there interests which are so racist, sexist or otherwise unacceptable that they should never be represented? And simply decentralizing power in an otherwise unequal society inevitably means devolving power to those who already disproportionately benefit from its exercise.

Secondly, how should the work of these various agencies be coordinated? Hutton resists the idea that an unreconstructed Treasury should be responsible for this, but if not the Treasury then who should secure effective financial control over the state, who should mediate between public agencies with conflicting objectives, and who should set targets, monitor outcomes and provide redress against public incompetence or corruption?

Both of these lacunae reflect the same profound optimism: the belief that political leadership can infuse the state with a sense of purpose and shared understanding within which a revitalized British state could be forged. The belief that this can be created through a consensus amongst 'reasonable people' is underlined by the emphasis given to the 'pre-modern' nature of the state. Who, after all, but the most truculent conservative is opposed to modernization? However, it is not clear that, by the mid-1990s, the British state was straightforwardly archaic in the sense implied by Hutton.

By the mid-1990s, Whitehall had experienced more or less continuous change since 1979 with 62 per cent of civil service staff transferred to agencies and a further 17 per cent planned. There were 102 executive agencies, thirty-one executive units of HM Customs and Excise and thirty-three executive offices of the Inland Revenue (Price Waterhouse, 1994; Next Steps Review, Cm 2750, quoted in Talbot, 1995, p. 46). Geoffrey Fry was to insist in 1995 that '(R)eformism has given way to a revolution in the Civil Service at large' (Fry, 1995,

p. 151). In addition, the application of some 2500 performance and output measures in the public expenditure process is suggestive of a wider shift in management practices (see Flynn, 1993, p. 111). Furthermore, the sprouting up of new agencies populated by an overwhelmingly pro-Conservative – but not necessarily archaic – 'new magistracy' is further evidence of change (see Weir and Hall, 1994, p. 32). Every aspect of the British state was exposed to significant changes during the 1980s and 1990s.

Hutton's aim was to democratize and flexibilize the British state and this is a worthy aspiration but, in a sense, it presupposed what it hoped to create. It may help to persuade others of the good sense of such changes to describe them simply as 'modernization' but from an academic viewpoint we should be more wary. We have seen that state management necessarily involves privileging the participation of some groups over others, it requires that priorities be established amongst competing objectives, it obliges state managers to decide on the statutory, financial and political framework within which the work of state agencies will be coordinated.

What role, for example, should be given to the representatives of transnational corporations and how should their interests be represented and met by the state (presumably no one is suggesting that their interests should be ignored). What should be the balance between the representatives of the consumers of public services and the workers who produce these services? How will Britain secure a cadre of officials with the skills, authority and honesty required to operate such a state? These are the questions which indicate why managing the state is profoundly political (and not just neutral 'public administration'). But they are also the questions which indicate that the 'republican opportunity', as Hutton calls it, requires not only a shared rejection of the antics of the new right in office but also a clear conception of which interests should be privileged, how these should be expressed through the management of the state and how this can be fitted to an electable party programme.

Towards a post-Fordist state?

Often sharing a concern with the relative decline of Britain, analysts writing from a Fordist perspective offer an alternative account of the changes currently taking place within the British state. They are impressed by what they take to be a restructuring of the British state in ways which 'fit' (more or less) with a wider restructuring of the political economy from Fordism to post-Fordism. Here we will focus on what is meant by such a transition, what this might imply for the management of the state and whether or not this is an adequate or persuasive account of the contemporary British state.

Theories of post-Fordism derive their strength from three rather separate sources (see Bagguley, 1991; Williams, 1994). The first is the French regulation school which focuses on the way in which the potentially self-destructive forces of capitalism are contained and managed within historically specific regimes. Such regimes are not an inevitable consequence of the development of capitalism and each contains within it its own limits which, over time, will eventually undermine and transform that regime. Frequently, as in the work of Aglietta (1979), this approach adopts an international focus. The second approach is based on more institutionally focused analysis of the changing structure of markets and the organizational response to this (see Piore and Sabel, 1984). Thirdly we have the managerialist school which is seeking to prescribe the managerial changes made necessary by the new focus on flexibility: managing the emergent core and periphery workers, new information technologies, new production technologies and the reorganization of the labour process (see Atkinson and Meager, 1986; Peters and Waterman, 1982).

Perhaps because of this rather mixed bag of influences, the terms 'Fordism' and 'post-Fordism' have been taken to represent rather different phenomena. Jessop distinguishes four alternative referents:

> 1 the labour process considered as a particular configuration of the technical and social division of labour;
> 2 an accumulation regime, i.e., a macro-economic regime sustaining growth in capitalist production and consumption;
> 3 a social mode of economic regulation, i.e., an ensemble of norms, institutions, organizational forms, social networks, and patterns of conduct which sustain and 'guide' a given accumulation regime; and
> 4 a mode of societalisation, i.e., a pattern of institutional integration and social cohesion which complements the dominant accumulation regime and its social mode of economic regulation and thereby secures the conditions for its dominance within the wider society (cf Jessop 1992a; 1992b). (Jessop, 1994, p.14)

Jessop goes on to suggest that, whilst each of these is relatively independent of the others, they can all enter into relatively stable relationships which have a certain congruency and provide a period of stability. 'Fordism' describes both a particular quality to Jessop's four referents and describes the relationships amongst them. It also

Table 8.3 The differences between Fordism and post-Fordism

	Fordism	*Post-Fordism*
Production	Mass production of identical goods using inflexible production processes	Batch production of varied goods using a flexible production system
Consumption	Mass marketing; everyone consumes increasing quantities of the same products	Niche marketing; everyone consumes increasingly finely differentiated products
Social relations	Largely homogeneous 'citizenries'	Fragmented identities
Culture	Mass culture spread through a mass media providing multiply reproduced identical messages	Fragmented culture reproduced through diverse media providing a wide choice of highly differentiated messages
Economic policies	National strategies of maintaining high and stable levels of demand	Strategies aimed at enhancing particular aspects of competitiveness in the global economy
Social policies	Universal welfare provided through nationally coordinated bureaucracies	Conditional welfare provided through locally responsive mechanisms intended to enhance economic competitiveness
Political strategies	'One nation' appeals for mass support	Alliances of multiple identities behind symbolic and largely simulated strategic differences

refers to the period in which they were dominant. This might be summarized as the economics, politics and culture of mass production and mass consumption.

More particularly, most theorists working within this tradition would distinguish between Fordism and post-Fordism in the terms set out in table 8.3. Focusing more closely on the state within this transition, Jessop suggests that it could be characterized in terms of:

1 the nature of the labour process within the state sector itself (e.g. Hoggett, 1987);
2 the state sector's direct economic role in a Fordist accumulation regime (e.g. Overbeek, 1990, pp. 114–19);
3 the state's wider role in the social mode of economic regulation linked to such a regime (e.g. Moulaert *et al.*, 1988; Painter, 1991)
4 its role in securing the institutional integration and social cohesion of a social formation within which Fordism in one or more of its possible guises is dominant (Hirsch and Roth, 1986). (Jessop, 1994, p. 16)

From within this framework, we might therefore consider current changes taking place in the form and function of the state:

1 The greater use of part-time staff, short-term contracts, perform-ance-related pay, the growing preference for quasi-contractual over hierarchical relationships, job descriptions giving managers more con-trol and the wider use of appraisal and 'human resource management' in general (see chapter 6) all support the claim that the state labour process is indeed changing in ways consonant with the wider changes of post-Fordism. Post-Fordism is held to produce the parallel devel-opment of a flexible work-force in an attempt to overcome 'the alienation and resistance of the mass worker, the relative stagnation of Taylorism and mass production, competitive threats from low-cost exporters in the Third World, and the relative saturation of markets for standardised mass-produced products . . . ' (Jessop, 1994, p. 19)

2 The state's direct economic role under post-Fordism could be seen as one of securing greater flexibility and innovation from former nationalized industries and public utilities either by privatizing them under conditions designed to secure such enhanced flexibility or through the importation of management techniques designed to achieve the same thing. Key polyvalent public sector workers with the approp-riate commitment to flexibility, and key managers capable of im-plementing such a shift, would be highly rewarded irrespective of the impact this may have on older differentials and conceptions of 'fair comparisons'; there would emerge a growing gap between core work-ers and periphery employees. The public sector would then reinforce post-Fordist economic trends towards a growth strategy based upon increasing flexibility, process innovation and an increasingly differen-tiated market for products and services. As we have seen, there is at

least some evidence to support the claim that the British state is (in this sense) becoming more post-Fordist.

3 Jessop regards changes in the state's wider role in the social mode of economic regulation as the most fertile of his four characterizations of the post-Fordist state. He describes this new role as the Schumpeterian workfare state which he contrasts with the Keynesian welfare state. Of the Schumpeterian workfare state, Jessop writes 'its distinctive objectives in economic and social reproduction are: to promote product, process, organizational, and market innovation in open economies in order to strengthen as far as possible the structural competitiveness of the national economy by intervening in the supply-side; and to subordinate social policy to the needs of labour market flexibility and/or to the constraints of international competition' (Jessop, 1994, p. 24). Once again, we can see evidence of the emergence of social security policies intended to flexibilize the bottom end of the labour market (see Ling, 1994b), the re-articulation of the education system and the labour market, the increased role for the private sector in providing a growing variety of insurance and pension schemes, the re-commodification of housing and the role of more varied housing associations in social provision. All of this has some degree of 'fit' with post-Fordist claims.

4 The pursuit of a flexibilized economy, associated with process innovation, product differentiation and global competition is an accepted part of Hutton's vision for the 'modern' British state. His social market preferences, it will be remembered, were based not only on the claim that they were fairer but also on the claim that they were more efficient. This should remind us that, even if we subscribe to post-Fordist theory, there is no obvious and singular social and cultural context within which a post-Fordist economy might thrive. The preferences of Conservative governments in the 1980s and 1990s expressed a very different vision of a post-Fordist Britain. This lack of an obvious relationship between any particular social and cultural set of preferences and post-Fordism more generally need not, of course, undermine the whole project of post-Fordist theory.

Is this excursion into post-Fordist theory helpful? At the abstract level of the theoretical integrity of the post-Fordist approach as a whole, there are problems if the concepts of Fordism and post-Fordism are used as causal explanations rather than loose descriptions which generate interesting questions. In particular, we have seen how the processes of change taking place within the state are conditioned by agencies, interests and calculations which are only distantly related to the wider regime of accumulation. As Jessop readily acknowledges, any attempt to read off a necessary relationship between the form of the state and the accumulation regime or the social mode of economic regulation is bound to fail unless it takes into account so many independent variables as to make the elegant claims of post-Fordism as a general explanation (rather than just a suggestive description) of late capitalism either unconvincing or unenlightening. In particular, it substantially under-explains the peculiarities and consequences of state management which lie at the heart of this book.

However, the project stimulates a number of important questions and generates potentially fruitful research agendas (whether or not this could be achieved with less theoretical complexity is another question). It is beyond the scope of this book to do more than to suggest the research programme which might arise from a confluence of state-focused and post-Fordist arguments. Amongst other issues, post-Fordist accounts prompt us to explore other research agendas.

1 managing state employees posed problems from the outset of the modern state and, as we have seen, these problems were particularly acute by the 1970s. How did new information technologies, new management practices and new labour processes being devised in the most overtly 'post-Fordist' sectors influence the new managerialism in the public sector? To what extent was there really a fragmentation of market demand for public goods and services which putatively lay behind the introduction of more flexible working practices in the public sector? To what extent is it possible to have a vibrant, internationally competitive economy with a hierarchical, bureaucratic state? If the economy in some sense 'requires' a post-Fordist state, how is the pressure for change transmitted to key players within the public sector?

2 Is there any necessary reason why the state can only play a neo-liberal, minimalist role in pursuit of a flexibilized economy? Are there circumstances in which public agencies might prove to be more flexibilizing (with training systems, for example)? Is the politics of regulation a likely outcome? Whatever the direct economic role of the state, how are public agencies (including regulators) to be so managed to produce post-Fordist outcomes; what interests should be incorporated, what calculations dominant and what forms of coordination applied?

3 The Schumpeterian workfare state, as envisaged by Jessop, is interesting (especially in the British case) but it is only one of a number of possible strategies each of which might be compatible with

a broad and vigorous post-Fordism. What other varieties of state form are possible today and what normative and theoretical arguments might help us discriminate amongst them?

4 The repertoire of political, cultural and economic responses and possibilities is wider than is allowed for by the theorists of post-Fordism. In particular, the globalization is insufficiently homogenizing and the variety of equally competitive options too great to accept the more universalizing claims of post-Fordist theory. However, during the 1950s–1970s there clearly was some coherence across the policies and practices of full employment, welfarism, universalism, mass consumption, free collective bargaining and the state agencies which supported and ran these policies. This 'virtuous circle' broke down and the limits to corporate strategies, state management and cultural leadership appeared to be reached. Can we identify any other potentially stable set of policies and practices which could provide the basis for a new period of economic growth and political freedom? What role should we give to the state in this?

Communitarian and neo-constitutionalist responses

The evidence presented here suggests that the way in which the British state has been managed since 1945 has had significant implications for its economic, social and political history. The changes associated with what we might loosely describe as post-Fordism, have posed further problems for British state management. And amidst the enthusiasm for unsubstantiated nonsense such as the new medievalism or the alleged disappearance of the nation state, more sober commentators accept that nations will continue to be governed over by a state which claims sovereignty over a geographical area, which can mobilize massive coercive powers against its own population and which enjoys at least some degree of popular affection (if not for the government of the day then at least for the state's association with the symbols of nationhood). Certainly, the tensions and pressures facing states are great, and may even be taking novel forms, but they remain the fundamental agency through which politics is conducted. The question of what the future state should look like therefore arises.

Concern with the apparently growing inability of states to meet the various expectations placed upon them is widespread. Such discontents have often been directed towards the conventional institutions and practices of politics of the past two hundred years and there is by now a standard set of criticisms about their bureaucratic, unresponsive and overburdened aspects (see Mulgan, 1994). Often traditional political parties have reacted to this situation by simulating politics in a political theatre in which sincerity, outrage and dubious accounts of history are paraded before an increasingly jaded public. This theatre and occasional blood-letting will not be enough to sustain popular interest (far less popular support). There have been at least two important responses to the perceived problems of the state. We might see these as the communitarian response and the neo-constitutionalist response. These are considered in turn.

The heart of the communitarian stance is to stress that the appropriate response to the weakening of the democratic structures of the state, and its increasing inability to satisfy widely held expectations, is to pull power and responsibility 'downwards' into the community. This is desirable, it is claimed, both because people in communities 'ought' to take responsibility for each other and because the state is simply not able to deliver the combination of freedoms and rights which is currently being demanded of it. Support for the idea of societies characterized by a high degree of trust, as proposed by, amongst others, Fukuyama, is warmly approved of in Hutton's introduction to the second edition of *The State We're In* (1996) and writers such as Putnam (1993) have developed the idea of social trust still further. Trust, for communitarians, places individuals in positive, creative and efficient relationships with each other (see Lowe, 1996, pp. 104–5). Such an approach, clearly, could become simply another form of anti-statism but, particularly in Britain, the communitarian approach has stressed the role of the state in creating partnerships with communities and helping communities to police and manage their own affairs more effectively*.

There are obvious and well-rehearsed problems about how 'the community' should be represented and what should happen if one part of 'a community' shows an enthusiasm for imposing its values on another part, and how inequalities and differences between different communities should be managed. Similarly, how can barriers to the abuse of trust be (cheaply) set up and how can social trust be positively rewarded? In practice, these are problems which inherently cannot be solved at the community level. Their solution presupposes

---

* Henry Tam and the Communitarian Forum have attempted to avoid an anti-statist position but they may then be open to accusations of supporting a rather authoritarian form of statism. Tam, in particular, has sought to avoid each of these. See the occasional publication *Democratic Communities*, published by the Communitarian Forum.

some sort of mechanism which enjoys widespread legitimacy, which is capable of securing a level of agreement about the most appropriate response to these problems and which is capable of imposing agreed solutions by force if necessary. In other words, in the absence of consensual and self-supporting communities, the communitarian approach requires a state, albeit one which is driven by different priorities.

Furthermore, 'communities' are not the only political players. At the very least, other agents for change include corporations (often transnational), which are driven by a logic very different from the logic of empowered communities. Many of the most thorny problems of contemporary politics concern the optimum way to balance the continued and expanded operation of (often globalized) private sector corporations with the need to satisfy popular and community aspirations. Communitarianism is less helpful on these. However, its concern with the texture of daily life and the pursuit of a meaningful and fulfilling social life is something which, in my view, is worth pursuing.

The second response to the current condition of the state is to criticize existing state institutions and call for neo-constitutionalist reforms. In Britain there is a widespread view that the executive is beyond the reach of Parliament, that civil servants are operating in a constitutional vacuum, that the public sector is traversed by quangos run by appointees many of whom lack both representativeness and expertise and that the judicial process has been called into question by well-publicized miscarriages of justice. Meanwhile, the Royals add their own touch of class to the 'end of an era' atmosphere.

Under such circumstances, it is tempting to see the neo-constitutionalist position as a peculiarly British phenomenon. However, it coincides with similar movements elsewhere. The nub of the issue is that, in order to carry out the responsibilities expected of it, the executive of the modern state requires a degree of power and flexibility which exceeds what is tolerable in liberal constitutional theory. The communitarian instinct is to reduce those responsibilities. The neo-constitutionalist response is to establish more effective constitutional devices to ensure political accountability and judicial oversight. The endemic inability of the executive of the modern state to achieve goals which it sets for itself, can (neo-constitutionalists argue) be overcome with improved constitutional arrangements. This may reflect either a neo-liberal preference for small government or it may reflect a concern with civil liberties and the institutional preconditions for progressive politics.

A constitution lays down the formal relationships which should exist between the state and society and it also establishes the relationships which should exist between the different parts of the state system (the judiciary, executive, local government and so forth). Whilst it cannot encompass the range of factors which goes to make up the activity of state management, it clearly provides part of the institutional basis within which state management occurs. There are certain aspects where constitutional considerations have great significance (including the judicial protection of the individual from the state). However, looking at the overall weaknesses of British governance since the Second World War, to what extent are the peculiarities of the British constitution responsible? At the very least a written constitution might have limited the constant *ad hoc*-ery of British institutional change and required a more careful consideration of the purpose and organization of the public sector. It might also have prevented the widespread sense that public agencies are not effectively accountable. But since many of the weaknesses of state management identified in this book are not explicitly constitutional, expectations of what can be achieved by a new constitutional settlement should be muted (although perhaps the process of debating and encoding the constitution would encourage a wider agreement about the purpose and form of the British state). Even these more muted claims suggest that any new political settlement should include a clarification and codification of the relationships between the state and the people and the relationship between the various parts of the state system.

State management for the twenty-first century

The view put forward here emphasizes the limits of any one form of coordination and control (hierarchical, quasi-contractual, financial, legal etc.). An over-dependence on any one form of coordinating will eventually undermine the purpose of that coordination. The example of the post-war British state also points to the inherent conflicts amongst the different ways of securing participation (parliamentary, corporatist, citizen's charters etc.). This is true for states operating in both socialist and capitalist conditions of production. The search for a single form of state which provides a permanent and optimal institutional form through which politics can best be conducted is futile. State management in the context of the modern nation state is therefore inherently a process of multiple, overlapping strategies of inclusion and exclusion, of reshaping the bases of participation, of restructuring the agencies of intervention and of exhausting one mode of coordination before shifting to another. Single solutions to these problems are inevitably doomed to (at best) only fleeting success, and the first prescription for state management in the twenty-first century is therefore to embrace mongrelism and diversity within the state.

Consequently, the conventional liberal democratic argument that the fundamental mechanism of democratic accountability should be the periodic election of competent elites is unconvincing. We have seen throughout this book evidence that state agencies adopt calculations different from those of the parliamentary leadership and incorporate interests very different from those dominant at the centre. Excluding all such calculations and interests and leaving only the values of the parliamentary elite alone within the state is hardly a recipe for extended democracy or more efficient government. The need is to give such intra-state diversity a democratic content and public accountability.

Consequently, the proposals implicit in Habermas's position (that all should feel included in democratic deliberations and all feel equally able to question and argue) provide a useful guide (see Habermas, 1990). This would require a public sector which enabled multiple, competing and overlapping discourses and identities to have an equal claim on the 'public interest' (a term to which we will return). Such a public sector would not seek to impose any particular way of conducting politics (save for basic requirements of probity and non-exclusivity). Rather it would seek to work with and empower freely formed associations and mutual organizations (see Hirst, 1994). In order to suggest how this might work in practice, and how it relates to current institutions and practices, I use the example of user-participation in the National Health Service. I make these prescriptive suggestions in the hope that they stimulate discussion and debate rather than be treated as a manifesto which must be either swallowed whole or ignored.

User-participation in the National Health Service

The example of user-participation in the NHS is examined because as a large complex service, with powerful producer interests, it manifests many of the most acute problems associated with democratizing the public sector. It is also a sector in which, by the mid-1990s, government policy was firmly to encourage some form of user-participation and this rhetoric enjoyed broad support from across the political spectrum. However, behind this consensus, fundamental questions had been avoided, and important distinctions elided, in relation to at least four issues.

- if patients are to participate in the NHS should they do so as *'consumers'* (or 'customers')?
- in what respects, if any, should users of the health service be seen as *citizens*?
- to whom is the Health Service *accountable* and how are these accountabilities best institutionalized?
- as *owners* of the assets of the NHS, how best might the public express their rights of ownership?

By the 1990s, the NHS had faced a more or less constant sequence of institutional changes over the fifty years since its establishment. However, these were overwhelmed by an agenda for change which claimed (amongst other things) to empower health service users by entrenching their rights as consumers. This followed from the implications of the 'customer-focused' reforms which culminated in the Citizen's Charter and its various more institutionally specific offspring, such as the Patient's Charter (see chapter 6).

What was wrong with the conventional view of the citizen?

As we saw in chapter 1, implicit in the establishment of the NHS in 1948 was the view that all citizens were entitled to participate fully and equally in society and that such an entitlement should not be undermined by idleness, avoidable ill-health, poverty, ignorance and squalor. As we have seen, this view was articulated in the Beveridge Report (HMSO 1942) and in the writings of academics such as Marshall and Titmuss. The agreed institutional mechanism for supporting such rights was that Parliament should fund large-scale, centralized organizations which would be hierarchically accountable upwards. Within these, in areas of welfare such as health and education, professionals would be left to determine priorities, coordinate agencies and manage processes within the financial and statutory framework laid down by Parliament.

In many ways these arrangements served the nation well and at the very least it provided a symbolic expression of mutual interests and concerns. However, the reforms of the 1940s presupposed a largely uniform and widely agreed set of health needs which a centrally directed and professionally dominated health service was thought to be well equipped to assess and meet. As we have seen, by the 1970s such a presupposition was becoming progressively less easy to defend. The implications of these trends included:

- a heightened sense of ethnic, gender, regional and social difference which weakened support for a system predicated upon an assumed transparency and similarity of health needs across the whole nation;
- a separate but related process in which a rapidly growing disposable income led to greater levels of sophistication in consumers' expectations (these expectations may have originated in response to the marketing techniques of the private sector but they quickly created changed expectations of the public sector, too; for example, many more women expected to have their needs taken more fully into account during childbirth);
- the (largely) middle class revolt against uniformity, often allied to a more radical critique of professional power and, indeed, the 'medical model' of health care itself; the confluence of an overtly radical sociological and philosophical position and a more old-fashioned assertion of petty-bourgeois 'freedoms' produced a new consensus around the need to limit professional power.

Such a diversity of identities and needs does not necessarily conflict with the liberal democratic model which has always implied that a civil society should provide a realm in which diverse interests and identities could flourish (albeit that all identities would share certain rights and interests in freedom of property, freedom of speech, freedom of person and so forth). However, once these individuals met within the confines of the state they would be transformed into citizens, each carrying identical formal rights of citizenship. Liberal politics presupposes the formal equality of all citizens.

By the 1970s, however, as private identities washed over the state, and as citizenship rights (to welfare, for example) reshaped civil society, this liberal transformation was no longer feasible. I wish to argue below that this liberal insight – that the state has the capacity to establish a terrain of equality of citizenship and a shared commitment to the 'public interest' – should not be abandoned in the face of the problems of liberal democracy. Rather, it should be entrenched and extended in new ways.

Furthermore, during the 1970s downward pressure upon public

expenditure combined with rising health needs. The confluence of these trends inevitably provoked some reconsideration of the legitimate expectations of the citizen in relation to health care. This might have prompted a socialist-inspired re-examination of the traditional concept of 'citizenship' and promoted an alternative model showing how the rights of all to participate as equal members of a society might be compatible with the equal rights of all to be different (although neither the political nor the cultural resources needed for this were present in the 1970s). It did not do so and the broader 'meaning' of citizenship was to be given a very different inflexion. As we saw in chapter 6, the 1980s and 1990s saw a progressive redefinition of the concept of the 'citizen' in terms of her or his rights as a consumer.

A brief aside on the new managerialism and the 'new consumerism'

Part of the justification for the new managerialism in the public sector is that the consumer has become more sophisticated and his or her needs more complex. A more flexible, niche-oriented public sector is therefore required to meet these new needs. This claim derives from a broader claim which is that the nature of consumption is changing. Two different reasons are suggested for this. First, the postmodernist reason is that the new reflexive individual with multiple identities and limited social attachments constructs his or her identities in a fluctuating and wilful way through the commodities which she or he buys and consumes. Consumption is thus an expression of the freedom offered in the postmodern world (see Baumann, 1988, p. 61). The second argument is that (as in regulation theory) production and consumption are closely interlinked and the emergence of post-Fordism heralds a new pattern of consumption as much as a new pattern of production (Urry, 1990, pp. 13–14; Warde, 1994, pp. 233–4). The new consumer consumes according to ethical, political, environmental and sexual criteria (amongst others) and, to match this fine grain of consumer demand, producers are compelled to develop new information flows from the consumer and a new flexibility of production to meet these complex needs. The state, therefore, must match this complexity.

These two arguments, whilst influential, ignore substantial continuities, exaggerate changes and, in relation to public sector change at least, completely fail to specify the mechanisms which are supposed to connect the new managerialism with the new consumer (and this is especially true in the case of health care). Briefly, consumption continues to be an expression of group membership and social belonging; it is still characterized by class differences; the homogeneity of the so-called 'mass-consumption' of the Fordist era is exaggerated; the idea that the drive towards the new managerialism was driven by a 'new consumerism' is empirically unfounded. Justifications for entrenching the rights of the consumer in any future public sector change (and there are many) require more persuasive arguments.

Public health care and the consumer

In relation to health care, there are obviously problems with both a neo-liberal conception of the consumer as the knowledgeable driver of change and with the postmodernist conception of the shopper as hero, fearlessly constructing shifting and multiple identities from the commodities on sale (for more on the consumer as hero, see Featherstone, 1991, p. 86; for a critique of this position, see Warde, 1994, pp. 228–31). However, even Warde's more social model outlined in chapter 6 of this book recognizes that consumers make choices which reflect their personal preferences and understandings of their current and future needs (even if these choices are shaped by wider social processes). Furthermore, the opportunity to make such choices may reinforce desired social outcomes, such as a plurality of acceptable and feasible lifestyles. However, accounts of the consumer as socially bounded in space and time also suggest that consumers' choices cannot be the sole basis upon which NHS resources are allocated and deployed. Such calculations and choices are shaped by social processes which may deny an individual access to information necessary for an informed choice; or lifestyles may encourage damaging choices; or that health fashions and fads come and go and may not be based on sound evidence; or the immediate circumstances of an individual may make the exercise of consumer choice impossible.

Yet despite such limitations, there is every reason to argue that, as far as possible, since individuals by and large manage their own health care most of the time (choice of diet, exercise, administering medicine etc.), the role of the health service should be to empower the individual to make informed health choices with adequate access to care and support. This much is common ground. Therefore at least part of a complex package of user-participation should include a focus on empowered consumers in their social context.

However, there remain compelling reasons for believing that even this 'enriched' conception of consumerism is not a sufficient basis upon which to organize health care. First, the consumer of health services is not always well placed to recognize the quality of the treatment. Secondly, the legitimacy of liberal democracies is partly based upon a notion of fairness which is compromised when it is believed that those randomly suffering from ill-health will not be cared for. Thirdly, the market mechanism for rationing scarce re-sources is price. Since this is not available in a health service free at the point of demand, alternative rationing mechanisms are required (and if these are not formalized, informal rationing mechanisms will emerge). Fourthly, there is no consensus over what should count as a 'legiti-mate' illness and what should be funded out of public money and what should count as vanity or a foible and therefore be privately funded. The range of services to be made freely available to consum-ers cannot therefore be determined solely through quasi-market mecha-nisms. Consequently, despite occasional rhetoric, no detailed proposals for a health service primarily driven by, and solely accountable to, the consumer have been (or will be) produced. This has at least three consequences for the management of the health service.

1 Where it is accepted that ability to pay should not be the only criterion determining access to health care, other mechanisms are required when coordinating a health-care service.
2 If the allocation of resources across different aspects of public expenditure is not to be determined by consumer preference, then overall priorities have to be determined through an essentially political process.
3 If it is accepted that individual consumers of health services are not always able to discriminate between poor treatment and good treatment then some other checks must be introduced to balance the potential misuse of power by those delivering the health service. Even where it is accepted that, in some circumstances at least, consumers will recognize maltreatment, those consumers still need some mechanism to make their complaint (other than simply exit-ing from the public health service).

Possible mechanisms of user involvement in the NHS

It is widely accepted that there must be mechanisms which permit a degree of public participation in the running of a publicly funded health service. The question is how this might best be achieved in a way which secures meaningful participation without 'gridlock' in which disproportionate resources are deployed in managing the large number of overlapping, mutually incompatible and partially conflicting objectives expressed through different forms of representation. There are a number of possible mechanisms for such representation.

1 Parliament   In setting up the NHS, Bevan believed that such were the benefits of a centrally planned and directed health service (as opposed to one which was fragmented and locally accountable) that the benefits of a ministerially-led NHS were self-evident. Many neo-constitutionalists would also like to see the 'restoration' of effective parliamentary scrutiny and ministerial responsibility in the hope that this would secure a meaningful and democratic accountability.

2 Local government   Prior to the creation of the NHS it was widely supposed that local authorities should have a significant role in ensuring a democratic input to health service management and throughout the years of the Keynesian welfare state there existed sedimented elements of this belief within the NHS structure.

3 Community health councils   As a single-purpose agency a revived and democratically accountable community health council is claimed by some to have advantages over the multi-purpose local authorities whose councillors inevitably have to satisfy a wide range of statutory and political demands.

4 Ombudsman   An easy-to-operate and user-friendly ombudsman service is also put forward as a way of empowering individuals in relation to the NHS. Some would advocate widening the ombudsman's brief to include, for example, the opportunity to look into a whole class of dispute (e.g. women's complaints about their institutionalized treatment during pregnancy). Others would suggest giving bodies such as local government a wider role in investigating complaints of maladministration.

5 User groups and advocacy groups   Yet others insist that particular groups of users require separate forms of representation. Disability rights groups, mental health groups, groups based on gender and race, and many others, have all asserted their right to be represented as a distinct interest within the broader 'public' interest. This is both because in a wider society which routinely discriminates against them, and one which frequently denies them access to the resources needed to live autonomously and with dignity, such groups have little confidence that they will be well represented through the 'public interest'. Different groups tend to adopt a different view of the relative merits of direct user representation and more indirect advocacy.

6 Corporatism The advocates of trades union and professional representation within the NHS rarely limit themselves to the claim that they can best represent the sectional interests of their members. They also insist that they are well placed to represent the wider public interest, particularly because of their detailed knowledge of how the service works. This is particularly true of claims made by general practitioners (GPs).

7 A GP-led NHS With their detailed knowledge of local health issues, and their personal contacts with the local community, some believe that the locally accountable general practice should lie at the heart of the NHS (although how such accountability would work is controversial). Such representation would, presumably, be entrenched at the level of practice management through a users' committee or equivalent.

8 Citizens' juries The distinctive feature of the citizens' jury is that 'jurors' are given the evidence and information to allow them to make more informed choices. They may also be involved over a longer period of time than with, say, a focus group in a marketing exercise. This would allow them to develop their skills and understanding over a number of days. Presumably, the justification for having a representative sample of the local population rather than an elected body is that politics is too important to be left to the politicians.

Undoubtedly many others (such as the press, political parties and pressure groups) would also claim that they had a valid role to play in securing an accountable health service. Is there an optimum 'democratic' or 'progressive' position which self-evidently emerges from these possibilities? I suspect not.

The mixed economy of representation

The problem is that any single form of representation has its own limits and excludes certain interests as well as including others. There is at least a case, therefore, for suggesting that there should be as wide a variety as possible of forms of representation within the NHS. Obviously, different levels of representation would be appropriate in different levels of decision-taking (overall decisions on public expenditure can only be made at a national level, for example). This might be seen as combining many forms of representation in the hope that some kind of democratic equilibrium will emerge. More likely, however, is that such a range of processes of representation would encourage competing and conflicting calculations and turn the NHS into a battlefield of competing interests rather than a service committed to the public interest (however defined). The range of possible health discourses is now too wide, and groups with a perceived interest in the operation of the health service too varied, to suggest that a health consensus would automatically flow from the democratization of health care.

Apparently, the NHS is therefore caught between either representing narrow, sectional interests or becoming gridlocked by congested lines of representation and accountability. This apparent impasse can only be overcome through clear political leadership. If the choice is for equality and diversity then this establishes some parameters. If the choice is to privilege an evidence-based approach to funding one treatment rather than another then this further defines the parameters (this is the preferred management solution). If the diagnostic skills of the medical profession and professions allied to medicine are to be respected then this, too, would further establish the context within which the decision-making process took place. Delivering this would then be a matter of political leadership and would, in particular, involve politicians in securing a degree of support for a particular conception of the public interest in relation to health care. The one area in which national politicians could play a crucially important role is the one area which they seem most determined to avoid.

State Management, the Public Interest and Diverse Private Interests

In health care, as throughout the public sector, effective state management is substantially facilitated where there is at least some shared concept of the public interest. This is called into question by a consumerist model which aims to maximize private need-satisfaction, by establishing quasi-contractual relationships throughout the public sector in which 'success' is measured against narrowly defined targets, and through a culture which privileges outcomes over the fairness of the deliberative processes. The importation of neo-classical economic assumptions through the new managerialism legitimizes a view that bureaucrats and consumers may have interests but the public does not.

Consonant with this neo-classical view is the postmodernist assertion of the importance of difference and of the implied importance of refusing to recognize any conception of the public interest on the grounds that it denies the legitimacy of the myriad identities in society and becomes a vehicle for the exercise of hegemony. Power, according to this view, will always be smuggled in and, in the name of 'the public interest', the powerful will triumph. This is a 'zero-sum' view of the world in which mutuality is a sham and 'solidarity' simply another vehicle for oppression.

This view is fallacious for at least two reasons. The first, practical, reason is that if individuals atomistically refuse to join with others in pursuit of a shared vision of the good society, if all disempowered individuals join the (Foucauldian or other) 'great refusal', it is not at all clear that the consequence will be that the state, or indeed other powerful agency, will thereby be constrained. Indeed, by denying the possibility of organized resistance, power inequalities would be reinforced.

The second fallacy is that it exaggerates the novelty of its own position. It is as if 'diversity' and 'difference' have been discovered for the first time. Yet liberal discourse has always regarded the purpose of the state as being the protection of a diverse civil society in which individuals were free to pursue their private interests and express their private identities. Indeed, according to a liberal perspective, the only way to protect such diversity is through a right-conferring state. The alternatives to the state as the guarantor of diversity is either the anarchic communitarian image of a stateless, homogeneous community or the transformation of human subjects into an improbable combination of multiple identities, maximum tolerance of transgressors and universal non-joiners of social movements.

Better, therefore, would be a recognition of the limitations of the role of the liberal democratic state in protecting diversity and to consider ways of extending this. Feminists, for example, have not only demonstrated the relative lack of representation of women and women's interests but also shown how the (formally equal) citizenship rights of women lock them into their roles as mothers and carers (whilst the citizenship rights of men lock them into their roles as workers and soldiers) (see, for example, Phillips, A., 1992). However, as feminists are quick to point out, a pattern of representation for women and of women's interests which failed to take account of the great variety and diversity amongst women would be but a very limited victory. Therefore an extension of liberal democratic argument would take us towards a conception of the state as a guarantor of multiple identities. For socialists, the task is to establish the practical limits imposed by class and to identify strategies which unite class opposition to the power of capital without denying the variety of identities which make up each working class as a historical entity.

The Hobbesian critique of the representative state was that divisions within civil society would simply be duplicated (or represented) by divisions within the state. Divisions in a divided society would therefore be writ large within the representative state. A model of deliberative democracy, on the other hand, is predicated upon the assumption that the process of representation should involve the transformation of non-state interests. The 'rules of the game' would require that, in return for the right to participate, all representatives should accept the principles of trust, solidarity and security. They should start from the assumption that they may trust the other participants, they should be solidaristically looking to influence and shape the pursuit of mutual goals and they should feel secure that any attempt to threaten the core interests and identities of any one group would be resisted by the state with all its coercive power.

In such an account, this is the public interest: the protection of the procedures and conditions required to allow all sections of society to deliberate peaceably, to differ without oppressing and to pursue mutual interests where possible. The public interest would not only involve finding ways in which we can pursue common collective objectives but also ways in which we can resolve conflicts over the pursuit of mutually incompatible sectional objectives. It would not require a commitment to a shared vision of a homogeneous society for us to share a commitment to a set of procedures and principles through which our collective and sectional interests may be negotiated and pursued.

The change of government in May 1997 did not produce a simultaneous change in the British state. The ambitions of the incoming government cannot be detached from the question of the state. The achievement of these ambitions will be fundamentally shaped by the answers to the three questions of state management which have shaped this book:

- who is represented and on what terms?
- what agencies of intervention are created and with what capacities?
- how will the overall coordination of the state system be secured?

State Theory, the Public Interest and the State

State theory poses at least two problems for this cosy image of the state as the guarantor of deliberative democracy. The first is the pressure on the state to sustain a degree of legitimacy and the second is the need to avoid fiscal crises (or, at least, to address such crises when they arise). We will look at these in turn.

Legitimation, through which the state comes to be regarded as a legitimate source of authority and thereby avoids the need for coercion as a routine part of governance, is not guaranteed by the sort of deliberative principles outlined above. The need for legitimacy amongst some interests is more pressing than others. Key opinion-formers and key sections of the media, and military, police or administrative elites, are all amongst those groups whose support will be more carefully sought by governments and without whose support the maintenance of democracy might be compromised. The capacity of the state to function as a terrain within which all interests can deliberate equally is clearly limited by the degree of inequality found in society as a whole. The liberal dilemma is that the protection of a diverse civil society can guarantee social inequalities which then infiltrate the operations of the whole state and thereby compromise the political equality of all citizens.

The need to respond to actual or potential fiscal crises also constrains the deliberative process. It compels state managers to establish financial control systems to monitor and manage expenditure. Furthermore, just controlling expenditure is insufficient. States must also maintain their tax base. Notwithstanding our earlier insistence that there remains a case for believing that national governments will continue to enjoy significant economic functions, increasingly this capacity will be shaped by the investment decisions of transnational corporations. The maintenance of the tax base compels states to pay at least some attention to the representatives of the organized working class where they have the capacity to disrupt profitability. But more particularly, it requires states to consider how best to ensure continued investment, employment and profitability. Whilst the strategies available to governments to sustain profitability are greater than is suggested by the most ardent globalization theorists, such strategic options have nevertheless clearly been changed and in some ways narrowed by trends towards economic integration.

For these two reasons at least, government cannot be simply about the governance of a system of deliberative democracy. Judgements about the extent to which the public interest is compromised by well-organized interests and the power of capital are a matter not only of normative choice. They also depend upon an assessment of the alternatives to an economic system based upon the capitalist enterprise and of the extent to which compromises can be secured through bargained outcomes in which capitalist corporations gain but so do other interests in society. As new problems arise and old ones change (the question of environmental degradation, for example), then this calculation will change.

In this scenario, however, the question of state management remains. Legitimation, capital accumulation and representation can only occur if there are public sector administrative structures, financial systems and modes of calculation coming together to form a state. It is clear that an understanding of how these are managed is fundamental both to analyses of the past conduct of politics and to decisions about their future. The state remains one of the most remarkable creations of the modern world. Our capacity to understand it, and collectively to use it, will condition our whole experience of late modernity.

Summary

The modern capitalist state is necessarily a terrain upon which a variety of interests and world-views compete. Historically it has shown an institutional preference for the interests and calculations of the more powerful and organized. Understanding how particular states do this is an important theoretical and historiographical task. However, states also have their own calculations and institutional competences which contribute directly to the politics of their age.

The task of reform is not to replace the systematic privileging of the powerful with an alternative homogeneous set of interests. Rather it is to sponsor a variety of organizational forms and political activities through which diversity can be protected. This would only be possible, however, in the context of a political leadership which set the protection of the equal rights of all to participate at the centre of its conception of the public interest.

Bibliography

Addison, P. (1975) *The Road to 1945*. London: Cape.

Adler, M. (1992) 'Realising the potential of the operational strategy', *Benefits*, April/May 1992.

Aglietta, M. (1979) *A Theory of Capitalist Regulation*. London: New Left Books.

Allan, M., Bhavnani, R. and French, K. (1992) *Promoting Women: Management Development and Training for Women in Social Services Departments*. London: HMSO.

Allen, J. and Massey, D. (eds) (1988) *The Economy in Question*. London: Sage.

Althusser, L. (1971) 'Ideology and ideological state apparatuses' in *Lenin and Philosophy and Other Essays*. London: New Left Books.

Anderson, J. (1988) 'The new right and Enterprise Zones'. Unit 23 of *Social Problems and Social Welfare*. Milton Keynes: Open University Press.

Anderson, P. (1992) *English Questions*. London: Verso.

Atkinson, J. and Meager, N. (1986) *Changing Work Patterns: How Companies Achieve Flexibility to Meet New Needs*. London: NEDO.

Audit Commission (1989a) *Better Financial Management*. Management Paper no. 3. London: HMSO.

Audit Commission (1989b) *The Probation Service: Promoting Value for Money*. London: HMSO.

Audit Commission (1989c) *Sport for Whom? Clarifying the Local Authority Role in Sport and Recreation*. London: HMSO.

Audit Commission (1989d) *Urban Regeneration and Economic Development: the Local Authority Dimension*. London: HMSO.

Audit Commission (1991) *Assuring Quality in Education: the Role of Local Education Authority Inspectors and Advisors*. London: HMSO.

Audit Commission (1992) *The Community Revolution: the Personal Social Services and Community Care*. London: HMSO.

Bagguley, P. (1991) 'Post-Fordism and enterprise culture: flexibility, autonomy and changes in economic organisation' in Keat and Abercrombie (1991).

Banham, R., Barker, P., Hall, P. and Price, C. (1969) 'Non-plan: an expression in freedom', *New Society*, 20 March 1969.

Barker, A. (ed.) (1982) *Quangos in Britain: Governments and Networks of Public Policy Making*. London: Macmillan.

Barnett, C. (1986) *The Audit of War*. London: Macmillan.

Barnett, J. (1982) *Inside the Treasury*. London: Deutsch.

Batley, R. (1989) 'London Docklands: an analysis of power relations between UDCs and local government', *Public Administration*, 67, 2.

Bauman, Z. (1988) *Freedom*. Buckingham: Open University Press.

Beechey, V. (1985) 'The shape of the workforce to come', *Marxism Today*, August 1985.

Bellamy, C. and Taylor, J. A. (1994) 'Introduction exploiting IT in public administration: towards information policy', *Public Administration*, 72, 1.

Benefits Agency (1992) *Benefits Agency Annual Report 1991/1992*. Leeds: Benefits Agency.

Benn, C. and Fairley, J. (eds) (1986) *Challenging the MSC on Jobs, Education and Training*. London: Pluto Press.

Bleaney, M. (1985) *The Rise and Fall of Keynesian Economics*. London: Macmillan.

Boddy, M. (1987) 'High technology industry, regional development and defence manufacturing: a case study from the UK sunbelt' in Robson (1987).

Bogdanor, V. (1988) *Against the Overmighty State: a Future for Local Government in Britain*. London: Federal Trust for Education Research.

Bogdanor, V. (1993) 'Ministers, civil servants and the constitution: a revolution in Whitehall?' Speech to the Institute of Advanced Legal Studies, printed in *IALS Bulletin*, issue 15.

Bradbury, B. (1988) *Municipal Journal*, 20 May 1988.

Bridges, Lord (1950) *Portrait of a Profession*. Cambridge: Cambridge University Press.

Bridges, Lord (1964) *The Treasury*. London: Allen and Unwin.

Brivati, B. and Jones, H. (eds) (1993) *What Difference Did the War Make?* London: Leicester University Press.

Bromley, S. (1996) 'Feature Review of Hirst, P. and Thompson, G. (1996) *Globalization in Question: The International Economy and the Possibilities of Governance*', *New Political Economy*, 1, 1.

Brown, M. (1985) *Introduction to Social Administration in Britain*. 6th edn, London: Hutchinson.

Buchanan, J. (1968) *The Demand and Supply of Public Goods*. Chicago: Rand McNally.

Burrows, R. and Loader, B. (eds) (1994) *Towards a Post-Fordist Welfare State?* London: Routledge.

Buxton, T., Chapman, P. and Temple, P. (eds) (1994) *Britain's Economic Performance* London: Routledge.

Cabinet Office (1993) *The Citizen's Charter Mark Scheme 1993: Guide for Applicants.* London: Cabinet Office and Central Office of Information.

Cadman, D. (1982) 'Urban change, Enterprise Zones and the role of investors', *Built Environment,* 7, 1.

Cairncross, A. (1985) *Years of Recovery: British Economic Policy 1945–51.* London: Allen and Unwin.

Callaghan, J. (1987) *Time and Chance.* London: Collins.

Campbell, C. (1987) *The Romantic Spirit and the Spirit of Modern Consumerism.* Oxford: Blackwell.

Campbell, H. (1959) *Housing: a Co-operative Approach.* London: Co-operative Union.

Carter, D. and Stewart, I. (1981) *YOP, Youth Training and the MSC: the Need for a New Trade Union Response.* Manchester Employment Research Group.

Carter, N. and Greer, P. (1993) 'Evaluating Agencies: Next Steps and Performance Indicators', *Public Administration,* 71, 3.

Carter, P., Jeffs, T. and Smith, M. K. (eds) (1991) *Social Work and Social Welfare Yearbook 3.* Milton Keynes: Open University Press.

Castle, B (1980) *The Castle Diaries, 1974–6.* London: Weidenfeld and Nicolson.

Cawson, A. (1993) 'High technology industries' in Maidment and Thompson, (1993).

Cawson, A. (ed.) (1985) *Mesocorporatism: the State and Sectoral Interests in Policy Formation.* London: Sage.

CBI (1968) *Supplement to CBI Education and Training Bulletin.* London: CBI.

CDP (1975) *Final Report; Part 1: Coventry and Hillfields; Prosperity and the Persistence of Inequality.* CDP in association with the Institute of Government Studies.

CDP (1977) *Gilding the Ghetto.* Newcastle upon Tyne: CDPPEC.

CDP (1980) *Back Street Factory.* Newcastle upon Tyne: CDPPEC.

CDP (1981) *West Newcastle in Growth and Decline.* Newcastle upon Tyne: Benwell CDP.

CDP (undated; 1976?) *Community Work or Class Politics?* North Shields: CDP Collective.

Civil Service Statistics (1986). London: HMSO.

Clarke, J. and Langan, M. (1993) 'The British welfare state: foundation and modernisation' in Cochrane and Clarke (1993).

Clarke, J., Cochrane, A. and McLaughlin, E. (1994a) 'Introduction: why management matters' in Clarke, Cochrane and McLaughlin (1994b).

Clarke, J., Cochrane, A. and McLaughlin, E. (eds) (1994b) *Managing Social Policy.* London: Sage.

Clarke, R. (1971) *New Trends in Government.* London: Civil Service Department.

Clarke, R. (1973) 'Mintech in Retrospect – II', *Omega,* 1, 2.

Clout, H. and Woods, P. (eds) (1986) *London.* Harlow: Longman.

Coates, D. (1995) *Running the Country.* London: Hodder and Stoughton.

Cochrane, A. and Clarke, J. (eds) (1993) *Comparing Welfare States: Britain in International Context*. London: Sage.

Cockburn, C. (1977) *The Local State: Management of Cities and People*. London: Pluto.

Collingridge, D. and Margetts, H. (1993) 'Can government information systems be inflexible technology? The operational strategy revisited', *Public Administration*, 71, 4.

Colville, I., Dalton, K. and Tomkins, C. (1993) 'Developing and understanding cultural change in HM Customs and Excise: there is more to dancing than knowing the Next Steps', *Public Administration*, 71, 4.

Cooper, Sir F. (1983) 'Freedom to manage in government'. RIPA Winter Lecture Series, March 1983.

Coopey, R. (1995) 'Industrial policy in the white heat of the scientific revolution' in Coopey, Fielding and Tiratsoo (1995).

Coopey, R., Fielding, S. and Tiratsoo, N. (eds) (1995) *The Wilson Governments*. London: Pinter.

Cronin, J. (1991) *The Politics of State Expansion: War, State and Society in Twentieth Century Britain*. London: Routledge.

Crook, S., Pakulski, J. and Waters, M. (1992) *Postmodernization: Change in Advanced Society*. London: Sage.

Dale, R. (ed.) (1985) *Education, Training and Employment*. London: Pergamon Press.

Dalton, H. (1935) *Practical Socialism for Britain*. London: Routledge and Kegan Paul.

Davidson, J. O. (1994) 'Metamorphosis, privatisation and the restructuring of management and labour' in Jackson and Price (1994).

De Swann, A. (1988) *In Care of the State*. Cambridge: Polity.

Deal, T. E. and Kennedy, A. A. (1982) *Corporate Culture*. Reading, Mass.: Addison-Wesley.

Dearlove, J. (1974) 'The control of change and the regulation of community action' in Jones and Mayo (1974).

Delafons, J. (1982) 'Working in Whitehall: changes in public administration 1952–82', *Public Administration*, 60, 3.

Demirovic, A. (ed.) (1992) *Akkumulation, Hegemonie und Staat*. Munster: Westfalisches Dampfboot.

Department of Health (1989) *Working for Patients*. London: HMSO.

Desai, M. (1996) 'Debating the British disease', *New Political Economy*, 1, 1.

DHSS (1972) *Management Arrangements for the Reorganised National Health Service*. London: HMSO.

DHSS (1976) *The NHS Planning System*. London: HMSO.

DHSS (1982) *Social Security Operational Strategy: a Framework for the Future*. London: HMSO.

DHSS (1983) *The NHS Management Inquiry* (the Griffiths Report). London: HMSO.

DoE (1987) *An Evaluation of the Enterprise Zone Experiment*. London: Inner Cities Research Programme, DoE.

Donnison, D. (1982) *The Politics of Poverty*. Oxford: Martin Robertson.

Dowding, K. (1993) 'Managing the civil service' in Maidment and Thompson (1993).

Dowding, K. (1995) 'Model or metaphor? A critical review of the policy network approach', *Political Studies*, 43, 1.

Downs, A. (1957) *An Economic Theory of Democracy*. New York: Harper and Row.

Drewry, G. and Butcher, T. (1988) *The Civil Service Today*. Oxford: Blackwell.

Duncan, G. (ed.) (1989) *Democracy and the State*. Cambridge: Cambridge University Press.

Dunleavy, P. (1981) *The Politics of Mass Housing in Britain, 1945–1975: a Study of Corporate Power and Professional Influence in the Welfare State*. Oxford: Oxford University Press.

Dunleavy, P. (1990) 'Government at the centre' in Dunleavy, Gamble and Peele (1990).

Dunleavy, P. (1991) *Political Power and Rational Choice*. Brighton: Wheatsheaf.

Dunleavy, P., Gamble, A. and Peele, G. (1990) *Developments in British Politics 3*. London: Macmillan.

Dunsire, A. and Hood, C. C. (1989) *Cutback Management in Public Bureaucracies*. Cambridge: Cambridge University Press.

Durbin, E. (1940) *The Politics of Democratic Socialism*. London: Routledge and Kegan Paul.

Efficiency Unit (1988) *Improving Management in Government: the Next Steps. Report to the Prime Minister*. London: HMSO.

Efficiency Unit (1993) *The Government's Guide to Market Testing*. London: HMSO.

Elcock, H. (1991)*Change and Decay? Public Administration in the 1990s*. Harlow: Longman.

Elcock, H. (1993) 'Local government' in Farnham and Horton (1993).

Esping-Andersen, G. (1990) *The Three Worlds of Welfare Capitalism*. Cambridge: Polity.

Esping-Andersen, G. and Friedland, R. (eds) (1981) *Political Power and Social Theory* vol. 3 Greenwich, Conn.: Jai Press.

Evans, P., Rueschemeyer, D. and Skocpol, T. (eds) (1987) *Bringing the State Back In*. Cambridge: Cambridge University Press.

Ewald, F. (1988) 'The law of law' in Teubner (1988).

Fairbrother, P. (1989) 'State workers: class position and collective action' in Duncan (1989).

Farley, M. (1985) 'Trends and structural changes in English vocational education' in Dale (1985).

Farnham, D. (1993) 'Human resources management and employee relations' in Farnham and Horton (1993).

Farnham, D. and Horton, S. (eds) (1993) *Managing the New Public Services*. London: Macmillan.

Featherstone, M. (1991) *Consumer Culture and Postmodernism*. London: Sage.

FECDRU (1981) *Vocational Preparation*. Further Education Curriculum and Review Development Unit, London: HMSO.

Feinstein, C. H. (1972) *National Income, Expenditure and Output of the United Kingdom 1855–1965*. Cambridge: Cambridge University Press.

Field, F. (1982) *Poverty and Politics*. London: Heinemann.

Field, F. (1983) *Guardian*, 28 October 1983.

Finn, D. (1984) *The Employment Effects of New Technologies*. London: Unemployment Unit.

Finn, D. (1985) 'The Manpower Services Commission and the Youth Training Sceme' in Dale (1985).

Finn, D. (1986) *Half Measures: Recent Developments in Special Measures for the Unemployed*. Unemployment Unit Bulletin, no. 19, February 1986.

Finn, D. (1987) *Training Without Jobs: New Deals and Broken Promises*. London: Macmillan.

Flynn, N. (1993) *Public Sector Management*. 2nd edn, London: Harvester Wheatsheaf.

Foot, M. (1975) *Aneurin Bevan*, vol. 2, 1945–60. London: Granada.

Foster, D. and Taylor, G. (1994) *Privatisation and Public Service Trade Unionism*. University of the West of England, Occasional Papers in Sociology, no. 11. Bristol: University of the West of England.

Foucault, M. (1969) *Discipline and Punish*. London: Tavistock.

Foucault, M. (1978) *The History of Sexuality: an Introduction* (translated by Hurley, R.). Harmondsworth: Penguin.

Friedman, M. and Friedman, R. (1980) *Free to Choose: a Personal Statement*. Harmondsworth: Penguin.

Fry, G. K. (1986) 'The British career civil service under challenge', *Political Studies,* 34.

Fry, G. K. (1995) *Policy and Management in the British Civil Service*. Hemel Hempstead: Prentice Hall/Harvester Wheatsheaf.

Gamble, A. (1988) *The Free Economy and the Strong State: the Politics of Thatcherism*. London: Macmillan.

Gamble, A. (1995) 'The new political economy', *Political Studies*, 43, 3.

Gibson, T. (1984) *Counterweight: the Neighbourhood Option*. London: Town and Country Planning Association.

Giddens, A. (1979) *Central Problems in Social Theory: Action, Structure and Contradiction in Social Analysis*. London: Macmillan.

Giddens, A. (1985) *The Nation State and Violence*. Cambridge: Polity.

Goldblatt, D. (1995) 'The paradox of power: globalisation and national government', *Missionary Government: Demos Quarterly*, 7.

Goldsmith, M. (ed.) (1986) *New Research in Central–Local Relations*. Aldershot: Gower.

Gough, I. (1979) *The Political Economy of the Welfare State*. London: Macmillan.

Graham, C. and Prosser, T. (eds) (1988) *Waiving the Rules*. Milton Keynes: Open University Press.

Grant, W. (1993) *Business and Politics in Britain.* London: Macmillan.

Gray, A. and Jenkins, W. (1982) 'Policy analysis in British central government: the experience of PAR', *Public Administration,* 60, 4.

Greater London Council (1985) *The London Industrial Strategy.* London: GLC.

Green, H. (1985) *Informal Carers.* London: OPCS/HMSO.

Greenwood, J. R. and Wilson, D. J. (1984) *Public Administration in Britain.* London: George Allen and Unwin.

Greer, P. (1992) 'The Next Steps Initiative: an examination of the agency framework documents', *Public Administration,* 70, 1.

Habermas, J. (1975) *Legitimation Crisis.* London: Heinemann.

Habermas, J. (1990) *Moral Consciousness and Communicative Action.* Cambridge: Polity Press.

Hall, P. (1981) 'Economic planning and the state' in Esping-Andersen and Friedland (1981).

Hall, S. and Jacques, M. (eds) (1983) *The Politics of Thatcherism.* London: Lawrence and Wishart.

Halsey, A. H. (ed.) (1988) *British Social Trends since 1900: a Guide to the Changing Social Structure of Britain.* 2nd edn, London: Macmillan.

Ham, C. (1996) *Public, Private or Community: What Next for the NHS?* London: Demos.

Harden, I. (1988) 'Corporatism without labour: the British version' in Graham and Prosser (1988).

Harris, L. (1988) 'The UK economy at the crossroads' in Allen and Massey, (1988).

Harrow, J. and Talbot, C. (1994) 'Central government: the changing civil service' in Jackson and Lavender (1994).

Hay, C. (1996) *Re-stating Social Change.* Cambridge: Polity Press.

Hayek, F. A. (1960) *The Constitution of Liberty.* London: Routledge and Kegan Paul.

Hayek, F. A. (1986) *The Road to Serfdom.* London: Ark Paperbacks.

Heclo, H. and Wildavsky, A. (1981) *The Government of Public Money.* London: Macmillan.

Hennessy, P. (1990) *Whitehall.* London: Fontana.

Hennessy, P. (1993a) *Never Again. Britain 1945–51.* London: Vintage.

Hennessy, P. (1993b) 'Never Again' in Brivati and Jones (1993).

Hennessy, P. and Arends, A. (1983) *Mr. Attlee's Engine Room: Cabinet Committee Structure and the Labour Government 1945–51.* Strathclyde Papers on Government and Politics, no. 26. Glasgow: University of Strathclyde.

Hennessy, P., Morrison, S. and Townsend, R. (1985) *Routine Punctuated by Orgies.* Strathclyde Papers on Government and Politics, no. 31. Glasgow: University of Strathclyde.

Hewart, G. (1929) *The New Despotism.* London: Benn.

Higgins, J., Deakin, N., Edwards, J. and Wicks, M. (1983) *Government and Urban Poverty.* Oxford: Basil Blackwell.

Hill, M. (1993) *The Welfare State in Britain: a Political History since 1945*. Aldershot: Edward Elgar.

Hills, S. J. (ed.) (1990) *The State of Welfare: the Welfare State in Britain since 1974*. London: Oxford University Press.

Hinings, C. R., Leach, S., Ranson, S. and Skelcher, C. K. (1982) *Policy Planning Systems in Central–Local Relations*. London: Social Science Research Council.

Hirsch, J. and Roth, R. (1986) *Das neue Gesicht des Kapitalismus*. Hamburg: VSA.

Hirst, P. (1994) *Associative Democracy: New Forms of Economic and Social Governance*. Cambridge: Polity.

Hirst, P. and Thompson, G. (1996) *Globalization in Question: the International Economy and the Possibilities of Governance*. Cambridge: Polity.

HMSO (1942) *Social Insurance and Allied Services* (the Beveridge Report). Cmnd 6404. London: HMSO.

HMSO (1951) *Report of the Committee on Social Workers in the Mental Health Services* (the Mackintosh Report). Cmnd 8260. London: HMSO.

HMSO (1955) *Royal Commission on the Civil Service 1953–55* (the Priestly Report). Cmnd 9613. London: HMSO.

HMSO (1959) *The Working of the Monetary System* (the Radcliffe Report). Cmnd 827. London: HMSO.

HMSO (1961) *The Control of Public Expenditure* (the Plowden Report). Cmnd 1432. London: HMSO.

HMSO (1967) *Report of the Committee on the Civil Service*. (the Fulton Report). Cmnd 3638. London: HMSO.

HMSO (1968) *Report of the Committee on Local Authority and Allied Personal Social Services* (the Seebohm Report). Cmnd 3703. London: HMSO.

HMSO (1968) *The Civil Service Vol. 1 Report of the Committee 1966–68* (the Fulton Report). Cmnd 3638. London: HMSO.

HMSO (1969) *Management of Local Government* (the Maud Report). Cmnd 4040. London: HMSO.

HMSO (1971) *The Reorganization of Central Government*. Cmnd 4506. London: HMSO.

HMSO (1977) *Policy for Inner Cities*. Cmnd 6849. London: HMSO.

HMSO (1983) *Streamlining the Cities*. Cmnd 9063. London: HMSO.

HMSO (1987) *Britain An Official Handbook*. London: COI.

HMSO (1988) *Action for Cities*. London: HMSO.

HMSO (1991) *Annual Report of the CAO for 1990–91 on Adjudication Standards*. London: HMSO.

Hoggett, P. (1987) 'A farewell to mass production? Decentralisation as an emergent private and public sector paradigm' in Hoggett and Hambleton (1987).

Hoggett, P. and Hambleton, R. (eds) (1987) *Decentralisation and Democ-*

racy. Occasional Paper 28. Bristol: School for Advanced Urban Studies, University of Bristol.

Hogwood, B. (1987) *From Crisis to Complacency?* Oxford: Oxford University Press.

Holland, P. (1981) *The Governance of Quangos*. London: Adam Smith Institute.

Hood, C. (1976) *The Limits of Administration*. Chichester: Wiley.

Hood, C. (1982) 'Governmental bodies and governmental growth' in Barker (1982).

Hood, C. (1991) *Beyond the Public Bureaucratic State*. Inaugural Lecture. London: London School of Economics.

House of Commons (1977) *Eleventh Report from the Expenditure Committee, 1976–77: the Civil Service*. London: HMSO.

House of Commons (1980) *First Report from the Select Committee on Employment*. London: HMSO.

House of Commons (1982) *Third Report from the Treasury and Civil Service Committee: Efficiency and Effectiveness in the Civil Service*. London: HMSO.

House of Commons (1983) *Second Report from the Environment Committee: the Problems of Management of Urban Renewal*. London: HMSO.

House of Commons (1986) *Report from the Public Accounts Committee: Enterprise Zones*. London: HMSO.

House of Commons (1988) *Third Report from the Employment Committee, Session 1987–1988*. London: HMSO.

House of Commons (1988a) *Eighth Report from the Treasury and Civil Service Committee: Civil Service Management Reform: the Next Steps*. London: HMSO.

House of Commons (1988b) *Third Report from the Employment Committee: the Employment Effects of Urban Development Corporations*. London: HMSO.

House of Commons (1989) *Twentieth Report from the Public Accounts Account Committee*. London: HMSO.

House of Commons (1990) *Eighth Report from the Treasury and Civil Service Committee: Progress in the Next Steps Initiative*. London: HMSO.

House of Commons (1991) *Seventh Report from the Treasury and Civil Service Committee: 'The Next Steps Initiative'*. London: HMSO.

House of Lords (1981) *Report from the Select Committee of the House of Lords on the Docklands Development Corporation (Area and Constitution Order 1981)*. London: HMSO.

Howarth, D. (1995) 'Discourse theory' in Marsh and Stoker (1995).

Howells, P. G. A. and Bain, K. (1994) *Financial Markets and Institutions*. 2nd edn, Harlow: Longman.

Hutton, W. (1995; 2nd edn 1996) *The State We're In*. London: Jonathan Cape.

Incomes Data Services (1983) *Youth Training Scheme*. Study 293. London: IDS Ltd.

Ingham, G. (1984) *Capitalism Divided? The City and Industry in British Social Development*. London: Macmillan.

Ingham, G. (1988) 'Commercial capital and British development', *New Left Review*, 172.

Jackson, P. (1995) 'Macroeconomic policies and prospects' in Jackson and Lavender (1995).

Jackson, P. and Lavender, M. (eds) (1994) *The Public Services Yearbook 1994*. London: CIPFA.

Jackson, P. and Lavender, M. (eds) (1995) *The Public Services Yearbook 1995/96*. London: Chapman and Hall.

Jackson, P. and Lavender, M. (eds) (1996) *Public Services Yearbook 1996–97*. London: Pitman.

Jackson, P. M. and Price, C. M. (eds) (1994) *Privatisation and Regulation: a Review of the Issues*. London: Longman.

Jacobs, S. (1985) 'Race, empire and the welfare state: council housing and racism', *Critical Social Policy*, 5, 1.

Jay, D. (1937; new edn 1947) *The Socialist Case*. London: Faber.

Jessop, B. (1982) *The Capitalist State: Marxist Theories and Methods*. Oxford: Basil Blackwell.

Jessop, B. (1990) *State Theory: Putting the State in its Place*. Cambridge: Polity Press.

Jessop, B. (1992a) 'Fordism and post-Fordism: a critical reformulation' in Scott and Stormper (1992).

Jessop, B. (1992b) 'Regulation und Politik: Integrale Okonomie und Integraler Staat' in Demirovic (1992).

Jessop, B. (1994) 'The transition to post-Fordism and the Schumpeterian workfare state' in Burrows and Loader (1994).

Jessop, B. (1996) 'The governance of complexity and the complexity of governance: preliminary remarks on some problems and limits of economic guidance'. Personal communication.

Jessop, B., Bonnett, K., Bromley, S. and Ling, T. (1988) *Thatcherism: a Tale of Two Nations*. Cambridge: Polity.

Jones, D. and Mayo, M. (eds) (1974) *Community Work One*. London: Routledge and Kegan Paul.

Jordan, A. and Richardson, J. (1987) *British Politics and the Policy Process*. London: Allen and Unwin.

Joshi, S. and Carter, B. (1985) 'The role of Labour in the creation of a racist Britain', *Race and Class*, 25, 3.

Kaufman, G. (1992) 'Privatising the Ministers', *Guardian*, 7 December 1992.

Kaufman, M. (1986) 'The MSC and the national training system' in Benn and Fairley (1986).

Kavanagh, D. (1992) 'The postwar consensus', *Twentieth Century British History*, 3, 2.

Keat, R. and Abercrombie, N. (eds) (1991) *Enterprise Culture*. London: Routledge.

Kellner, P. and Crowther-Hunt, Lord (1980) *The Civil Servants: an Inquiry into Britain's Ruling Class*. London: Routledge.

Kelly, A. (1991) 'The "new" managerialism in the social services' in Carter, Jeffs and Smith.

Kelly, J. (1987) *Labour and the Unions*. London: Verso.

Keohane, R. and Nye, J. S. (1977) *Power and Inter-dependence: World Politics in Transition*. Boston: Little, Brown.

Kessler, I. (1993) 'Pay determination in the British civil service since 1979', *Public Administration* 71, 3.

King, A. (1975) 'Overload: problems of governing in the 1970s', *Political Studies*, 23, 2 & 3.

King, D. S. (1993) 'The Conservatives and training policy 1972–92: from a tripartite to a neo-liberal regime', *Political Studies*, 41.

King, R. (ed.) (1983) *Capital and Politics*. London: Routledge and Kegan Paul.

Klein, R. (1989) *The Politics of the NHS*. 2nd edn, London: Longman.

Klein, R., Buxton, M. and Outram, Q. (1976) *Constraints and Choices*. London: Centre for Studies in Social Policy.

Krugman, P. (1995) *Peddling Prosperity: Economic Sense and Nonsense in the Age of Diminished Expectations*. New York: W. W. Norton.

Laclau, E. and Mouffe, C. (1981) 'Socialist strategy – where next?', *Marxism Today*, January 1981.

Langan, M. and Clarke, J. (1994) 'Managing in the mixed economy of care' in Clarke, Cochrane and McLaughlin (1994b).

Lash, S. and Urry, J. (1987) *The End of Organized Capitalism*. Cambridge: Polity.

Lawless, P. (1988) 'British inner urban policy: a review', *Regional Studies*, 22, 6.

Levacic, R. (1992) 'Running schools: co-ordination of the school system' *Running the Country*, D212. Milton Keynes: Open University Press.

Leys, C. (1986) 'The formation of British capital', *New Left Review*, 151.

Leys, C. (1989) *Politics in Britain: from Labourism to Thatcherism*. Revised edn, London: Verso.

Liekerman, A. (1982) 'Management information for Ministers: the MINIS system in the Department of the Environment', *Public Administration* 60, 2.

Lindberg, L. N., Alford, R., Crouch, C. and Offe, C. (1975) *Stress and Contradiction in Modern Capitalism*. Lexington, MA: D. H. Heath.

Ling, T. (1991) 'The Management of the British State in the Transition from the Keynesian Welfare State to Thatcherism'. Unpublished PhD thesis, University of Essex.

Ling, T. (1994a) 'Case study: the Benefits Agency – claimants as customers' in Tam (1994).

Ling, T. (1994b) 'The new managerialism and social security' in Clarke, Cochrane and McLaughlin (1994).

Lovenduski, J. and Stranger, J. (eds) (1995) *Contemporary Political Studies*. Belfast: The Political Studies Association.

Lowe, T. (1996) 'Communitarianism as a blind alley? A reply to Lacey and Frazer', *Politics*, 16, 2.

McInnes, J. (1987) *Thatcherism at Work: Industrial Relations and Economic Change*. Milton Keynes: Open University Press.

McKay, D. and Cox, A. (1979) *The Politics of Urban Change*. London: Croom Helm.

Maclean, M. and Groves, D. (eds) (1991) *Women's Issues in Social Policy*. London: Routledge.

Madgwick, P. J., Steeds, D. and Williams, L. J. (1982) *Britain Since 1945*. London: Hutchinson.

Maidment, R. and Thompson, G. (eds) (1993) *Managing the United Kingdom*. London: Sage.

Margetts, H. (1996) 'Information technology in government' in Jackson and Lavender (1996).

Marquand, D. (1988) *The Unprincipled Society: New Demands and Old Politics*. London: Fontana.

Marsh, D. (1991) 'Privatisation under Mrs. Thatcher', *Public Administration*, 69, 4.

Marsh, D. and Rhodes, R. A. W. (eds) (1992) *Implementing Thatcherite Policies: Audit of an Era*. Buckingham: Open University Press.

Marsh, D. and Stoker, G. (eds) (1995) *Theory and Methods in Political Science*. London: Macmillan.

Marshall, T. H. (1950) 'Citizenship and social class' in Marshall, T. H. and Bottomore, T. (eds) (1950) *Citizenship and Social Class*. London: Pluto.

Massey, D. and Meegan, R. (1983) 'The new geography of jobs', *New Society*, 17 March 1983.

Mathews, R. C. O. (1968) 'Why has Britain had full employment since the war?' *Economic Journal*, 78.

Mercer, H. (1991) 'The Labour governments of 1945–51 and private industry' in Tiratsoo (1991).

Metcalfe, L. and Richards, S. (1990) *Improving Public Management*. 2nd edn, London: Sage.

Middlemas, K. (1979) *Politics in Industrial Society*. London: André Deutsch.

Middlemas, K. (1986) *Power, Competition and the State, Vol. 1: Britain in Search of Balance, 1940–61*. London: Macmillan.

Middlemas, K. (1990) *Power, Competition and the State, Vol. 2: Threats to the Postwar Settlement*. London: Macmillan.

Middlemas, K. (1991) *Power, Competition and the State, Vol. 3: the End of the Postwar Era*. London: Macmillan.

Middlemas, K. (1993) 'Commentary Two' in Brivati and Jones (1993).

Mitchell, B. R. and Deane, P. (1962) *Abstract of British Historical Statistics*. Cambridge: Cambridge University Press.

Moran, M. (1977) *The Politics of Industrial Relations*. London: Macmillan.

Moran, M. (1983) 'Power, policy and the City of London' in King (1983).

Morgan, D. and Evans, M. (1993) 'The road to nineteen eighty four: Orwell and the post-war reconstruction of citizenship' in Brivati and Jones (1993).

Morgan, K. (1984) *Labour in Power 1945–51*. Oxford: Clarendon Press.

Morgan, K. (1990) *The People's Peace: British History 1945–1990*. Oxford: Oxford University Press.

Moulaert, F., Swyngedouw, E. and Wilson, P. (1988) 'Spatial responses to Fordist and post-Fordist accumulation and regulation', *Papers of the Regional Science Association*, 64.

MSC (1977) *Young People and Work* (the Holland Report), London: MSC.

MSC (1980) *Outlook on Training: a Review of the 1973 Employment and Training Act*. London: MSC.

MSC (1983) *Scheme Design and Content: Youth Training Scheme*. YTS B12. London: MSC.

MSC (1984) *Notes of Guidance: Occupational Training Families*. London: MSC.

Mulgan, G. (1994) *Politics in an Anti-Political Age*. Cambridge: Polity.

Myrdal, A. and Klein, V. (1956) *Women's Two Roles, Home and Work*. London: Routledge and Kegan Paul.

Nairn, T. (1981) *The Break-Up of Britain*. London: Verso.

National Joint Advisory Council (1958) *Training for Skill: Recruitment and Training of Young Workers in Industry* (the Carr Report). London: HMSO.

Newman, I. and Mayo, M. (1981) 'Docklands', *International Journal of Urban and Regional Research*, 5.

Newman, J. (1994) 'The limits of management: gender and the politics of change', in Clarke, Cochrane and McLaughlin (1994).

Next Steps Unit (1993) *Next Steps Briefing*. London: Next Steps Unit.

NHS Executive (1996) *Patient Partnership: Building a Collaborative Strategy*. London: Department of Health.

Niskanen, W. (1971) *Bureaucracy and Representative Government*. Chicago: Aldine-Atherton.

Niskanen, W. (1973) *Bureaucracy: Servant or Master?* London: Institute of Economic Affairs.

O'Connor, J. (1973) *The Fiscal Crisis of the State*. New York: St Martin's Press.

Offe, C. (1975) 'The theory of the capitalist state and the problem of policy formation' in Lindberg, Alford, Crouch and Offe (1975)

Offe, C. (1980) 'The separation of form and content in liberal democratic politics', *Studies in Political Economy*, 3, Spring.

Offe, C. (1984) *Contradictions of the Welfare State*. London: Hutchinson.

Offe, C. (1985) *Disorganized Capitalism*. Cambridge: Polity.

Olson, M. (1965) *The Logic of Collective Action: Public Goods and the Theory of Groups*. Cambridge, Mass.: Harvard University Press.

Osborne, D. and Gaebler, T. (1991) *Reinventing Government: How the Entrepreneurial Spirit is Transforming the Public Sector*. New York: Plume.

Overbeek, H. (1990) *Global Capitalism and National Decline*. London: Unwin Hyman.

Painter, J. (1991) 'Regulation theory and local government', *Local Government Studies*, November/December 1991.

Panitch, L. (1976) *Social Democracy and Industrial Militancy*. Cambridge: Cambridge University Press.

Panitch, L. (1980) 'Recent theorizations of corporatism: reflections on a growth industry', *British Journal of Sociology*, 33.

Pascall, G. (1986) *Social Policy: a Feminist Analysis*. London: Tavistock Publications.

Peters, T. and Austin, N. (1985) *A Passion for Excellence*. New York: Harper and Row.

Peters, T. and Waterman, R. (1982) *In Search of Excellence: Lessons from America's Best Run Companies*. New York: Harper and Row.

Phillips, A. (1992) 'Must feminists give up on liberal democracy?', *Political Studies*, special issue Held, D. (ed.), 40.

Phillips, M. (1992) 'The tender trap of the civil service plc', *Guardian*, 21 July 1992.

Pimlott, B. (1989), 'Is the postwar consensus a myth?', *Contemporary Record*, 2, 6.

Piore, M. and Sabel, C. (1984) *The Second Industrial Divide*. New York: Basic Books.

Pliatzky, L. (1980) *Report on Non-Departmental Public Bodies*. London: HMSO.

Pliatzky, L. (1985) *Paying and Choosing: the Intelligent Person's Guide to the Mixed Economy*. Oxford: Basil Blackwell.

Pliatzky, L. (1992) 'Quangos and agencies', *Public Administration*, 70, 4 .

Poggi, G. (1990) *The State: its Nature, Development and Prospects*. Cambridge: Polity.

Pollitt, C. (1984) *Manipulating the Machine*. London: George Allen and Unwin.

Pollitt, C. (1992) 'Running hospitals: the rise and fall of planning', Unit 16 of *Running the Country*, D212. Milton Keynes: Open University Press.

Pollitt, C. (1993a) 'Running hospitals' in Maidment and Thompson (1993).

Pollitt, C. (1993b) *Managerialism and the Public Services*. 2nd edn Oxford: Blackwell.

Ponting, C. (1985) *The Right to Know: the Inside Story of the Belgrano Affair*. London: Sphere Books.

Poole, M. (1994) 'Britain's managers' views on the role of government in the economy and industrial activity: a longitudinal analysis', *Public Administration*, 72, 3.

Porter, D. (1995) 'Downhill all the way: thirteen Tory years 1951–64' in Coopey, Fielding and Tiratsoo (1995).

Price, C. M. (1994) 'Economic regulation of privatised monopolies' in Jackson and Price (1994).

Price Waterhouse (1994) *Executive Agencies – Survey Report 1994*. London: Price Waterhouse.

Prime Minister (1991) *The Citizen's Charter: Raising the Standard*. Cmnd 1599. London: HMSO.

Putnam, R. D. with Leonardi, R. and Nanetti, R. Y. (1993) *Making Democ-*

racy Work: Civic Traditions in Modern Italy. Princeton: Princeton Univeristy Press.

Pyper, R. (1991) *The Evolving Civil Service*. Harlow: Longman.

Randall, A. (1992) 'Service planning – an agenda for the Benefits Agency', *Benefits*, April/May 1992.

Randall, S. (1986) *Manpower – Serving Whose Interests?* Bristol: SAUS, Bristol University.

Ranson, S. (1980) 'Changing relations between centre and locality in education', *Local Government Studies*, 6, 6.

Ranson, S. (1982) 'Central–local planning in education' in Hinings, Leach, Ranson and Skelcher (1982).

Reich, R. B. (1993) *The Work of Nations: Preparing Ourselves for the 21st Century*. New York: Simon and Schuster.

Rhodes, R. (1986) '"Power-dependencies" theories of central–local relations: a critical assessment' in Goldsmith(1986).

Rhodes, R. (1988) *Beyond Westminster and Whitehall: the Sub–Central Governments of Britain*. London: Hyman.

Rhodes, R. (1991a) 'Policy networks and sub-central government' in Thompson, Frances, Levacic and Mitchell (1991).

Rhodes, R. (1991b) 'Theories and methods in British public administration: the view from political science', in *Political Studies*, 39, 3.

Rhodes, R. (1995) 'The changing face of British public administration', *Politics*, 15, 2.

Riddell, P. (1983) *The Thatcher Government*. Oxford: Martin Robertson.

Robson, B. (1988) *Those Inner Cities*. Oxford: Clarendon Press.

Robson, B. (ed.) (1987) *Managing the City: the Aims and Impacts of Urban Policy*. London: Croom Helm.

Robson, W. A. (1928) *Justice and Administrative Law*. London: Macmillan.

Rose, R. (1979) 'Ungovernability; is there fire behind the smoke?', *Political Studies*, 27, 3.

Rueschemeyer, D. and Evans, P. (1985) 'The state and economic transformation' in Evans, Rueschemeyer and Skocpol (1987).

Salt, J. (1986) 'Population trends in London: problems of change' in Clout and Woods (1986).

Salveson, P., Tansley, S. and Colenutt, B. (1990) 'Urban regeneration: local authorities have the key role', *Local Work*, Centre for Local Economic Strategies, February/March 1990.

Savage, S. and Robbins, L. (eds) (1990) *Public Policy under Thatcher*. London: Macmillan.

Schein, E. H. (1985) *Organisational Culture and Leadership*. London: Josey-Bass.

Schlote, W. (1952) *British Overseas Trade from 1700 to the 1930s*. Oxford: Blackwell.

Schultz, R. I. and Harrison, S. (1983) *Teams and Top Managers in the NHS: a Survey and Strategy*. London: King's Fund Project Paper no. 14.

Scott, A. J. and Stormper, M. (eds) (1992) *Pathways to Industrialization and Regional Development*. London: Routledge.

Sharpe, L. J. (1985) 'Central coordination and the policy network', *Political Studies*, 33, 3.

Shell, D. (1993) 'The British Constitution 1991–2', *Parliamentary Affairs*, 1993.

Short, C. (1986) 'The MSC and special measures for unemployment' in Benn and Fairley (1986).

Shutt, J. (1984) 'Tory Enterprise Zones and the Labour movement', *Capital and Class*, 23.

Sleeman, J. F. (1979) *Resources for the Welfare State: an Economic Introduction*. London: Longman.

Smellie, K. B. (1950) *A Hundred Years of English Government*. London: Duckworth.

Smith, M. (1995) 'The changing nature of the British state, 1929–59: the historiography of consensus' in Brivati and Jones (1993).

Stones, R. (1990) 'Government–finance relations in Britain 1964-7: a tale of three cities', *Economy and Society*, 19, 1.

Strinati, D. (1982) *Capitalism, the State and Industrial Relations*. London: Croom Helm.

Summerfield, P. (1993) 'Approaches to women and social change in the second world war' in Brivati and Jones (1993).

Swann, D. (1988) *The Retreat of the State*. Hemel Hempstead: Harvester Wheatsheaf.

Talbot, C. (1995) 'Central government reforms' in Jackson and Lavender (1995).

Tam, H. (ed.) (1994) *Marketing Competition and the Public Sector: Key Trends and Issues*. Harlow: Longman.

Temple, P. (1994) 'Overview: understanding Britain's economic performance: the role of international trade' in Buxton, Chapman and Temple (1994).

Teubner, G. (ed.) (1988) *Autoptoietic Theory*. Berlin: de Gruyter.

Thompson, G., Frances, J., Levacic, R. and Mitchell, J. (eds) (1991) *Markets, Hierarchies and Networks: the Coordination of Social Life*. London: Sage.

Thompson, H. (1995) 'Globalisation, monetary autonomy and central bank independence: the case of the British government and the Bank of England' in Lovenduski and Stranger (1995).

Thomson, P. (1992) 'Public sector management in a period of radical change', *Public Money and Management*, 32, 3.

Thurow, L. (1992) *Head to Head: the Coming Economic Battle among Japan, Europe and America*. New York: Nicholas Brealey.

Tiratsoo, N. (ed.) (1991) *The Attlee Years*. London: Pinter.

Titmuss, R. M. (1958) *Essays on the Welfare State*. London: Allen and Unwin.

Tomlinson, J. (1990) *Public Policy and the Economy since 1900*. Oxford: Oxford University Press.

Tomlinson, J. (1991) 'The Labour government and the trade unions 1945–51' in Tiratsoo (1991).

Tomlinson, J. (1992) 'Running the Economy'. Unit 23 of *Running the Country, D212*. Milton Keynes: Open University Press.

Treasury (1991) *Competing for Quality: Buying Public Services*. Cmnd 1730. London: HMSO.

TURC (1986) *The Great Training Robbery Continues: a Follow-up Investigation of the Role of Private Training Agencies in Birmingham/Solihull*. West Midlands YTS Research Project, Birmingham: TURC.

Tym, R. and Partners (1983) *Monitoring Enterprise Zones, Year Two Report*. London: DoE.

Tym, R. and Partners (1984) *Monitoring Enterprise Zones, Year Three Report*. London: DoE.

Tym, R. and Partners (1986) *Trafford Park Industrial Strategy*. London: DoE.

Urry, J. (1990) *The Tourist Gaze*. London: Sage.

Vickerstaff, S. (1985) 'Industrial training in Britain: the dilemmas of a neo-corporatist policy' in Cawson (1985).

Walby, S. and Greenwell, J. (1994) 'Managing the National Health Service' in Clarke, Cochrane and McLaughlin (1994b).

Ward, C. (1985) *When We Build Again Let's have Housing that Works!* London: Pluto.

Ward, H. (1995) 'Rational choice theory' in Marsh and Stoker (1995).

Warde, A. (1994) 'Consumers, consumption and post-Fordism' in Burrows and Loader (1994) *Towards a Post-Fordist Welfare State?* London: Routledge.

Warner, G. (1993) 'The impact of the Second World War on British foreign policy' in Brivati and Jones (1993).

Webster, C. (1988) *The Health Service since the War, Vol. 1: Problems of Health Care*. London: HMSO.

Webster, C. (1991) 'Conflict and consensus: explaining the British health service', *Twentieth Century British History*, 1, 1.

Weir, S. and Hall, W. (eds) (1994) *Ego Trip: Extra-governmental Organisations in the United Kingdom and their Accountability*. London: Charter 88 Trust.

Wiener, M. (1981) *English Culture and the Decline of the Industrial Spirit 1850–1880*. Cambridge: Cambridge University Press.

Wilks, S. and Wright, M. (eds) (1987) *Comparative Government–Industry Relations: Western Europe, the United States, Japan*. Oxford: Oxford University Press.

Williams, F. (1989) *Social Policy: a Critical Introduction*. Cambridge: Polity Press.

Williams, F. (1994) 'Social relations, welfare and the post-Fordism debate' in Burrows and Loade (1994).

Wilson, J. R. and Greenwood, D. J. (1984) *Public Administration in Britain*. London: George Allen and Unwin.

Woodward, N. (1995) 'Labour's economic performance, 1964–70', in Coopey, Fielding and Tiratsoo (1995).

Woytinsky, W. S. and E. S. (1953) *World Population and Production: Trends and Outlooks.* New York: The Twentieth Century Fund.

Wright, M. (1977) 'Public Expenditure in Britain: the crisis of control', *Public Administration,* 55, 3.

Zysman, J. (1983) *Governments, Markets, and Growth.* New York: Cornell University Press.

General Index

Action for Inner Cities, 194–5, 200–1
Attlee, C., 23–4
Audit Commission, 159–61

Bains Report, 93
Bancroft, Sir Ian, 129
Bevan, N., 32
Beveridge Report, 30–4, 102, 109, 241
Black Papers, 110
Blunkett, D., 206
Bridges, Sir Edward, 23
British Medical Association, 31

Carr Report, 63
Central Information Technology Unit, 146
Central Policy Review Staff, 81–2
Chester, N., 22–3
Citizens' Charters, 149
civil service, fragmentation of, 130
Communitarian Forum, 237n
communitarianism and neo-constitutionalism, 236–9
Community Care Act, 114
compulsory competitive tendering, 142, 151–2, 155
consumerism and citizenship, 241–4
consumers of public services (models of), 139–41
corporate management, 93–4

corporatism, 39–42
training, 179–82
Crowther Report, 109

Denning, Lord, 154
Department for Economic Affairs, 57–8
Derbyshire, Sir Andrew, 204
Docklands Joint Action Group, 202
Docklands Joint Committee, 202

economic decline, 223–30
balance of payments 48–54
central planning, 55–62
City and, 225–7
definition of, 45–6
devaluation, 48–54
and the state, 46–8
economic policy, 45–71
foreign trade, overseas investments, 48–54
Keynesianism, 68–71
public sector and, 228–30
structural economic change, 65–8
training policy, 62–5
see also corporatism; Fordism
Education Act, 31
Efficiency Unit, 126, 128, 151
Employment and Training Act, 64, 172
Employment White Paper, 34–9, 41
Enterprise Zones, 195–9

Financial Services Act, 165
Fordism and post-Fordism, 230–6
Fulton Report, 80, 81, 121, 122,
   124–5

globalization, 221–3
Griffiths Report, 107, 142
Guillebaud Committee, 77n, 92, 106

Haldane Report, 121
health reforms, 142–6
Hunt, D., 206

IMF loan, 61–2
Incomes Policy; the Next Step, 55
Industrial Relations Act, 60
Industrial Reorganization Committee,
   59–60
Industrial Training Act, 63
Industrial Training Boards, 63,
   172–3
Industry Act, 61
information technology, 146–9

legitimation crisis, 220
Lloyd, S., 51

Mackintosh Report, 113, 115
Manpower Services Commission,
   64–5, 108–10, 172–88, 209–10
   central control over, 182–6
   corporatism and, 179–82
   market testing, 151–2
   markets, competition and customer
      focus, 139–52, 243–4
Marshall, T. H., 241
Maud Report, 93
Milner Holland Report, 111
MINIS, 127–8
Ministers of the Crown (Transfer of
   Functions) Act, 29
Monopoly and Mergers Commission,
   162
Morrell, D., 85–6
Morrison, H., 38

National Economic Development
   Committee, 56–7
National Health Service Act, 31, 105
National Plan, 58–9

new managerialism, 118–37, 138–70
   Benefits Agency, 146–59
   beyond Whitehall, 133–6
   citizens' charters, 150
   fragmentation of civil service, 130
   health reforms, 142–6
   Keynesian welfare state and, 136–7
   managing public employees, 152–7
   market testing, 151–2
   markets, competition and customer
      focus, 139–52, 243–4
   origins of, 122–5
   performance indicators, audit and
      quality, 157–61
   Thatcherism and, 125
neo-constitutionalism and
   communitarianism, 236–9
Newsom Report, 109
Next Steps, 130–3, 128–9
NHS and Community Care Act, 114
Northcote-Trevelyan Report, 21,
   122

Office of Fair Trading, 162
overload, 220
overseas investments, 48–54

Paterson Report, 93
*Patient Partnership: building a
   collaborative strategy*, 145
Plowden Report
   education, 112
   public expenditure, 77–9, 121–2,
      153
Plowden, Lord, 24
Policy for Inner Cities, 191–2, 197,
   201
post-Fordism *see* Fordism
post-war settlement
   citizenship, 32–4
   civil service and, 21
   core institutions of, 20–1
   corporatism, 39–42
   economic strategies, 34–42
   international context of, 17–20
   key organized interests, 15–17
   levels of analysing, 26–7
   nationalization, 38–9
   power and, 27–9
   welfare state and, 30–4

Priestly Report, 153
Public Expenditure Survey, 78–80
public and private interests, 248–52

quangos, 133–6

Radcliffe Report, 53
Rayner Reviews, 127
Rayner Unit *see* Efficiency Unit
Rayner, D., 123, 126
regulation, 162–8
*Reorganization of Central
   Government*, 123
Royal Commission on Technical
   Instruction, 62

Sanderson, P., 162
Schumpeterian workfare state, 234,
   235
Seebohm Report, 112, 113–15
self-regulation, 165–6
Selsdon Man, 60
state
   bringing the state back in, 218–20
   British state and economic decline,
      223–30
   and capitalism, 3–5
   coherence of, 10–12
   communitarianism and neo-
      constitutionalism, 236–9
   contingency theory, 212–13
   core and periphery, 5–6
   current theories of, 212–23
   globalization and, 221–3
   importance of, 6–9
   interpretations and prospects,
      211–52
   nature of, 1–6
   post-Fordism and the British state,
      230–6
   public choice theory, 214–15
   public interest and private interests,
      248–52
   public sector discourses, 215–18
   state crises, 220–1
   user involvement, 240–8
Streamlining the Cities, 199

tendering, compulsory competitive,
   142, 151–2, 155

*The Reorganization of Central
   Government*, 81
Titmuss, 241
Training and Enterprise Councils,
   187–8
Training for the Future, 63, 172
training policy, 172–88
trust, 237

Urban Development corporations,
   200–9
   London Docklands Development
      Corporation, 201–6
   Merseyside Docklands
      Development Corporation, 205–6
urban policy, 188–210
   inner city policy, 188–93
   reorganization of (1980s), 193–5
user involvement in health-care,
   240–8

Ward, R., 203
welfare state, 72–96
   community development projects,
      82–95
   crisis of, 76, 115–17
   education, 107–10
   expenditure on, 74–5
   health care, 105–7
   housing, 110–12
   managing social expenditure, 76–82
   participation, 85–6
   personal social service, 113–17
   post-war welfare states, 72–4
   poverty, 83–5
   professional interests in, 97–117
   racism in, 100–1
   sexism in, 100
   social base of, 99–102
   social security, 102–4
Whitleyism, 152–7
Wilson, H., 40, 55
Working for Patients, 105–6,
   143–4

Younghusband Report, 113
Younghusband, E., 113–15
Youth Opportunities Programme,
   173–5
Youth Training Scheme, 175–9

Author Index

Addison, P., 16, 26, 31
Adler, M., 148
Aglietta, M., 231
Althusser, L., 215
Anderson, J., 33, 196, 197
Atkinson, J. and Meager, N., 231

Bagguley, P., 231
Banham, R., Barker, P., Hall, P. and
   Price, C., 195
Barnett, C., 19, 69, 228
Barnett, J., 78
Batley, R., 190, 200
Bauman, Z., 243
Beechey, V., 184
Bellamy, C. and Taylor, J. A., 146
Bleaney, M., 68
Bogdanor, V., 81, 132
Bradbury, B., 201
Bridges, Lord, 23, 78
Bromley, S., 222
Brown, M., 111
Buchanan, J., 150

Cadman, D., 197
Cairncross, A., 49
Callaghan, J., 86, 89, 91
Campbell, C., 141
Campbell, H., 111
Carter, D. and Stewart, I., 175
Carter, N. and Greer, P., 157
Clarke, J. and Langan, M., 75, 103

Clarke, J., Cochrane, A. and
   McLaughlin, E., 156
Clarke, R., 60, 136
Coates, D., 224
Cockburn, C., 89, 92, 93
Collingridge, D. and Margetts, H., 146
Colville, I., Dalton, K. and Tomkins,
   C., 157
Cooper, Sir F., 129
Coopey, R., 59, 60
Cronin, J., 30, 33
Crook, S., Pakulski, J. and Waters,
   M., 222

Dalton, H., 43
Davidson, J. O., 166
De Swann, A., 73
Deal, T. E. and Kennedy, A. A., 160
Dearlove, J., 91
Delafons, J., 83
Desai, M., 220
Donnison, D., 104
Dowding, K., 21, 22, 126, 212n
Downs, A., 214
Drewry, G. and Butcher, T., 124, 126–8
Dunleavy, P., 110, 129, 214
Dunsire, A. and Hood, C. C., 214
Durbin, E., 43

Elcock, H., 23, 151
Esping-Andersen, G., 212
Ewald, F., 10

Fairbrother, P., 156
Farnham, D., 153
Featherstone, M., 244
Feinstein, C. H., 77
Field, F., 85, 111
Finn, D., 174–81
Flynn, N., 158, 230
Foot, M., 32
Foster, D. and Taylor, G., 155
Foucault, M., 3, 216, 218
Friedman, M. and Friedman, R., 150
Fry, G. K., 23, 125, 129, 229

Gamble, A., 187, 212, 217
Gibson, T., 111
Giddens, A., 3, 212
Goldblatt, D., 221–2
Gough, I., 76, 85
Graham, C. and Prosser, T., 25
Grant, W., 212n
Gray, A. and Jenkins, W., 81, 123
Green, H., 100
Greenwood, J. R. and Wilson, D. J., 25, 78, 93
Greer, P., 131

Habermas, J., 220, 240
Hall, P., 190
Ham, C., 105, 116
Harden, I., 200
Harris, L., 67, 68
Harrow, J. and Talbot, C., 131, 151, 152
Hay, C., 33, 76, 220
Hayek, F. A., 25, 150
Heclo, H. and Wildavsky, A., 78
Hennessy, P., 23, 24, 29, 34, 36, 38, 55, 79, 125, 130
Hennessy, P. and Arends, A., 28
Hennessy, P., Morrison, S. and Townsend, R., 82
Hewart, G., 25
Higgins, J., Deakin, N., Edwards, J. and Wicks, M., 112
Hill, M., 32, 77, 105
Hills, S. J., 102
Hirsch, J. and Roth, R., 233
Hirst, P., 70, 240
Hirst, P. and Thompson, G., 222
Hoggett, P., 233

Hogwood, B., 128
Holland, P., 134
Hood, C., 8, 121, 134, 136, 208
Howarth, D., 10n
Hutton, W., 50, 213, 223, 225, 228, 237

Ingham, G., 225, 226

Jackson, P., 224
Jacobs, S., 101, 110
Jay, D., 43
Jessop, B., 3, 5, 27, 104, 212, 213, 218, 221, 231, 233, 234
Jessop, B., Bonnett, K., Bromley, S. and Ling, T., 212
Jordan, A. and Richardson, J., 82
Joshi, S. and Carter, B., 101

Kaufman, G., 131–2
Kaufman, M., 172
Kavanagh, D., 16
Kellner, P. and Crowther-Hunt, Lord, 125
Kelly, A., 120, 154
Keohane, R. and Nye, J. S., 27
Kessler, I., 156, 157
King, A., 220
King, D. S., 187
King, R., 106
Klein, R., 85
Krugman, P., 213

Laclau, E. and Mouffe, C., 215
Langan, M. and Clarke, J., 114, 160
Lash, S. and Urry, J., 66–7
Lawless, P., 193–4
Levacic, R., 108
Leys, C., 18, 19, 21, 60, 62, 226
Liekerman, A., 127, 128
Ling, T., 103, 149, 183, 234
Lowe, T., 237

Madgwick, P. J., Steeds, D. and Williams, L. J., 56
Margetts, H., 147
Marquand, D., 16, 41, 225
Marsh, D., 167
Marsh, D. and Rhodes, R. A. W., 119
Marshall, T. H., 30, 101

Massey, D. and Meegan, R., 184
Mercer, H., 36, 40, 55
Metcalfe, L. and Richards, S., 132
Middlemas, K., 16, 20, 26, 27, 36,
    41, 44, 52, 53, 59, 70, 212, 225
Mitchell, B. and Deane, P., 18
Moran, M., 57
Morgan, D. and Evans, M., 33
Morgan, K., 23–4, 28, 36–7, 43, 54
Moulaert, F., Swyngedouw, E. and
    Wilson, P., 233
Mulgan, G., 237

Nairn, T., 225, 226, 228
Newman, I. and Mayo, M., 202
Niskanen, W., 214

O'Conner, J., 76
Offe, C., 8, 76, 220, 221
Olson, M., 214, 227
Overbeek, H., 233

Painter, J., 233
Panitch, L., 40
Pascall, G., 100
Peters, T. and Austin, N., 160
Peters, T. and Waterman, R., 231
Phillips, A., 250
Phillips, M., 132
Piore, M. and Sabel, C., 231
Pliatzky, L., 127, 131, 133
Poggi, G., 9
Pollitt, C., 29, 105–7, 143–4, 156
Ponting, C., 125, 129
Poole, M., 157
Porter, D., 51, 52, 53
Price, C. M., 162, 163
Putnam, R. D., 237
Pyper, R., 123

Randall, A., 148
Randall, S., 180
Ranson, S., 108
Reich, R. B., 225
Rhodes, R., 11, 107, 109, 121, 135,
    153, 189, 212, 212n

Riddell, P., 128, 176
Robson, B., 189, 200, 206
Robson, W. A., 24
Rose, R., 220

Salt, J., 192
Salveson, P., Tansley, S. and Colenutt,
    B., 204
Schein, E. H., 160
Schlote, W., 19
Schultz, R. I. and Harrison, S., 106
Sharpe, L. J., 208
Shell, D., 150
Short, C., 108
Shutt, J., 196
Sleeman, J. F., 75
Smellie, K. B., 21
Smith, M., 31
Stones, R., 226
Strinati, D., 181
Summerfield, P., 33

Temple, P., 224
Thompson, H., 54
Thomson, P., 119
Thurow, L., 225
Tomlinson, J., 40, 49, 50
Tym, R. and Partners, 192, 196

Urry, J., 243

Vickerstaff, S., 65, 181

Walby, S. and Greenwell, J., 145
Ward, C., 110, 111
Ward, H., 214
Warde, A., 141–2, 243
Weir, S. and Hall, W., 228, 230
Wiener, M., 69, 225, 228
Wilks, S. and Wright, M., 212n
Williams, F., 100, 231
Woodward, N., 52
Woytinsky, W. S. and E. S., 19
Wright, M., 78

Zysman, J., 56